This book is dedicated to Rose, B.D., David and your families, for all you have taught me and for all you will teach many.

Cover design by Maria Blon through Canva.com

 Hearts Blooming symbol designed by Anna Blon

All proceeds from the sale of this book are donated to the HEART in Haiti School. The reason is, there is funding for mentoring and education of young adults with special gifts in the United States, but in Haiti, there isn't even free public education. Our school provides jobs, education and hope to the people who live in the Merger and Sibert communities. May the students at the HEART School be empowered through their education to reach their full potential.

Table of Contents

Foreword 8

Introduction 9

    Find Your Heaven on Earth....................................... 16

    How to Use this Book... 19

    Welcome New Opportunities 21

Earth Angel ROSE 23

    Create a Fresh Start 23

    Bond With People.. 26

    Follow the Leader.. 28

    Foster Patience 31

    Set Goals... 33

    Validate Achievements.. 35

    Be Silly 36

    Listen and Offer Possibilities 37

    Think Outside the Box... 39

    Respond Rather than React 41

    Uncover Passions.. 42

    Know When the Party is Over.................................. 43

    When to Step Back or Forward 44

    Learn to Manage Bureaucracy................................. 45

    Show Understanding with Challenging Habits 47

    Recognize Endearing Habits 50

    Receive Compliments.. 51

    Do Less, Allow More 52

    Teach With Humor.. 54

    Speak Directly to the Worry................................... 56

    Address Feelings Creatively.................................... 58

Find Your Heaven on Earth 62

Recognize Being Out of Balance 64

Balance Uncertainty with Play 68

Shift Focus 72

Build Trust with New People and Situations 73

Set Clear Intentions 75

Explore Without an Agenda 79

Teach and Model Respectful Behavior 81

Find Meaning in Every Situation 83

Accept Disappointment 85

Dance as if Nobody is Watching 87

Get Organized 88

Honor Friendships 90

Decide When or if to Speak 92

Share Thoughtful Gifts 94

Give Yourself Credit 95

Embrace Silence 97

Face Fears 98

Offer, Then Let Go 102

Finishing Remarks 105

Perseverance Pays Off for B.D. 106

Observation 106

Pay Negotiation 108

Start Where You Are 109

Support Growth 112

Have Fun with Learning 113

Switch Your Focus 114

Ask for Help 116

Set Boundaries 118

Be a Detective 120

Dig Deeper 121

Compliment Sandwiches 122

Learning Opportunities 125

Create an Inspirational Quote 128

Evaluate Messages Shared 130

Circle of Support 131

Dream Reflections 132

Be Vulnerable 133

Expand Social Circles 135

Reduce Stress as Much as Possible 136

Network 137

Be Open to Differences 138

Let Someone Else Be In Charge 140

Celebrate 142

Practice In Order to Succeed 143

Recognize Lessons Learned 144

Allow People to Make their Own Decisions 146

Support the People You Work With 148

Share Appreciation 150

Respect and Hear People's Stories 151

Don't Give Up if You Believe in Something 153

Admit What You Don't Know 155

Know When to Step In and Out 156

Balance Silence With Talking 158

Get In Synch 160

Value Incubation Time 161

Set Boundaries with Family Members 162

Encourage Leadership Skills with Compassion 163

Lean into Trust.. 166

Be Persistent, Yet Flexible 167

Acknowledge Your Own Needs 170

Manage Your Emotions... 172

Design Your Own Definition of Mentoring 173

Manage Finances 176

Go With the Flow 179

Focus on Strengths... 182

Celebrate Blooming... 184

David: King of Books and Humor... 185

Find a Good Fit... 185

Get to Know Each Person and Their Goals 187

Apply Learning with One Person to Another Person 189

Commit to Passions 190

Joyfully Connect Through Humor...................................... 195

Manage Unexpected Events 196

Remain Calm 199

Create Adventures 201

Respond in a Positive Way... 207

Seek Spiritual Guidance 209

Discuss Emotions 210

Delve into Stories Shared 212

Slow Down 214

Be Your Own Support System 217

Seek Training... 218

Find Space to Work Together... 220

Eat Healthy Food... 221

Pay Attention to Your Feelings 223

Observe Family Dynamics 226

Offer Ideas 227

Be Spontaneous 228

Use Stories as Teaching Moments 229

Be Open to Inspiration... 234

Keep Trying Different Methods 237

You Are Important 243

Foster Social Connections 244

Communicate With Members of the Team 246

Address Anxiety During Low Stress Times 250

Talk Or Write It Out.. 251

Decompress to Allow More Positive Communication 253

Be Understanding When Being Ignored................................. 257

Take a Break.. 260

Fostering Leadership Skills 262

Take Action to Care for Yourself... 263

Embrace Openings... 268

Recognize When You Come Full Circle 270

Appreciate the Efforts of Caregivers 274

Notice the Fruits of Learning 275

Our Work Carries On 278

Epilogue... 279

Appendices 281

Hearts Blooming Mottos 281

Simple Ways to Express Feelings Creatively......................... 282

Connecting Spiritually with Evan 286

Contributors... 288

Foreword

by Day Howell

Hearts Blooming is a book about one woman's journey as a mentor to young adults with special gifts, but it could just as easily be a book about awakening the soul.

Through stories of her time spent with three inspiring young people with different challenges and abilities, Maria delicately guides us down a path of discovery, teaching us not only how to be mentors, but how to get in touch with the divinity that courses through us all.

Maria has a gift for recognizing when passion is in the room, and she offers tools and perspectives to the reader that coax us to open our hearts and minds so that we, too, can recognize the light of passion in others as well as in ourselves. By introducing us to these inspiring young adults and leading us through typical mentoring activities with them, Maria unveils the magic that can happen when one's calling is identified and nurtured. Her candid stories are engaging in their authenticity and vulnerability. Full of celebration, challenge, and hilarity, each one contains within it a deep wisdom that can be used to guide mentors and laypeople alike to find creative and intuitive ways to lead.

A glimpse into the bond between mentor and young adult, this beautiful book is about more than techniques and life skills. It is a tribute to the immense power of deep listening and the willingness to become a student of a power greater than ourselves. In the end, this book is a living example of how, by helping another to find their way, we just might end up finding our own.

Introduction

I had already quit my job as a college professor to start my own yoga business, written a book, done volunteer work in Haiti, yet I still couldn't put my finger on what was wrong. With no clear idea of what to do next, I felt depressed and confused. Then a glimmer of hope shined through when I received an invitation to mentor a lovely young lady named Rose, whom I had known a very long time. I discovered that my lifelong passion to help people, most especially people who are differently abled, was a key to improving my state of mind. I also discovered in serving others, I learned much about myself and have been profoundly transformed by these experiences. I have come to realize sharing these stories may help those working with differently abled people not only to effectively mentor them, but also to feel better in their own lives. This book is my way of relating what I've learned.

Creative expression has been a tremendous gift for me. When facing the depression and confusion I experienced, I discovered many ways to shift and shake loose what felt like a dark cloud in my mind which was keeping me from looking at situations from a wise, inspired perspective. For me, the most effective ways to view a challenge in new ways involves creativity through writing, especially poetry, dancing, making jokes or teaching in unique ways. In some cases, these creative expressions become alternate communication methods in situations when words alone are not enough. You may not find writing, dancing or making jokes to be the creative outlets which help you shift yourself to see new perspectives. This is completely understandable, because each person has their own unique creative outlets, and it is important to remember you don't need to be professional status at any of them. I enjoy dancing, yet I am certainly not ready or willing to perform on a stage. I enjoy being able to process my feelings and communicate with people through poetry, but I don't aspire to be a poet laureate. As far as humor, I could never imagine myself as a stand-up comic, and still, there are lucky times when I am funny. When you are reading these stories, notice how creativity is woven through them and reflect on what inspires creativity to shine through you.

Not only do I receive spiritual nourishment from creativity, it comes to me from a variety of sources. Nature has always been a source of inspiration and spiritual connections. For this reason, I am lucky to be born into my family, who first drove me out of Manhattan for a camping trip when I was still in my mom's belly. Outdoor adventures have continued throughout my life when I went to Girl Scout Camp with my best friend, sitting by the river while my dad fished or swam in a mountain pond with my mom and brother. I also like to tune in to the natural balance of my body through yoga. Imitating dad's yoga poses as a child was play, yet after becoming a mom, I was strongly called to this practice which connects my body, mind, and spirit. Daily yoga and meditation practice led to lots of soul searching, reading, learning, and becoming a yoga teacher, a yoga therapist, a life coach, and an energy healer. The more I take really good care of myself by getting massages on a regular basis, spending time in nature, eating healthy food, and immersing myself in creativity, the more inspired I feel. I also am guided by a spiritual teacher, Dechen Rheault, who has helped by repeatedly reminding me to rest, play, believe in myself, and enjoy the moment. She offers such depth of insight and patience as she witnesses the internal challenges I face from present and past lives, struggles from which I have been healing and growing stronger from each and every day. There were times when I would receive guidance and healing from her every two weeks, but recently, I went almost three months before I needed to check in, to understand why on the inside I felt like I was doing so much wrong, when on the outside, I was contributing in many different ways. She could see right to the core of what was happening energetically and after just thirty-five minutes, I felt like I would be okay and could find a way to believe in myself more fully again. You will briefly witness Dechen's help in Rose's, B.D.'s, and David's stories, just a glimpse you might think, yet Dechen's teachings shine through each moment where you can feel Divine Love asserting itself to help heal the situation.

Writing this book has helped me see how the seeds of mentoring people with special gifts has been in me from the beginning of my life, but it was up to me to notice and nurture these innate passions. Following is a scan of my life, filled with clues as to why mentoring was the perfect career for me at this time in my life.

I was born in New York City on November 18, 1964. When I was six months old, my Mom and Dad moved us all to Bronxville, a one square mile village a short train ride from the city. We lived in a lovely apartment building made magical by the community atmosphere the residents created there. Inabelle, who was like the Pied Piper for us children, invited us all to her apartment to play, create art, cook, and have fun together every Sunday afternoon. She also organized us to plant flowers in the gardens and play outside. We were fortunate to live in a safe area, and our parents allowed us a lot of freedom to explore the big field surrounded by woods across the street from our apartment, where we could frolic and play, even past dark. What lucky kids we were to have such freedom to live and explore!

A deaf teenager, who was ten years older than me, was a member of our lively community. I felt bad not being able to communicate with her, so I picked up a book on sign language at the library and learned a little bit of this language. I remember practicing the alphabet over and over again on my own. To be honest, I don't think I ever had the courage to attempt speaking sign language to the young woman, and yet I was passionate about learning with the intention of speaking with her. From an early age, I saw the value of reaching out to others, even if it meant investing extra time and effort to do so.

After I finished third grade and my brother Paul completed Kindergarten, my family moved to Churchill, a suburb of Pittsburgh, because of my father's job. I felt shocked to be in a house where we were so far away from our neighbors, each family having a big lonely yard. Neighborhood kids were spread out and there weren't any common playing areas. While I did form a close friendship with Amy, who joined girl scouts and went to camp with me every summer, there was never the community atmosphere I so cherished in Bronxville.

In fifth grade at my new school, another clue emerged about my inclination towards helping people with special gifts. Melanie, a blind girl, joined our class. I was fascinated with her braille typewriter. I wanted to be an angel who swooped in to make everything feel better and lighter for people with special gifts. I just didn't quite know where to begin. I was young and had so much to figure out for myself at that time. I remember some kids laughing at Melanie when she ate really ripe bananas which were dark and mushy. I wasn't sure what to do about this teasing, and I still feel some regret that I did not find a way to help Melanie more. I didn't have much confidence in my ability to make a difference in her life, but I wanted to help somehow.

One of the most important events in my life happened near the end of eleventh grade. I was at a sunrise service in a historic stone church singing, "This Little Light of Mine", with the youth group I belonged to. This is my favorite song because it is so easy to sing and the message resonates with the little light inside of me. When we walked out of the church, the minister, Renny Domsky, told me my baby brother was born while we were singing. How exciting! I loved babies and couldn't wait to meet him. Mom and Dad hadn't decided on a name yet. They liked names which couldn't be shortened. My Mom's name is Susan, so people call her Sue. My Dad's name was William, and people called him Bill. They asked my brother Paul and me for suggestions, and I offered Evan, the name of a peaceful, kind friend in my youth group. Everyone liked the name, even though dad was not quite sure and debated about changing his name even after it was written on the birth certificate. At the time, my feelings were hurt by this, and I took his hesitation as a personal insult.

Looking back, I wonder if dad may have had worries, at the age of forty-seven, about being prepared for the challenges which were ahead of him and us as a family. Evan was a beautiful baby with dark brown hair, big blue eyes, and long dark curly eyelashes. Oh, was he ever charming! I loved helping care for him, which it turned out was something we would do for the rest of his life. Evan progressed normally for the first three months of his life, sitting up and even rolling over, but when Evan was three months old, he started changing, going backwards in development. There was no more rolling over. Sitting up was not getting easier, but harder, for him. I didn't recognize the problems like my worried parents because as a seventeen-year-old, I wasn't familiar with typical baby development stages. Although I did comment to mom after babysitting that the baby I cared for, who was younger than Evan, was doing more things than he was. One night when we were out to dinner as a family, Evan started having seizures. We didn't know what they were at the time. I just remember being scared of what was going on. This started a series of doctor visits both near and far, as everyone did their best to figure out what was happening with Evan and what could be done to help him. We discovered Evan had cerebral palsy, epilepsy, and developmental delays. Evan would stay at the level of a three-month-old baby his entire life and developed scoliosis because of his low muscle tone. How heartbreaking it was to witness this beautiful baby grow older, without gaining more skills and freedom.

When Evan was young and we weren't yet certain about what he would be able to do, I would walk with him on the beach when we were on vacation at Cape Cod, carrying him in a front pack, a "bug snuggly" we called it. I begged him to talk, to tell us what he was thinking, things he would like to do and how we could help him, but of course, there was no response. The only time Evan communicated with me in a way I was aware of was shortly before he died. (This story is included in the Appendix.) Since I loved caring for babies, I was happy to feed, bathe, dress, and change Evan's diapers, especially when he was younger. As Evan grew and gained weight, caring for him became more and more challenging, but my parents were physically fit and handled these hurdles with kindness, strength, and determination.

Evan had a really good life. My mom and dad loved spending time outside swimming, walking, fishing, skiing, and so much more. Whatever we did, Evan came along, first being carried and then in a baby jogger, which went on many hiking trails and beach dunes. Dad always felt it was important to bring Evan with us everywhere as people with special gifts were often hidden from society and many times sent away to homes. I remember being young and overhearing (more like listening in on) a conversation spoken in hushed tones between my grandmother, mom, and aunt about one of our relatives who had a child who was a "vegetable." "How on earth could a person be a vegetable?" I wondered. I believe the child was probably a lot like Evan who could not walk, talk, or even sit up on his own. Thankfully, language related to people with special gifts has become more sensitive since those days. At the time, Evan was diagnosed as being retarded—I prefer to explain he was at the developmental level of a three-month-old his whole life. I like the term "specially gifted" better than "disabled" because while a person may not have the same abilities as others, sometimes not having a skill can lead to other important strengths. Despite his challenges, Evan was delivered to us all to teach very important lessons. He was the only one of us three kids that could calm dad down. There was nothing dad could do to change or fix Evan, despite his very best efforts. All dad could do was to accept Evan for who he was. Dad would hold Evan and visibly relax, hence his nickname: "Evan from Heaven". Dad would whistle to Evan, who would smile and make happy noises.

Unlike many others, Evan was blessed with wonderful services and education available for him close to our home. He attended an Easter Seals Preschool, which was on the grounds of the church where I sang "This Little Light of Mine" on the day he was born. Evan was picked up in a bus with a wheelchair lift from our house each day, attending schools designed for his ability level. My mom found a lovely babysitter, Pam,

13

who was always happy to watch Evan when mom was taking classes in accounting, or doing other activities where she couldn't care for him. When mom and dad swam or played tennis, Evan would go the baby nursery at the Racket Club, where he fit right in. There was no respite money to cover Evan's care beyond the time he was in school, but after Evan moved to Allegheny Valley School, all of his needs were paid for by the government. The facility was a huge mansion converted into a beautiful home for people with special gifts. There was a heated pool on the ground floor, which Evan loved as it helped his tight muscles relax. There was a lovely garden where we would bring Evan in his wheelchair to feed him when visiting. Later in the book, I will discuss the expanded support now available to families and their children with special gifts.

My baby brother had a profound effect on me. When I taught Math and Yoga at Orange County Community College for over twenty years, anytime I saw someone attending school in a wheelchair, I would say in my head, "You are so lucky." Thankfully I had enough sense not to say this directly to the person because they would think I was a bit bonkers. It seems kind of a strange thing to think this when seeing someone with special gifts, yet as I compared their skills to Evan's, they could do so very much more than he could. Deep down, I wished that person was my brother. I really missed being able to speak to Evan, to play with him and to know what he was thinking and feeling. Throughout my teaching career, I have used holistic methods to help people with differing abilities to learn. Having Evan as a brother heightened my gratitude for the skills and abilities each of us has, even when a few are missing. I feel even more thankful for what I do have. Evan's challenges were so profound that when I had a student in my class with special gifts, I felt privileged to be able to help and develop a relationship with them.

Eventually, I got to the point in my teaching career when I wanted a change. I began studying Yoga Therapy and decided to take a break from my full-time job to study and start a yoga business. Around this same time, my daughter Carina wanted to travel to Haiti after the devastating earthquake of 2010. I had time to go on this trip with her, the first of many visits where we went to volunteer. This was an opportunity for me to mentor and be mentored by people who were very different from me culturally and linguistically. During this time, I was trying all kinds of new experiences to see if there was some place I felt I belonged and my talents could be helpful. My daughter and her husband eventually founded a school in Haiti, called the Haiti Education and Resource Team, HEART for short (www.heartinhaiti.org), and I did all I could to support their efforts there. I offered some teacher training at HEART and served in a few different positions on board, but most of my volunteer work involved fundraising and sharing the story of the school. I did so many new, scary and exciting things, traveling back and forth to Haiti over a dozen times, learning different energy healing techniques, starting and stopping a few different businesses and writing the book *Living Passionately: 21 People Who Found Their Purpose and How You Can Too*. I learned a tremendous amount from these explorations, picking up valuable skills in a variety of areas. Despite having great experiences and completing meaningful service, there came a time when I didn't find myself in a place where I felt I belonged, other than in our gardens, where no matter what is happening around me, I know I am welcome and nourished. Feeling uncertain about how I could use my skills and experience to contribute in a meaningful way, I was floundering. This book is the story of how I found a career I am passionate about where I could help people discover and follow passions of their own, some of which were similar to mine and some of which were not. In this process, I grew to appreciate how very much I have to offer. Now I invite you to take time to consider reviewing your life as I just have.

♥ **Take a Life Scan:** Make time to reflect on what has been consistently important to you throughout your life. What are your passions and what are the passions of people who you work with? What clues are there to help unlock the secret gifts you have had throughout your life? Healing gifts are often disguised as things we do with great ease, or passions we have. Even if we are not proficient in these areas as a child, they are still where we are being called by our soul to contribute.

Find Your Heaven on Earth

I have been guided many times by different people to make this book focused on teaching and learning by using the stories to illustrate how these transformation tools can be used. I have resisted this guidance time after time because I haven't felt like a master quite yet: I feel like I need more practice in order to be an authority. Yet, when I read these stories, I am surprised and delighted by what an amazing amount of transformation happens for myself and the people I work with. Am I a "super mentor," an "ultra-expertly trained know- it-all" who made these changes happen? Not at all! I am a humble mentor who approached each moment with an open heart and stumbled my way through the best I knew to do at the time. Because I didn't feel like or act like a know-it-all expert, I was open to guidance from, well, I don't quite know who guided us: could be soul, spirit, angels, fairies, Goddess/God, the Flying Spaghetti Monster, a quantum field. I just don't know how to describe who or what my guiding force is because as much as I would like to, I don't hear, see, or feel any of these in a concrete, definitive way. Yet I feel some sense of peaceful, joyful calm where magical, inspiring things seem to happen, where it seems (but I can't clearly see) an energetic chord is plugged into a wise, intuitive Source of Guidance, which surrounds myself and those in my presence. I believe on our best days, the people I work with sense this wise presence in our midst, which helps them trust me and trust themselves in order to be open to new possibilities. I would love to be in this peaceful, open, joyful space all the time and have been searching for ways to do this for many years. I am learning to experience "heaven on earth" more and more often using the very techniques shared here. The times when I feel off balance, uncertain, and fearful are important as I learn to lean into and glean wisdom from the confusion.

Western society teaches us we are most valuable when producing, doing, contributing outwardly, in a way which can be seen by others, which in Eastern philosophy is described as yang, who like father sky, invites tree branches to spread up and out, encouraging us to express ourselves openly in the world. Western society discourages resting, gestation, nurturing, intuition, which in Eastern philosophy is described as yin, who like mother earth, welcomes a tree's roots deep into her womb for nourishment, comfort and stability. It is said, these opposing forces of nature are complimentary, in us all, and both are needed for balance. Yet, I have learned to hold up branching out as better than rooting down. This is what I am unlearning in order to come into greater balance, honoring the inward, feminine, dark, intuitive energy, the life force of the earth. For me, I feel most whole and connected with my soul when spending time in nature walking, observing, gardening, swimming, taking pictures, soaking in the regenerative energy of the earth. There are times when branching out, producing, contributing outwardly is nourishing and fulfilling, but if the emphasis is solely on this aspect, I get exhausted, make mistakes, hurt myself, and nothing in my life looks or feels right. When I allow enough time to grow energetic roots through meditation, resting, observing, or simply "chilling out," I gain the wisdom and perspective to get into motion once again. Unfortunately, I often judge myself as "less than" when I slowdown, which is something I have partially unlearned through mentoring both the people I work with and myself. When reading this book and considering the challenges in your life, take time to reflect on whether you are being called to send more roots down and out or branch up and out. Is it time to exhale or inhale more deeply? I share stories of when I have tried both of these strategies and what their outcomes have been.

I find mastery can be a process often based on repetition rather than a destination in which every skill is "check-marked" off a list. For that reason, the same learning points may appear in different examples, because many people, like me, need lots and lots of repetition to gain confidence in using these techniques. I am learning all the time, and I intend to keep expanding my heart and mind throughout my life. For example, in New York, there is a six-month program which is offered to become a "Master Gardener." I have met many people who have graduated from this program and who wear "Master Gardener" nametags. When people see my gardens, they ask, "Are you a Master Gardener?" My answer is always, "No, I am always learning something new from my gardens and don't ever imagine myself achieving master status." Maybe I might know some things another person doesn't, but I am sure that person knows something I don't. When hosting a garden tour in our yard, one visitor asked me, "Do you plan everything out before planting?" I replied, "No, I put a plant in and care for it as best I can. If it seems happy in this location, it stays there. If it doesn't look happy because of one reason or another, I move it to another location. For me, gardening, like life, is a process of trying things out to see how they work and the only thing which is constant is change each and every second of every day.

This flexible approach brings beautiful surprises in both gardening and mentoring. Flowers create seeds which the wind, birds, and, most likely, fairies spread around to different spots. I call these plants which show up in places where I haven't planted them "volunteers." I am thrilled with the beauty of our gardens, which I credit to a mix of the nurturing efforts of my husband, Tom, and me with the magical inspiration and seeming randomness of nature. This is the way I view mentoring as well. Often, I am not sure what will happen on any given day, yet I stay open to seeds of magical inspiration which blow in, some taking root and growing to fruition and some just popping in for a quick visit before flying off in search of the perfect location. Gardening and mentoring provide me opportunities to experience heaven on earth. This book is called Hearts Blooming because I feel like Rose, B.D., David, and I all experienced our hearts opening and flourishing in ways we never expected. Sometimes, there are resting stages in plants during which flowers do not bloom, yet, each time our hearts expand a bit, we sense that blossom ripening and unfolding because we feel so vibrantly alive.

♥ **Find Your Heaven on Earth:** Where and when do you experience "heaven on earth"? What beliefs do you have about the balance of growing roots and branches in your life? Where is that place where you always feel welcome and as if you belong?

How to Use this Book

Many of the stories and learning tips in this book about mentoring young adults with special gifts serve as examples of how we and those we work with might learn, grow, and bloom into our best selves. Navigating through life challenges is fertile ground for transformation, yet it can also be a scary time filled with uncertainty. When using the suggested techniques shared in this book, my hope is you feel a helpful presence guiding you to open your heart and mind to new possibilities. Sometimes, you may not recognize how much you have grown, so taking time to pause, give yourself credit, and recognize accomplishments is an important part of this process.

The stories in this book show readers what it is like working as a mentor both physically and spiritually. Real life situations in which we supposedly teach others often transform into spiritual learning for ourselves. Thus, in teaching others, we in-turn become students as our own lives are made richer, deeper, and more meaningful through contact with the people we spend time with. In order to help uncover the lessons hidden in interactions with the people I work with, a "Heart Blooming Tool" follows each story:

This symbol precedes each Hearts Blooming Tool or perspective which you may consider using in an area of your life, or with people you may be mentoring. These tools and views suggest different ways to approach a situation, possible questions to help foster growth, useful reminders, or encouragement. Often, a story will suggest lessons for improving the mentorship relationship as well as fostering self-knowledge. I hope you find the experiences in this book as useful for your growth as a person and as a mentor as I did when I experienced them!

When a flower blooms, we celebrate the miracle of its beauty. What comes before and after this glorious blossom may not appear to be as spectacular as the flower itself, and yet these stages are of utmost importance. Each day of a plant's life, important work is being done, and without each step, there will be no flower.

A seed in the earth, waiting to sprout
Water is needed to help life burst out
The shell cracks open
A root starts a comin'
A seedling reaches up, up, up to the sun
Growing every day. Isn't this fun?
As strength is developed both under and over the ground
Buds start appearing all around
With nurturing and care, some buds unfold
Showing their full glory for all to behold
There is singing and dancing and all kinds of praise
Until the petals fall as do the rains
And yet there is more as seeds and fruits form
Giving us hope as our heart feels warm
With excitement to eat a juicy sweet fruit
As we chant root a toot toot
The seeds in the middle are saved for the day
When they can be planted in a new way
Which honors the cycles and seasons
Plants show us the reasons
All stages of blooming are celebrated
For they are each part of life and we are elated.

Just as plants have all different stages in growth, so do we as people. When learning anything new, we are beginners, needing clean fresh energy to open us up. We send roots down into the ground, using our past learning as a foundation to reach up to new territory. If conditions are right, with love and support, in time buds will form, a sign of glory to come. When the flower blooms, there is great celebration, and even more follows when the fruits of our labors ripen for harvest. Even eating the fruit is not an ending as the seeds inside are saved to keep the circle of life going round and round in spirals of learning and growing together. May we all be aware of the importance of each stage of growth which occurs as our hearts are blooming together.

Welcome New Opportunities

During the winter of 2018, I became quite depressed as my beloved gardens rested and I searched to find meaning in my days. No work or leisure activities seemed interesting, and the idea of trying something, anything was terrifying. This was new territory for me because up to this point in my life, I fearlessly explored many different passions with great zest. I had plenty of degrees, experience, and skills, but I was having trouble imagining a career to fit who I was at this time. One day, despite feeling lost, I was looking forward to having lunch with my friend Patti. We had met almost twenty years earlier. At the time, my four-year-old daughter Carina and her son Thomas were in preschool together, and Patti and I were exploring elementary school options for them. We met at an elementary school tour with all of our children. I brought Carina and Anna who was two years old, while Patti brought Thomas, Patrick, and Rose (five years, four years, and six months old).

This was my first meeting with Rose, who had Down Syndrome. She was calm and happy at the time. Quite unexpectedly, I started bawling, tears rolling down my face as I said, "You are so lucky." I explained my youngest brother Evan was severely disabled and at the developmental level of a three-month-old his whole life. I knew Rose was headed for great things, since people with Down syndrome are able to learn and integrate with society in ways my brother never could. My reaction was surprising to Patti, but especially surprising to me. I didn't often share my feelings with people, much less break down in tears with someone I barely know.

Patti, the children, and I went on many adventures together over the next several years. We spent a lot of time outside because we all loved the outdoors. When they were old enough, Anna and Carina babysat for Rose. Rose loved playing hospital and would lie on a bed while the girls asked her what hurt, then wrapped her up with many layers of ace bandages. They patched Rose up countless times from a plethora of different pretend injuries. When Carina was in college in her early twenties, Patti asked her to work with Rose after school, driving her to basketball and other events. At the time, I remember thinking the work she was doing with Rose seemed like something I might enjoy.

But back to lunch with Patti in 2018. Despite feeling depressed, I had showered, put on nice clothes, and did my best to muster up a happy face. Patti started telling me about Rose's activities. She told me how much

Rose had been loving doing volunteer gardening work, whereas working at a clothing store was not appealing to her at all. Patti said she was looking for someone to mentor Rose with gardening and tentatively asked if I might be interested. I couldn't think of any reason why I wouldn't want to explore this option and shakily said I was open to learning more. Thankfully, I was brave enough, despite feeling despondent in general, to dip my toe into the waters of trying something new.

Welcome New Opportunities: If you feel stuck and uncertain about what to do, open your heart to new ideas and opportunities which arise, even if this might seem scary at first.

Earth Angel ROSE

Create a Fresh Start

I was beginning in a new career, wondering what would unfold and feeling grateful for this opportunity. Patti, being the devoted mother and efficient lawyer she is, got going right away to bring Rose and myself together. She began by paying me from her personal funds, until the complicated paperwork was processed. Since it was quite cold outside, I spent time getting to know the nineteen-year-old adult Rose in our greenhouse. I showed Rose around and taught her how to cut herbs, which I gave her to take home. We also worked together to make small plant arrangements in recycled jars for a monthly fundraising project for our HEART in Haiti School. From the beginning, I have always been careful that my work with Rose is done with integrity in that I never ask her to do tasks for my benefit. In order to teach her about weeding and planting, we often volunteer at other people's gardens. Whenever we work in my greenhouse, anything picked is for her to take home to her family.

Patti treated me with the utmost respect, applying for me to earn more than the minimum wage suggested by the organization, since I came into the job with a plethora of education and experience. This job really was a dream come true in so many ways. I never imagined I would have a job that utilized all of my varied skills. I found myself beginning a new career where all of my passions for teaching, gardening, adventuring, relaxing, and inspiring were relished and celebrated. How lucky am I to do what I love and to get paid and appreciated for doing it!

Note from Patti: I was so excited when Maria agreed to try to work with my Rose! I needed a calm loving person who could appreciate Rose's attributes and scattered skills, and who knew plants and yoga. I was also thrilled that Maria had wonderful ideas about ways Rose could work in the community. I never would have thought a retired college professor would be interested in mentoring Rose, but was thrilled she said yes!

The close relationship Patti and I have had provides both benefits and challenges, and I am often inspired by the work she has done to help other parents of children with special gifts. I have witnessed Patti's intense love and dedication to Rose over the years. From the time Rose was a little baby, Patti had physical therapists, speech therapists, occupational therapists and other helpers coming into her home to teach Rose important skills which many children learn on their own. I was at her house a few times when therapists came in during the intense early years; Patti was trying to foster Rose's development on top of raising two very active boys and caring for her mother-in-law, who had many health issues. To help the boys exercise and have fun on days when they couldn't go out and play, Patti's husband installed a swinging trapeze in the raised ceiling of the living room. Everyone in the family has lots of energy so Rose was immersed in lots of activities like swimming, hiking, skiing, bowling, basketball, and in her adult years, rowing. People with Down syndrome typically have low muscle tone, but the physical activities encouraged by her vibrant family have helped her grow exceptionally strong and fit. Inspired to help others, Patti started a family support group called "Angels Amongst Us" which helps families who have a child with Down syndrome. She provided hope and support, organized picnics and parties, and connected parents to services that could help them address the challenges of raising a child with special gifts.

As a family friend, I had some knowledge of what it had been like raising Rose. When Patti and I hiked, camped or kayaked together, she would talk about some of the challenges she faced, not only with Rose but also with her other children over the years. Every time I went home after a trip with Patti, I felt grateful for the relative calm of my life. Now I was choosing to work with Rose, to immerse myself in all of her simplicity and complexity. Another challenge coming to the forefront was now having my good friend suddenly become my boss. Being confident enough to say no when something doesn't feel right, while also respecting the family wishes was something I learned to balance.

After I agreed to work with Rose, Patti asked me if I wanted to read over Rose's evaluations before we began. I thought about this question for a moment and said, "No thank you." While knowledge is power, reading over all of Rose's challenges might leave me feeling discouraged or prejudiced about what she could or couldn't do—I wanted to begin our work together as fresh and open to possibilities as I could. I really was not sure of what we would do together or what this work would be like, and I was excited to see what she could achieve.

♥ **Create a Fresh start:** Entering a new relationship with some background is important, yet be alert to places where having an open mind is more important than gaining knowledge which might inhibit possibilities. This can be applied to new mentoring relationships as well as your relationship with yourself. We all have memories, mental and emotional records from our past. Consider setting those past stories aside and give yourself the opportunity to have a fresh start while welcoming new experiences.

Bond With People

When creating meaningful relationships with ourselves or another person, getting to know each other by discovering shared interests is the first step. This requires attention and deep listening with all of our senses. The program which pays me is called Encouraging Self Support (ESS). This program grants money to adults with special gifts to help them do what they enjoy in life, with the help of mentors who listen to their dreams and help these dreams become reality.

Rather than making decisions for her, I listen to what Rose does and does not want, then make suggestions for activities based on her own desires. Together we plan our time for adventures near and far. Right from the beginning of our work together, Rose and I bonded. Even though I had known and spent time with her throughout her life, this moment in time, beginning her nineteenth year of life, was different. We clicked so quickly, which felt magical, even divinely guided. Rose and I have a great deal in common. We both love digging in the dirt, growing plants, and learning. We also love warm rains, swimming, dancing, and spending time in nature. I am attentive to how Rose is feeling and adapt when I notice a change is needed. For example, we can make plans to weed a person's garden, but if the day is warmer than expected and Rose is in danger of overheating, we might need to leave that job early and take a dip in cool water. On the other hand, if we are volunteering at the community garden where we both have plots and a gentle rain cools us off, even if the other gardeners scatter, Rose and I happily stay to work, jump in puddles, dance, and sing to our heart's delight. Can you tell how much fun we have together? How lucky we both feel!

We garden at a number of different places:

- Private homes where we earn money for the HEART in Haiti School
- Community gardens where Rose has her own plot and helps with the shared gardens.
- Inspire Farm, which grows food for people in the Inspire Community of people with special gifts. This farm employs two full-time people with special gifts.
- Our family's greenhouse in the winter, where we prepare table arrangements to raise money for the HEART in Haiti School.

♥ **Bond with people:** Notice shared passions and connect through these vibrant interests, rather than trying to force your own interests onto the person you are mentoring. Often families or society may encourage us to choose interests based on our gender, culture, or other criteria. Take time to listen to what resonates strongly deep within. You will notice excitement, sparkling eyes, and big smiles from anyone discovering their passions.

Follow the Leader

Follow the lead of the person you are working with, even if they do things differently than you might. As a mentor, you may notice yourself wanting to offer suggestions, yet deciding instead to observe and allow the person you are working with to take the lead. After less than a year of exploring together, Rose told me, "It is time to step up my game. I want to start taking measurements, doing math, and working on getting a job." It took me some time to understand what she wanted to do with measurements and math, but she had her own vision of how she should use her time. When we visited the Inspire Community Greenhouse in the winter, Rose brought her journal and took notes on what we did to help with their microgreens program. She asked Jon-Jon, the program's director, for the measurements of the greenhouse and drew a huge diagram of the growing facilities. She also takes notes on what we plant in her community garden plot. These were Rose's ideas, which both Jon Jon and I supported and encouraged. The diagram and notes were her way of showing us in action, rather than words, "I am a professional. This is the way I have seen people do important things, they take measurements and notes." This became apparent in the confident way Rose showed her family the work she was doing through the diagram and notes. Rose was being a leader in this part of her life. I imagine this was a way to learn and understand what she was doing.

Inspire Farm is an amazing place and Jon Jon is a gentle giant. At six feet eight inches tall, with all the kindness and patience of Mister Rogers, Jon Jon lovingly guides people with special gifts to learn growing skills. Most importantly, he makes them feel welcome and valuable. Everyone who Jon Jon mentors feels special. He delights in teaching Rose how to greet the chickens and to collect and wash eggs. He is grateful for all the work she does, whether it is picking rattlesnake beans, weeding the onions, or harvesting the tomatoes. He always sends her home with some of the bounty, which helps her see results of her hard work.

I have learned a tremendous amount watching Jon Jon in action. He is tirelessly patient. One day, one of his long-time employees, Sam, was angry and frustrated with both the volunteers and the chickens, and we heard him angrily complaining about Jon Jon being late for work. Sam was having a bad day. Jon Jon patiently talked to Sam each time: "Sam, we've talked about not throwing food at the chickens. We treat them with respect, placing the food on the ground beside them. . . . Sam, I want the volunteers to do all of the steps. Please allow them to trim the plants and put them in the soil. . . . Sam, when am I late for work? Oh yes, the other day I had an appointment in the morning and came in a little late. Remember when I told you about that?" Yikes, I don't know how Jon Jon has the patience! Of course, as I said, this was just a bad day for Sam, who usually is quite helpful. Jon Jon's other full-time employee, Thomas, who is only half of Jon Jon's height, is the sweetest man. He clearly adores Jon Jon, doing his best to emulate his patient, encouraging teacher. Thomas is appreciative of the learning he receives and the volunteers who come to the garden. He is always excited to have Rose help out, guiding her gently and showing gratitude for her efforts. Watching this display of love and respect for Rose, my heart swells and I imagine her heart is swelling as well.

My time with Rose is filled with such great joy. She moves slowly and deliberately, which is relaxing for me. My playful spirit comes out with Rose as we splash each other in the water, dance in the rain, or skip down the sidewalk arm in arm. Since she wants to start a business involving gardening, we were working on finding a name. Rose's first ideas were: The Landscapers Volunteers and Rosetoga's Landscaping (followed by howling laughter because the name includes her name Rose, as well as the end of the name of the town Saratoga). There were many more suggestions, but finally, we agreed upon this one: Earth Angels.

The story of how this name was discovered is sweet. My Christmas present that year to Rose was a spirit rock, created by healer Lynne Newman. With guidance from angels, Lynne painted a rock to represent Rose's spirit and the work she is being called to do this lifetime. The angels referred to Rose as an Earth Angel. When I gave Rose her spirit rock, she was beside herself with gratitude. Rose could feel how the angels love and appreciate her for who she is. Tears were rolling down her face and she was so very grateful for this heartfelt and incredibly cool present. I realized if I wanted to help Rose achieve her own idea of the best version of herself, I would need to mirror this same loving acceptance of her and allow her to choose her own path.

Follow the leader: Even if a desire doesn't make sense, follow its lead and notice what opportunities arise. This is true both of working with others and working with ourselves. Often inspiration comes in to encourage us to look at a situation differently. New things can seem scary, so sometimes our fear will step in and say, "This is a really bad idea." This can happen when observing another person or ourselves do something differently. Notice who makes the suggestions in your head. Fear is usually a frantic feeling or words like, "Stop this now or something bad is going to happen." The wisdom of spirit provides calm suggestions like, "Why don't we just observe and see what happens here?".

Foster Patience

After the earthquake in Haiti in 2010, my daughter Carina and I traveled to Haiti with Shad St. Louis, a guidance counselor at Middletown High School, where she went to school, and where my husband Tom worked. This was a life changing experience for all of us, which I won't expand on now, because my first book, "Living Passionately" shares our stories there. We ended up starting the HEART in Haiti School in the community where Shad grew up, and I did some fundraising for the school. One monthly fundraising project was to put plant cuttings in small vases to place on the tables at the Something Sweet Restaurant in Middletown, NY. We used recycled spice jars to hold the plant cuttings. Rose enjoyed carefully putting water into each tiny jar and was better at this job than I was. I tended to rush and spill a lot of water, but Rose carefully poured water into each little jar, and if she spilled a bit, she quickly wiped it up. We used spiderwort cuttings Jon Jon allowed us to trim and placed them in these vessels. Rose counted a total of eighteen arrangements, writing this down in her notebook, then carefully placing them in a tub for us to deliver the next time we worked together. Breaking big projects down into the smaller parts was important for our work together. If I was doing this project on my own, I would work quickly, filling jars, spilling water, putting the plant cuttings in the jars and into the container in quick succession. With Rose, each step of this process was done meticulously, with explanations, awareness and celebration for each accomplishment. Delivering our creations would be done another day. Working with Rose slowed me down considerably, and part of me would feel quite impatient at this pace, whereas another part of me could breathe more deeply, relaxing into the moment, appreciating so much more than I would at my typical lightning speed pace. Since people with special gifts may work more slowly than the general population, they are often rushed, pushed to complete tasks at someone else's pace, which must be frustrating. Allowing the person you are working with to set the pace is empowering for them.

Another time, Rose inspired me by paying attention to small details which busy people might overlook. We were admiring the strawberry flowers in her community garden, when she realized she had stepped on a plant by mistake. She earnestly bent down, pulling the leaves up and asked me if I would get her some water. She gently watered the plant, which looked so happy being remembered and recognized after being stepped on by mistake. We all glowed in the beauty of this moment.

❤ **Foster patience:** Slowing down may seem less productive at first, yet notice what changes in you and the person you are working with when a slower pace is practiced.

Set Goals

On the day we were to deliver our creations to the restaurant, we were in the car with David, a classmate of Rose's at the program they attended at our local community college called "A Helping Hand". We drove David home once a week so he would have a break from taking the bus home. (You will learn more about David in the third section of this book because I also mentor him). These times when they were together in the car had moments which were rich with learning for all of us. After delivering the arrangements to Something Sweet, we returned to the car. I explained to Rose, the HEART in Haiti School earns $100 each time we make a delivery. Rose's eyes were so wide in surprise at the value of our work together. I explained she could start a project like this to earn money for her business.

Rose said, "I want to set some goals, but they didn't work out well the last time I tried." I asked her to explain what happened, and she tearfully told me how she had set goals at her "A Helping Hand" program, when her teacher told her they were trash and threw them away. My heart broke hearing how discouraged Rose felt and I vowed to help her set goals that she believes in and can accomplish. (I have met the teachers at "A Helping Hand" and can't imagine them saying or doing this, yet this is how Rose expressed how she felt.) Rose brightened and told me goals need to be "time- something, realistic, action-something and something else". With the help of David, because they were both learning these skills in their program, they pieced together the specific requirements for goals, which must be:

- **S**pecific

- **M**easurable

- **A**ction-oriented

- **R**ealistic

- **T**ime-bound

At Rose's home, we set to work brainstorming ideas for her business, estimating fees and expenses, listing possible clients and charities, and discussing business-building skills she might need. Rose was so thrilled with these goals and ideas we wrote down, she ran into her mom's office,

33

making copies for her parents and teachers. She was literally jumping up and down with joy and hugging me, ecstatic that these dreams really may come true.

♥ **Set Goals:** What SMART goals might you want to set in your life? Start by brainstorming ideas. There are no limitations, only possibilities to explore. An important part of brainstorming is the person put everything coming to mind on paper, without worrying about which ideas are great and which will not lead anywhere. This is part of the process, and the great ideas can be sorted from the impossible ideas later.

Validate Achievements

I have felt magical inspiration between Rose and myself, yet I didn't understand the impact of our work together until her mother Patti explained to me that in the past, anytime Rose was asked about working, she would hang her head way down and say in a quiet voice, "I can't work. That is too scary.". However, now when Rose is asked about work, she is filled with enthusiasm, knowing she can and will work. I am really happy our time together has given Rose confidence, and grateful Patti has shared this incredible transformation with me. The combination of Rose's learning in "A Helping Hand" and the close relationship we have developed has allowed Rose to feel safe, hopeful and enthusiastic, rather than fearful as she felt in the past.

I have learned this kind of feedback is rare when working with young adults with special gifts and it was a huge confidence boost for me. I felt excited working with Rose and being part of creating the future she wanted in her life. As a mentor, I am not able to help Rose with a money-earning job, but I am able to help her develop skills through volunteering. This is the perfect way for us to test out what Rose does and does not like to do and to learn business skills along the way, which will serve her well in the future.

❤ **Validate Achievements:** When hearing feedback which validates the important work you are doing, take time to receive this praise and appreciation fully with an open heart. These successes are important to recognize and celebrate. What successes have you and the people you work with achieved and how would you like to celebrate? For me, writing this book has been a way to honor and celebrate successes.

Be Silly

Every trip with Rose is an opportunity to be silly and have fun. Rose and I did a drive-by visit to the community garden and park surrounding it. We passed a nearby boat launch on the Wallkill River. The sun was shining, and I said the river had lots of angels shimmering in the sunlight. Rose asked if I knew a river song. When I said I did not, she grinned and started singing, "Row, row, row your boat…." We sang together, then she started singing with animal noises, "Bark, bark, bark-bark-bark… Meow, meow, meow-meow-meow… Moo, moo, moo-moo-moo…quack, quack, quack-quack-quack…" and on and on. We laughed and sang and laughed and sang some more. It was truly hilarious! When I took her home, she asked if we could put the garbage cans away, so we walked, skipped, and galloped down the driveway, kicking branches that had fallen from a windstorm off to the side as if they were soccer balls. We were helping out her parents and exercising with gusto, which was great and yet what stands out is the utter joy I experience spending time with Rose. This is a real gift for me.

 Be Silly: Allow some childlike play into your life and work.

Listen and Offer Possibilities

There is often quite a bit of planning needed when deciding how Rose and I spend our time together. The previous summer, Rose had a community garden plot next to mine, which was near where she went to school but a thirty-minute drive from her home. Rose's mom said it was challenging to take care of the plot on a regular basis and wondered if there were gardens closer to their home. We found a lovely community garden just a five-minute drive away. Rose, her mom and I attended a meeting with the gardeners. An article had been published in "Soil" magazine about the work Rose and I had done together, which she proudly showed everyone, while also offering to help them weed their gardens. Her generous spirit of wanting to help people was incredibly sweet. Rose decided she would like to rent her own community garden plot for the summer and work on it with me, her mom, and other mentors. We sat down to plan, and I asked Rose what she would like to plant. She said she wanted to grow organic vegetables because her mom needs to eat organic food. Rose wanted to grow hot peppers for her dad and tomatoes for her mom, emphasizing yet again, they need to be organic. I explained this community garden is organic so she didn't have to worry about anyone using non organic things in the garden (like pesticides or chemical fertilizers). Rose wanted to grow carrots, beans, and flowers. Since this was Rose's first garden, I was her guide, offering suggestions of what she might consider planting. Considering what she had already told me she wanted to grow and the twenty by twenty foot plot size, I asked if she would like to try these ideas:

- **rainbow flower garden**, with all the colors of the rainbow
- **sunflower house** where sunflowers are planted in a circle and the tops are tied together to form a house
- **three sisters garden** which is the Native American way to grow corn, beans and squash together. The corn provides a support for the beans to grow up and the squash growing at the base to keep the weeds down.

Rose said yes to all three of these ideas. We were also delighted to discover she had lots of strawberry plants and a blueberry bush in the garden plot she rented. Rose received gifts from her mom and aunt for her garden, like two angels and a windmill, which were great fun to install among the plants.

♥ **Listen and Offer Possibilities**: When you hear input from people, begin by honoring their ideas, then expand options available based on the foundation of their desires. The ideal solution might have a combination of both of your ideas.

Think Outside the Box

There were times we spent gardening together and other times, we worked on different projects. Since Rose loves music and singing along with her favorite songs, for her birthday, she wanted to sing and act out "Defying Gravity" from the Broadway show "Wicked." She was to play the part of Elphaba, the green "wicked" witch, and asked if I would play Glinda. At first, I suggested she ask her other mentor to be Glinda since they went to see "Wicked" in NYC together, but since she was unavailable, I agreed to play the part. Even though I promised to help her get ready for this performance, I didn't know much about acting or singing myself, so I felt both nervous and excited to see what would happen. Taking one step at a time, working from what I do know has made for a really enjoyable experience. First of all, I knew we needed help! I asked Patti if Rose and I could take a few singing lessons together, which she agreed to immediately. We scheduled two lessons before the grand performance, where we learned to do warm-up exercises for our voices and most importantly, got some guidance for learning our parts. Although Rose can read and has all the songs memorized, when she sings along with songs, her words echo after the performer's words, and she lags behind for the entire song. I wanted Rose to be able to sing the words on her own, without the confusion of echoing words of other singers, but I knew she needed extra time to clearly enunciate the lyrics and keep up with the music. Once we learned YouTube videos can have their tempo altered with ease, our teacher helped us find the right tempo: 0.5 or 50% slower than the original song. We would perform "Defying Gravity" in 10 minutes instead of the usual 5 minutes. This is a good example for thinking outside the box.

However, Rose was nervous about having to get all of her words correct and keep up with the pace of the karaoke screen, and she invested quite a bit of effort in trying to talk me out of this method. On our big breakthrough day, I suggested we record the song the two different ways: first singing with the professionals, echoing their words, and second with the karaoke at 50%. Despite being nervous about this new way of singing, Rose agreed to give this a try. I emphasized I wanted her to be the star of her birthday performance, which was exciting to her. During this decision-making time, I knew what I wanted her to choose, yet I didn't want to force any choice on her. I made an agreement with myself that no matter what her final decision was, I would go along with it, despite how much pain or embarrassment I might experience. After all, it was about her goals for her project.

With the echo method, Rose would often get mad at me for missing my cue or forgetting my line, because she kept choosing different versions and the words were not on the screen. Thankfully, she decided to be the star of her own show and to consistently use the same version of lyrics at 50% speed, which carried her to some amazing breakthroughs: she quickly learned her lines and the tempo. This way, I also had confidence to learn my lines, and when we sang together, were able to use the same tempo. I realized if I watched her, rather than the screen, it was easier to stay in synch. Rose excitedly put on her costume so we could record our dress rehearsal, using a stepstool for her to step up and fly for the end of the song. Oh, this was such a wonderful adventure!

♥ **Think Outside the Box:** Sometimes when accommodating special gifts, we need to look at options not typically used, like in this case, slowing the tempo of the music down. Where might you think outside the box when working with people with special gifts? Maybe there is a challenge you are facing in your life. Being open to options and thinking outside the box might lead you to exciting options.

Respond Rather than React

I get excited when the people I am mentoring make a breakthrough, and I often like to send messages to parents sharing our good news. The responses I receive are interesting. Often, there are tears of joy and gratitude for what we are doing together, but occasionally puzzling messages come my way. Here was a puzzling reply from Patti: "Now don't have too much fun. This is a job you know. Lol." How does one respond to this kind of message, when I am working to help their adult child find their passion? Our society is funny, isn't it? We aren't supposed to have too much fun in life. Work ought to be hard, a grind which we suffer through. This kind of outdated and sad attitude has caused so very much pain. Since she was my friend, I felt I could speak my viewpoint more freely. I responded to her in this bold way, "Jobs can be fun, my friend. A different way of living from many... ," and she responded, "Yes indeed. I am so happy for both of you!" Instead of stewing over her comment, I reflected and quickly addressed it with newfound confidence, then moved on to enjoy this time with Rose.

♥ **Respond Rather than React:** When you receive input which is confusing, consider taking time to check in with your thoughts and emotions. This allows time to respond, rather than react. A person's comment may tell you more about the person saying it and their state of mind rather than the actual situation. If the words don't really apply to you or the person you are working with, maybe it should be disregarded.

Uncover Passions

When I mentor people with special gifts, I feel like the divinity inside me meets the divinity inside them, like a spark from a sparkler jumping from one to the other and back again as each person remembers the reason they are here. This process has been transformative for all of us, and it is a tremendous honor for me. When we work on activities that aren't within their calling, exhaustion overwhelms me and I feel like I might fall asleep on the job. When we are doing activities inspired by their spirit, I feel alive as creative energy flows through and around us. We all become more alive as the promises made before this life began are being ignited and fulfilled. Their passions are emerging!

♥ **Uncover Passions:** When exploring possibilities, notice how your body feels or what you notice about how the other person seems to feel by listening to their tone and watching their body language. If an activity feels exhausting, look for other options. If you feel energized, this is a passion worthy of exploring.

Know When the Party is Over

I go on some really wonderful adventures with Rose. We plan our trips and activities together, making sure we explore what interests her most. Rose loves being in and around water, so we have gone hiking to waterfalls, swimming in pools, and splashing in lakes on hot summer days. When Rose and I are playing together, I know without a doubt, we are the luckiest people in the whole world. I check in with myself often to make sure we are following Rose's lead and not my lead: when she is tired and wants to head home, we do. There are occasions, however, when I will step in. For example, after two hours of being with Rose as she stands on the high dive at a pool, where she wanted to jump off, but was too afraid to take the plunge, I knew we needed to get ready to head home. The sun began to ride low in the sky, and both she and I needed rest time plus dinner. This was a decision made in her best interests, which she may not be happy about at the time, yet she is grateful when she gets home. Might she have worked through her fear of jumping if we stayed just a bit longer? This is a question we will never know the answer to, and that is okay for now.

🖤 **Know When the Party is Over:** Exciting adventures are wonderful, yet at some time, they come to an end and rest is needed. How do you know when it is time to end an activity and move on? What may happen if you don't switch gears?

When to Step Back or Forward

When I first started working with Rose, she would dash across streets and parking lots, which was really alarming and scary. Understandably, this was one of the first skills we successfully worked on together. How wonderful to see her now looking both ways as she leads us across streets and parking lots safely. If safety is in question, I have no problem stepping in and helping Rose understand and respond to dangers in wise ways. Once when we were hiking to a waterfall, there was a stray black dog running in the woods. Since we didn't know the dog, I didn't want her trying to pet it, as she typically would do. She was walking very fast toward the dog and despite the fact that I was asking her not to chase the dog, I saw she was increasing her pace rapidly. Finally, I had to grab her backpack and slow her down to explain this dog could hurt her. I felt badly about being physically forceful like this, but it seemed like the only option at the time. Once Rose slowed down to listen to me, even though she was disappointed, she said she was sorry and agreed to leave the dog alone. Thankfully, the dog ran away, and our path was cleared to make our way safely to the waterfall.

❤ **When to Step Back or Forward:** When a situation is safe for exploration, hanging back to allow independence is wonderful. However, when there is danger, taking preventative measures is important. Where do you need to step back or forward? Could it be your expectations might be changed? On the whole, can you step back more in order to allow the person you are working with to have more freedom in a safe way?

Learn to Manage Bureaucracy

Unfortunately, mentoring requires a lot of bureaucratic procedures and paperwork. Learning how to manage all this paperwork in the beginning can be very challenging. One day, Rose and I planned to watch a movie about feelings, which I hoped would help me understand the way Rose describes feelings and give us a platform to stand on for further discussions. Patti was at home this day and I was surprised by what she said to me: "I hope you know; you can't write on Rose's timesheets that you watched a movie together. I hear you having meaningful conversations. That is what needs to be recorded and it needs to be tied into her learning goals." I responded, "Of course, Patti," but I am thinking, "Yikes, what have I gotten myself into?!" Watching this movie with Rose is helping me get to know her and understand the phrases she repeats from movies. It helps me understand how her mind works and how she interacts with the world around her, but now I feel afraid to watch a movie with her. This job is challenging when it comes to establishing boundaries. I need to be clear of my intention for each activity we do together. There are times when Rose has worked hard and needs to rest: our rest time may include chilling out together, listening to music, or watching a movie. It is more fun watching a movie with a friend than it is watching a movie alone. There is so much integrity needed when working with people with special gifts within a bureaucratic system. At the end of the day, the question I ask of myself is if I feel confident in my heart about doing the best job possible with Rose, given her state of being. Here is a note from Patti:

Training a mentor is very challenging for the parent. It's impossible to share twenty-two years of Rose's life, passions, medical issues, scattered skills, etc. in a short period of time, so I find myself stepping back and letting the mentor make their own assessments of Rose. At the same time, there are guidelines from the State Office for People with Developmental Disabilities, which must be followed. To balance the reality of the mentor's role with the state guidelines requires a parent to be robotic and always try to place the activities Rose does with the mentor into a category. While it sounds cold, it is a necessary evil to maintain the funding to pay Rose's staff.

Looking back on this time after having experienced so much as a mentor, I understand why Patti said what she did about not just writing we watched a movie together, but to connect it with a category of Rose's learning objectives. This is the way the system understands we did something of value. There has to be accountability for our work together since the state is paying for it.

However, there are so many thoughts and feelings which come up when doing this work. This requires a lot of conversation, and also times with much silence in order to process those feelings. We often move slowly together and don't see measurable results on the outside. The internal work we accomplish as we bond and grow through simply being together is extremely important. Where on state forms have you ever seen a category for "bonding with person" or "magical moments"? In this way, there is a disconnect between what is necessary in order to effectively mentor a person and the paperwork which must be completed in order to be paid for this work. Over time, I have learned to follow the state-required protocols and not take this aspect of the job personally, allowing me to focus my energy on doing the important work of finding ways to deepen our relationship so Rose could feel safe opening her heart and mind to new possibilities. Through writing these stories, I recognize and value the intuitive work being done, honoring its importance for Rose. Authentic validation needed to come from myself as I witnessed Rose and my hearts blooming through our time together.

Learn to Manage Bureaucracy: When doing intuitive work under a bureaucratic system, it is important to understand the system you are working under in order to follow the requirements correctly. It is also important to recognize the purpose of filling out paperwork that proves to the state work is being done, in order for the mentor to be paid. Bureaucratic issues must be addressed, yet they do not come close to recognizing the deep soul connection which is essential for creating a trusting relationship. How do you do what needs to be done paperwork-wise, while recognizing and valuing the heart centered work which is absolutely essential? Try writing or sharing with a friend the deep connection and learning you notice and receive when mentoring yourself or others. They may be able to help you come up with ideas for how to satisfy the "powers that be", while also acknowledging the deeper spiritual transformations you are inspiring.

Show Understanding with Challenging Habits

The most challenging and perhaps most important part of my job is helping people change habits which are harmful to them. I want to have fun, laugh, witness breakthroughs, and enjoy this mentoring work, but there are times when challenging the status quo is necessary. Rose, who is delightful in so many ways, has one habit that drives me, and lots of people, crazy. She makes a loud snorting kind of noise with her tongue on the back of her throat, while her tongue is sticking out of her mouth. She has been doing this since her teen years. Her mom explains this habit is a comfort to her, especially when she is not feeling well. The problem is, this habit is quite annoying to many people, and when she is doing it, she looks confused and seems to have checked out, which leads people who don't know her to dismiss her. I accept Rose for who she is, and am able to tolerate her habit. Yet I worry mostly about what other people think of her when she is doing this habit. Despite speech therapists' and her family's efforts to help her break this habit, it persists. Part of Rose desperately clings to the habit for the comfort it provides her, and another part of Rose seems defeated, ashamed, defensive, and frustrated because she can't stop.

In the beginning of our work together, we made some progress because I also had a habit that annoyed Rose. I get seasonal allergies sometimes, which makes my nose run at an annoying rate. Instead of constantly blowing my nose to get rid of them, I will sniff, sniff, and then sniff some more to keep the clear liquid from dripping from my nose. This habit used to drive my dad crazy, and it certainly drives Rose crazy. When it happens, she reminds me quite strongly and impatiently, "You are doing it again." I always thank her for the reminders and say I will do my best to change. I am really truly grateful for this awareness because sniffing had just become second nature to me, an easier way to manage allergies, especially when driving, rather than blowing my nose every time. Since I had an annoying habit just like Rose had an annoying habit, this gave me a window to discuss her habit with a feeling of equity, as two equals struggling to fix a habit that annoyed the people in our lives. We made a bit of progress, which was encouraging.

Unfortunately, as she faced health challenges, her habit kicked in stronger than ever. At one point, Rose, her mom, her teachers, and mentors were all feeling quite defeated. We kept trying to come up with new ideas. One day, I counted the number of times she did this behavior in a minute and it was fifty-three one time, then twenty-four later after we had yet another discussion about her habit. I offered a suggestion to put the tip of her tongue on the roof of her mouth as this can be relaxing and would keep her tongue in her mouth. Giggles began as Rose touched her tongue to the tip of her nose, and we both busted out laughing. Comic relief is needed during these tense times. When we met up with her mom that day, I shared the counting and tongue-on-the-roof-of-the-mouth ideas, and we talked about them. Rose went off to the side, not wanting to be present, which I certainly understood.

When it was time to leave, Rose came over to me in the sweetest manner, stroking my face gently and she said, "You know Maria, I've got this. You don't have to worry about me." She was doing her best to tell me to leave her alone peacefully. Part of me was melting, melting with this gentle gesture, yet here is how I responded to Rose, "We are just making observations." She put her head down and walked away. Our goodbye routine vanished in the thin air of dejection. I feel really sad when this scene replays in my mind. Rose was just not open to changing her habit, and all of us were determined to change her mind. Patti offers her perspective:

. . . This habit we call 'suckling' seems to appear more strongly when Rose is sick, not feeling well, tired, or very relaxed. After years of trying to get her to stop, I did not think Maria would be successful either but gave her a chance to try. As a parent of a disabled child, one is humbled so many times during their life that eventually you stop focusing on what other people think and you embrace your child as they are with all of their habits and virtues. Our society puts a lot of pressure on us to be 'perfect', but the reality is, there is no such thing!

Rose's mom was correct. Rose felt comfort from this habit, and we just needed to accept her for who she is. Even though this habit annoys people, it is part of who she is. The gentleness with which she told me she did not want to work on getting rid of this habit shows how loving she is, even in the face of great distress. After this experience, Rose's mom asked us all to stop working on Rose's suckling habit, which I heartily agreed with as I shifted to focus on her strengths, instead of challenges. Rose was able to stand up for what she did and did not want with such gentle love and compassion. Imagine how the world could be if we all learned from Rose's example.

♥ **Show Understanding with Challenging Habits:** Are there any habits you or someone you know would like to change? Being kind during the process and noticing positive habits to accentuate helps shift behaviors with more ease.

Recognize Endearing Habits

Rose has some habits and routines which are absolutely endearing and this is important to recognize. Here is an example of the goodbye routine Rose gifts me with just about every time we work together:

After some shyness and silence, Rose says with a big smile on her face, "Gracias!"
Returning her big smile while waving my body and hand sassily, I say, "De nada mi amiga."
Rose responds to my sassiness with a big smile and lots of giggles each and every time.

Our hearts are united through the magic of our connection and love for each other. This little routine warms my heart every single time!

♥ **Recognize Endearing Habits:** What endearing habits do you or the person you are working with have? How might you recognize and celebrate these beautiful traditions?

Receive Compliments

Rose's mom says, "Rose likes how well you listen to her; how you help her to do the ideas she has; how you allow her to dream outside the box!" This compliment from Patti helped me to understand the effect I have on Rose and to gain confidence in the incredible power of listening. Here is an example of how attentively listening and being receptive, going deeply into the roots of what really matters to Rose helps her believe in herself and open to new possibilities. Rose looks at me with tears in her eyes and says, "Maria, you just make my whole world better, Maria, I love you so much." As Rose says this to me, she is speaking directly from her heart to mine. Nothing in the world matters more than how Rose's world feels better with me in her life. She isn't able to explain why her world is better or what I have done to make her world better, yet I feel deep in my soul how her heart has opened and bloomed, which allows my heart to open and bloom along with her.

♥ **Receive compliments** when they come your way and celebrate how wonderful you are!

Do Less, Allow More

Both on and off the clock, there are times I have helped the people I work with more than was absolutely necessary, and it actually worked against our progress. When I do too much, this leaves the person I'm mentoring out of part of the process of learning. At times, I have to admit, doing too much has also inspired resentment on my part. In this way, it is bad for both of us. I've also had to learn not to do too much work on my off time, when I am not getting paid, and more when they are with me. For example, when we are working on projects that involve coordination with people through emails and phone calls, I sometimes would take care of this correspondence off the clock, partly to save time, because I know I am so much more efficient time-wise doing these things. A phone call might take me five minutes from thought to action to completion. In contrast, when working with Rose, a phone call might take us thirty minutes. When I am short on patience, this inefficiency can seem torturous. But when I am calm and focused on teaching new skills, I have no problem taking the extra time to complete projects.

Managing this issue is all about keeping my mind on the true goals of mentoring. These goals are not about getting things done quickly, but allowing for learning along the way. It can be hard to shift into this gear because most of us live in a fast-paced world that is all about efficiency. The mission of mentoring involves working with each person at their level of proficiency. Even if a task with Rose takes fifty times the amount of time it would take me to complete, we have to turn the spotlight away from how much time it took and onto the progress Rose has just made on mastering a new skill.

One day, Rose's mom told me she noticed I was doing too much for Rose. I knew Rose was tired after doing a lot of gardening that day, so I did one of her chores for her to give her time to rest. However, when her mom went inside to get something for me, Rose had loud music on and was dancing up a storm. Wasn't this important information for me to hear? Rose was tired of structure and gardening, yet she was energized enough to freely dance her heart out. Okay, no more doing chores for Rose, and thank you, Mom, for this important guidance. I realize the more I do *with* people—but not *for* them—the more they learn. The pace of the process may be slower than feels comfortable for me, but that is all part of this work and is a good thing. I am learning the more I empower people through mentoring, the happier I feel and the more they grow. This is a win-win situation for us all.

♥ **Do Less, Allow More:** Where can you step back, allowing more to unfold while doing less? When does a person you are working with truly need help completing a task and when can they accomplish it alone?

Teach With Humor

Rose had a lot of health issues, which her parents and doctors were trying to figure out. She experienced episodes of adrenal failure and this would cause her heartrate to slow way down, leading to fainting, followed by complete exhaustion and confusion. These episodes would often happen without warning, making mentoring Rose pretty scary at times. Working with Rose on a day when she was recovering from an adrenal failure episode, she was moving especially slowly because she was feeling tired and confused. She was taking a long time getting ready and at the last minute remembered she had two DVDs to return to the library. I said, "Oh Rose, we are going to be really close to the Walden Library when we go to our singing lesson, so we can return your videos there." "Oh no!", Rose said emphatically, "We have to return them to the Pine Bush Library." I did my best to explain how all the libraries in the Catskill Ramapo system accept returns for any library, no matter where a patron checks them out. Rose, however, was having none of this nonsense, no matter how many different ways I tried to explain the system. She was convinced the DVDs had to be returned to Pine Bush, where her friend Rebecca worked. This discussion was going nowhere, so I let it go for the moment.

After gardening and having lunch among the flowers, we headed over to Walden. Upon parking the car in front of the library, I turned to Rose and said, "Rose, the Walden Library has a special delivery system and will send your DVDs straight to Pine Bush after you return them here." I was floored to hear her reply, "How cool is that? I didn't know they could do this." Imagine my shock and surprise at not only her openness but also her excitement and willingness to try this new way of returning books. How was this time different from all the other attempts at explaining this to her? I believe there are a few factors:

- Rose heard the idea previously and had some time to process this new information.
- She was feeling better after spending time in the garden and having lunch.
- I explained this new idea in a more magical way, saying they have a "special delivery system," as if Santa Claus himself would put the books in his sleigh and the reindeer would fly them on over to her beloved Pine Bush Library.

Whatever happened, Rose's acceptance of this method which was new to her became a magical way of returning items borrowed from the library. Her mom was thrilled she didn't have to return the DVDs and to hear from Rose about this wonderful way to return borrowed items.

♥ **Teach with Humor:** Since new learning may take time, repetition and different perspectives, how can humor be brought into the process so it feels like fun instead of drudgery?

Speak Directly to the Worry

Some days when leaving Rose at her house when nobody is there, I feel terror building up inside me. I fear she may keel over and die just after I am with her. I imagine deep and loud wailing, mourning her death with her parents. I am so distraught in this vision, her parents need to comfort me, despite their own grief. Where does this all come from? I snap myself out of this nightmare-like terror, and give Rose a call just to make sure she got inside the house safely. Whew, she is fine. Rose has serious medical issues; there is no doubt about that. Where my terror comes from is a mystery to me, so I sought out guidance from my spiritual teacher Dechen. This is what she sees looking at this situation:

In a past lifetime as sisters who lived together throughout their lives, I was Rose's caretaker at the end. I acted brave and did not share my feelings with Rose to spare her my burden in the hope this would allow her to live longer. In response, Rose did not share how tired she was and how she was ready to let go and transition. After Rose died, I suffered from severe depression and my will to live was really weak. Had I expressed my feelings with her, things may have been different, healthier emotionally for both of us. This lifetime, Dechen encouraged me to express my feelings with Rose.

As I prepared to see Rose after the weekend, I vowed to share my feelings with her. After this session with Dechen, the panic I had been feeling about Rose dying faded away, and I simply focused on each moment we had together. I looked forward to restful activities like offering Reiki and doing yoga together. If she was well enough to visit the garden, we could plant some blue flowers to complete her rainbow garden and enjoy the peace of nature.

🌿 **Speak Directly to the Worry:** You may not be interested in examining past life history, yet there is another technique to consider. Close your eyes and take a few deep breaths, bringing your attention to the present moment. Imagine your wisest self sitting comfortably in a chair and Worry, in the form of a person stands or sits in front of you to share their concerns. Notice how Worry looks and feels. Listen carefully and repeat back what you are hearing to make sure you understand what is being said. Then ask Worry if there is anything they would like your help with. Listen to Worry's request and discuss it with them, making a promise you can keep to follow through with Worry's request. Thank Worry for sharing their time and wisdom. Personifying strong emotions and speaking to them has been a powerful tool I have used many times with amazing healing results.

Address Feelings Creatively

Rose takes any kind of conflict hard, including conflict with me. Although it would be wonderful if we never had any disagreements, they can provide learning opportunities for Rose and myself. I realize part of my job as a mentor is to help her with personal communication issues, including learning how to process conflict in respectful, productive ways. For example, at one point, Rose didn't want me talking to her about food, but I couldn't figure out why, and it was quite confusing for me. This issue came out when her mom asked Rose questions about why she likes working with me and what she doesn't like about working with me. Her mom told me Rose struggled for something to say, then blurted out "Food. I don't like when Maria talks about food." No further details were given by Patti. She just said, "So don't talk about food," and nervously laughed a bit.

How do I avoid talking about food when we eat a fair number of lunches together, sometimes going out to a restaurant? One day, we had lunch at Something Sweet, where we fundraised for the HEART in Haiti School with the plants we prepare for their tables. Their food is absolutely delightful. Rose was eating a salad with raspberry vinaigrette and maple glazed walnuts, while I sipped on roasted red pepper soup. I was enjoying my soup and marveling at how Rose was open to eating this healthy food, which was a change from her usual gluten free PB&J sandwich. Losing myself in the glory of the moment, with a big smile on my face, I said, "How is your salad Rose?" Rose immediately frowned and said, "I don't want to talk about food." The smile disappeared from my face as my heart sank in confusion. I regained my bearings, explaining, "When eating yummy food with a friend who looks like they are enjoying themselves, I am in the habit of asking how they like their food to get some conversation going." After a long pause where Rose seemed to be deliberating about what to say, Rose explained, "I am fine with my family and some friends asking me how my food is. I just don't want mentors talking about food."

I was baffled by these words. What on earth to do at this point? Since I am teaching social skills in our work together, I felt this needed to be addressed. I gently said, "That is a bit hurtful Rose, if all those people can talk with you about food, but I am not allowed to." Immediately, her head went down into her hand and she said, "Oh no! I don't want to hurt you in any way. You are my friend and I just love you so much." Yikes, now

58

I felt badly seeing Rose upset. I explained, "We need to discuss these things in order to find ways for both of us to feel comfortable." I talked to her about how, although part of my job is to help her with healthy eating, when we go out to lunch, I am not there to try to teach her about healthy eating. I just want us to enjoy each other's company. Before leaving, Rose said to me, "Your kindness changes people's lives every time we go places." Oh how my heart does melt at times when Rose is so very sweet.

Later that day, I wrote her a poem to sort through the emotions whirling inside of me and show her how much I love her no matter what. Poetry helps me express emotions in a short amount of words and time. The rhyming brings joy and levity, even if the topic is not all sunshine and rainbows. I am able to smile and view situations from a more light hearted perspective, rather than feeling enmeshed in strong emotions. Messages shared with joy are the best of all.

My Friend Rose
We dance and sing, laugh and play,
making the very most of every day.

We can garden, swim, dance, sing, and hike,
finding the perfect activity, no matter what the weather is like.

When there is difference, confusion, or glum.
we talk things out, knowing our best effort will be done

We agree on so much,
most days we are one

Bonded with love and joy,
respect for the earth and oh boy
do we ever have fun!

I wasn't sure how Rose would receive the poem, which felt a bit scary. She didn't respond to the poem when I texted it to her, so I didn't know how it affected her, which was a bit unnerving. I hoped this poem would help us to communicate in a less uncomfortable way.

Soon after I gave Rose this poem, Patti had invited all of Rose's mentors to her Circle of Support meeting at their house. Mentoring young adults with special gifts is a team effort, including parents, mentors, and professionals who assist with obtaining funding, guiding the family through paperwork, making sure the myriad rules are followed, plus encouraging the participant to set goals and reach them. The best Circle of Support Teams are a dynamic group of people, who empower individuals to reach their full potential and be independent. When skills are mastered, needs change and Circle of Support members work together to create new, developmentally appropriate goals, which include appropriate support, so the person may continue to grow. I feel lucky being a member of Rose's team as we guide her in reaching higher than anyone ever imagined possible.

At this meeting, Rose shared my poem with everyone on her Circle of Support team with great joy and pride. Part of me felt so very special to have the poem I wrote her to be both received and shared with such enthusiasm. What an amazing celebration! Another part of me worried the two other mentors there would feel jealous of our closeness. I spoke to Patti about this later, and she told me not to worry. Each mentor has a unique relationship with Rose and a special role in her life. Her mom wrote me a note after the meeting:

. . . this poem really impacted Rose when she received it. She was filled with joy and shared it with me as she danced around. Some months later, while I was preparing a submission for Maria to be nominated for an Outstanding Direct Support Professional Award, I asked Rose's opinion of Maria and why she loved her as a mentor. Rose thought for a moment then quickly ran to get her phone, cruised through her text messages and showed me this poem. Then she said, "That's why I love Maria, Mom."

Can you feel the healing which happened through this poem for both Rose and myself? Even challenging situations that happen when working with people can lead to greater love and connection. I have the advantage of working part time with Rose anywhere from four to ten hours per week. The time for reflection, rest and rejuvenation in between our time together gave me the space to process creatively. This poem was a way for me to express both the loving and confusing parts of our relationship and in turn

60

became a wonderful connection between us. Bringing all aspects of our relationship out into the open was healing for both of us when done in this creative way. Rather than letting resentment fester, the truth was brought to light and released. Rose doesn't like to talk or listen a lot. This condensed form of communication through fun poetry turned out to be a wonderful way to connect intimately with Rose, without using too many words.

Address Feelings Creatively: To process feelings, consider using writing, painting, dance, or other creative outlets to express both the conflict and love you experience in a situation. How do you feel after expressing yourself? Consider sharing your creation if this seems right to you. Each person has unique creative outlets. If you don't know what kind of creativity you enjoy, keep experimenting until you find what works for you. See the Appendix: Simple Ways to Express Feelings Creatively for more ideas.

Find Your Heaven on Earth

One sunny summer morning, Rose and I went to volunteer at Inspire Farm on a day that promised to bring rain. Rose decided to work in the hoop house to stay dry, and what a wonderfully inspiring day we had. This work fills me with great joy. I love seeing the glorious plants in the hoop house with rows of colorful lettuce hugging a bed of majestic garlic, already bursting with scapes, next to luscious fava bean plants loaded with huge pods jutting out and framing the regal eggplant blooms and baby fruit beginning their growing cycle, surrounded by gloriously tall flowering chamomile and comfrey plants. There is such a riot of colors, shapes, and smells there. We both feel a sense of accomplishment when the few weeds intruding on the artistry are removed and clean lines are restored to this masterpiece of both nature and gardener.

Rose and I are most happy when working with the earth, as if a cloud of euphoria surrounds us. The hour and a half of driving is worth the confidence and joy Rose receives from working with this wonderful man. When I dropped her at home after our fun day, Rose said, eyes brimming with tears, "Oh and tell Jon Jon, he is the most pleasant man I have ever seen." I sent this message right away to Jon Jon, who said his eyes also filled with tears. His interactions with Rose were magical, heart-centered, and immensely important to her and the countless other people with special gifts he works with. Jon Jon gives a group of people who are ignored by much of society purpose and hope by teaching them how they can contribute in productive ways and be valued for their work. As Rose's mother wrote after reading this story, "This is why Rose loves Maria so much – she helps Rose find this purpose." Gardening is not only important for the special gifts population, but also for the mentors who work with them. Many people feel a sense of calm when spending time with plants and seeing their efforts pay off in great beauty plus healthy, delicious food. For me, time in the garden or in nature feels like I am in heaven.

🍂 ❤️ **Find Your Heaven on Earth:** When do you feel like you are doing exactly what you have come here for, where you know your purpose and you belong? Each person has unique passions and places they feel most at home. Explore what and where feels best to you. How can you bring more of these experiences into your life? How can you help more people experience heaven on earth?

Recognize Being Out of Balance

Sometimes, when I work with Rose more than usual, I noticed myself being out of balance. After having a fantastic day with Rose and Jon Jon, I experienced insomnia, which typically comes from anxiety, yet this time it was fueled by euphoria, excitement about something I couldn't quite put a finger on. I had the morning for my own gardening and came up with a plan: since Tom was making roast chicken and vegetables for dinner, food Rose enjoyed and could eat, she could come over for dinner after we worked in her community garden and then we could go see the newly released documentary movie, *The Biggest Little Farm*. Rose was excited for this adventure, and so was her mom. I learned later one of Rose's goals was to learn how to be a good dinner guest at someone's home, so this was the perfect opportunity for her. Since she wanted to help, I asked Rose to put the plates and forks around the table and she said, "Cool." How cool is that? She enjoyed most of the food, and at the end of the evening, she said, "Maria (pronounced Mawia), thank you so much for inviting me to eat at your house with your family." Aww, Rose is such a sweetheart. All of this is sounding great, isn't it? Well yes, there were really positive aspects to our time together so far. At this point, I would typically bring Rose home, and I would have the evening to myself and there would not be much more to share.

I made the decision to extend beyond our typical day, which might have been fine if I had slept well the night before and there hadn't been other stressors added to the mix. Rose continues to be challenged with her suckling habit. It is frustrating to her, as well as her family and mentors. As a team, we decided not to work on changing this habit anymore, but now there is an added complication. In addition to her suckling habit, Rose developed a new puzzling behavior of pulling the hair out of her head. Both of these behaviors had been escalating lately, and my patience was running thin. After having less sleep than usual, despite the wonderful activities of the day, I was a bit worn out. On our drive to the movies, I was stewing and feeling agitated, while Rose's habits were kicking in strongly in the car. The tumult inside me increased as Rose made especially loud suckling noises, alternating with passionately singing of songs from Pippin. At one point when we were driving on the highway, a truck veered over into our lane. I was alert, quickly avoiding an accident by swerving into the shoulder. Whew! This scary event was a wake up call reminding me to focus on the situation at hand so we could arrive at the movie theater safely.

There was tension at the movie theater as well. Right behind us, some young people squeezed by an older couple, knocking tea into the woman's lap. The man angrily scolded them. Oh, my nerves were quite frazzled at this point. Rose purchased a medium bucket of popcorn, which she heartily enjoyed eating. She began touching and rearranging her hair repetitively, to my absolute frustration and distraction. I gently touched her arm, guiding it away from her head and asked her to please stop touching her hair, suggesting she put her hood up. She refused to do this. I felt like I was barely holding on to a thin rope of patience and didn't know how to collect myself. I moved one seat away for a bit to gain my composure. She is really sensitive and while I knew this would be upsetting to her, I just couldn't figure out what else to do. I did move back and she apologized, which didn't even feel good because I knew she was struggling. A few times when the frustration built up too much inside me, I put my hands up at the sides of my eyes like blinders and this provided some relief. Reading this story now while doing final edits, I am chuckling at these various tactics I tried to calm myself down. I am not sure why her habit of touching her hair repeatedly was so very aggravating to me. I just think it was a buildup of frustration over time, combined with being tired and lacking my usual patience. Just to let you know, the movie was absolutely amazing and I highly recommend it.

What I didn't recognize until I had returned Rose home and arrived in my driveway at 11:00 pm was Rose had not done any suckling the whole time we were watching the movie. At the theater, I hadn't even noticed this wonderful break from the annoying habit that would have been disruptive to other moviegoers. Instead, I could only focus on her hair touching habit. This is less-than-stellar behavior on my part which I still regret. I am blessed to be a relatively patient person, but I sometimes falter. I am hard on myself when I don't meet my own standards. I have to work on forgiving myself for being human, for being tired and not as compassionate as I wish to be. I see mentors being impatient at times and can be critical of them, too. I know I don't typically work as many hours as they do, and the breaks I have in between sessions with Rose allows me to unwind. I chose to work longer hours over these last couple of days, which gave me a different perspective. I am now more understanding of mentors who work long hours and can relate to the challenges they face trying to muster up patience day after day. This has helped me realize the importance of taking time to balance work and rest. Even though I have amazing fun and joy much of the time I am working with Rose, there are also stressors. I need time to recover. I want to treat people with the utmost respect and kindness at all times. Forgiving myself for having a bad day is important as I find my way in this challenging work. Rose's mom's perspective helped me to understand the situation better:

Raising a child with a disability is unlike any job the average person undertakes. Raising a disabled child who suddenly has a mental health collapse is a nightmare and one questions every parenting move. The irrational behavior appears suddenly and there is no way to be prepared or to prepare a family member or staff. It's especially difficult when you cannot understand why the child is behaving this way and did not begin her life with these bizarre behaviors.

All of us who care for and love Rose struggle during these times. On a day filled with rain, I make time to write, reflect, and spend time in my gardens. I feel myself coming back into alignment, settling into the luxurious flow of life which envelops me when I am present with no expectations. On the other side of less than stellar, I feel grounded and safe, whole and complete. Here is a poem I wrote which helped me process the less-than-stellar times:

Patience
Sometimes I feel like the saint of patience, until I am not........ and it is time to rest................ patience graces my being once again..............until it is gone...........and it is time to rest.............and the cycle goes round and round................................

❤ **Recognize Being Out of Balance:** Remember how I spoke about balancing time to send down roots, resting, and restoring with branching out and taking action? The story I just told shows how I realized when I overextended myself and the results of this decision. How do you recognize when you are out of balance? Being honest about where you are is the most important first step. Take a moment to stand up. Feel your feet on the ground, scan from your feet up through your body to the top of your head. Imagine you are a tree with roots going down into the earth and branches up to the sky. At this moment in time, do you need to focus on sending down more roots or growing out your branches?

Balance Uncertainty with Play

After recognizing how I was out of balance the last time we worked together, along with the uncertainty of Rose's well-being, I needed to muster the courage to continue mentoring Rose. The night before working with Rose the following week, I woke up at 1:00 am, then thrashed and turned in bed before finally falling back asleep. I was unsure what my exact worries were, but I guessed they were Rose related. There was so little joy in that sweet young lady last week. Hopefully, the medicine her parents were trying would give her some relief from this hair pulling behavior. I want to tell Rose, "You are always Jesus' Earth Angel, no matter what challenge you are facing," mirroring language I have heard her speaking many times. Her faith is strong and she feels a close connection to Jesus. My faith is faltering a bit as I struggle to understand why this beautiful Earth Angel is tested so. I miss Rose's spontaneity, joy, and humor.

While writing this, I notice my hand is numb. Looking deeper, I realize I am holding my breath. I pause to take some deep breaths, allowing tension to flow through me and away. I contemplate what we will do together on this morning quenched with steady rain. This might be the perfect weather for us to practice yoga together before taking Rose to the magical massage therapist Mary Elizabeth. I let Rose know Mary loves angels and is excited to meet Earth Angel Rose. How wonderful it was for me to hear Rose and Mary giggling in the massage room. The smile on my face was wide with relief. When Mary finished the massage, she came down raving about Rose, her intelligence, clear knowing of what she does and does not like, plus strong communication skills. Rose fittingly told Mary, "The massage was heavenly."

We went to lunch afterwards at the Greek Grill, Opa! In addition to the food, Rose loved our server, who showered her with attention. She even mentioned wanting to bring her family here in the future. Then, she started talking about how her brother Patrick is obsessed with burgers, laughing about how much he likes them. I mentioned she just ordered a burger and Rose told me eating them sometimes is okay. I feel like she was worried about also becoming obsessed with burgers, yet didn't have the language to express this directly, so did this through a story about her brother.

Rose had a cheeseburger on a gluten free bun and a pile of French fries. I don't understand, even though I sat through the whole experience, how it could take her so very long to eat. She carefully picked all the lettuce, onion, and tomato off the burger first, then proceeded to empty half the ketchup bottle onto her plate and burger. She then started shoving large amounts of burger and fries into her mouth, followed by chewing and drinking water. I am a fast eater, so I sat and watched her eat for an hour. I suggested she bring some of the fries home, since there were so many. Rose definitely did not like this idea, which she shared with a strong "No" and head shake. I made this suggestion once more because I was asked to watch how much Rose eats since her family said they don't want Rose gaining weight on this new medicine.

What can I do about this as a mentor? I could only offer the suggestion to bring some food home. Since she refused, we moved on from there. I don't believe it is my job to take the food she is purchasing with her own money away from her. She is twenty-two years old, an adult making decisions for herself, decisions she will need to experience the effects of. There are times during mentoring when I just have to accept the choice a person makes, even if I feel this choice is not in their best interest, and I don't understand why they made this decision.

On our drive home, I asked Rose if she was going to tell her parents about Opa! and ask if they wanted to go there when they take her to camp. She got quiet then said with great uncertainty, "I don't know what they would say." I suggested she couldn't find out what they would say unless she asked them. She didn't respond. Something was bothering her that she couldn't express. She sat in silence, pulling more hairs out from her scalp. I repeated this prayer in my head a few times, "I bless you with all the peace and joy your heart desires." In a few moments, Rose somehow snapped out of her stewing mood and started telling me about how she collected and put out the garbage on the day after Father's Day. She asked if I would help her bring the garbage and recycling bins up to the house today.

By the time we got to her long winding driveway, the rain which had come down steadily all day long magically ceased. Rose asked if she could sit in the back of my trunk, hold onto the two large cans with wheels while I drive slowly. She asked me this before and I had said no. I didn't want to crush her good mood, so I suggested she show me what she had in mind. I opened the trunk on our SUV type car. She climbed into the trunk with bits of straw still scattered from when we purchased straw for her garden. I brought over the two rolling cans, asking her once again how this would work. She said she would hold onto the cans and I would drive up slowly and carefully like her mom does. Feeling very uneasy, I said, "I don't know Rose. This makes me nervous. I am going to leave the car parked here and am happy to help you roll these up the driveway." In this instance, I was not willing to engage in what I viewed as risky behavior, which I stated. Rose was able to engage in conversation and compromise. We were both honest and willing to be flexible. Contrasted with our discussion about bringing home some of her food, this negotiation was a great success.

Rose began organizing her things into her backpack, which took a long time. While waiting for her, I checked out the luscious puddles in their grass created by the drenching rains of the day. I began dancing in the warm puddles, which is one of my most favorite things to do on a hot summer day. I stopped dancing upon noticing Rose all packed up and ready for our adventure. She looked at me and said, "Did I ever tell you, you are crazy?" Laughing, I asked if I was a good kind of crazy. She laughed, then got really serious asking, "Can you do that again?" Both of us were howling as I gladly honored her request, leaping over to the puddle with joy, dancing around, then bouncing back to Rose. Oh, the frivolity and joy we share together is such a blessing! This moment is especially precious when contrasted with the silence and hair pulling from not so long ago on our travels. I basked in this glorious moment when Rose's joy returned and we reveled in silliness together.

Let me share a story which happened on another day, when Rose balanced a time of uncertainty with play. Rose just had a health scare at school and on top of that, had misplaced her planner. We searched everywhere we could think of, asking anyone we saw. Eventually, I told Rose it was time for us to leave so she could get home to rest. On our walk out, we passed the skeleton of a Mastodon that had been named Sugar. It sat in a lobby of her classroom building and was actually a skeleton which had been excavated in this area. How cool is that? Rose turned to Sugar as she passed it on our walk down the stairs, asking, "Do you know where my planner is?" The mastodon was silent. "Of course not. You don't speak," Rose said, followed by peals of laughter. I was impressed by her sense of humor, which eased the stress she was feeling. When we crossed the street on our way to the car, she asked a street sign, "Do you know where my planner is?" Silence. "Of course not. You don't speak," she said, once again followed by lots of laughs. I am not completely sure if she created this dialogue herself or if these were lines from a movie—it could be a combination or it could be a Rose original. You, the reader, might know more than I. Disney movies are her favorites and she knew lots of lines from them. Her humorous dialogue had both of us cracking up and feeling better after the worry of the health scare and lost planner.

♥ **Balance Uncertainty with Play:** When you experience challenging times, how can you find ways to bring play and frivolity into your life? This is a wonderful strategy because when we find ourselves in challenging situations, often our mind can shut down and block us from considering other options. A little bit of silliness can shake the stuck places in our mind loose, allowing more flow and options. You know how salt sticks together sometimes when it sits in the same spot for a long time? Then if you shake the container it is in, the salt loosens up and flows? This is similar to what happens with our minds, our thoughts get stuck together, but if we shake them up with fun, the stuck thoughts loosen up, and new ideas can flow in as old ideas flow through freely.

Shift Focus

Sometimes, one has to shift the focus of a conversation in order to avoid conflict. Rose and I spent the day at Minerals Spa, where there are beautiful pools, waterfalls, tunnels, and high jumps. As we walked to pick out lounge chairs to sit on, Rose said, "Camp was spectacular." I asked, "Can you share what was spectacular?" Rose responded, "Oh boy." With those two words, I realized this conversation had come to an end, which was disappointing to me. Later, I asked, "Rose, how is your ice cream?" Rose responded sassily, "So how is the nature around here?" We both laughed and I praised Rose. Rather than being mean and growling, "I don't want to talk about that now," when I asked her about her food, she had simply switched the subject. She responded, "I didn't want to be mean." We played and danced in the sprinkler park and she was delighted to pet a bunny, baby ducks, chicken and goats at the petting zoo. Rose said, "This is the best day of my life."

As you know by now, Rose takes a long time doing everything, including getting ready. With this new obsession of pulling out her hair, things take even longer and are more painful for me to witness. She was pulling out and breaking the hair on her scalp in the large mirror at the spa. I am dedicated to focusing on the positive with Rose. Not saying anything to stop this destructive habit is very difficult for me. Focusing on what she is doing well feels so much better.

I was ready and told her to let me know if she needed help in any way. Instead of watching her get ready, I decided to read my book until she got dressed. Because I took my focus away from trying to hurry her and was in fact directing attention away from her, she hustled to dress and was ready in no time. I was happy because I enjoyed a little bit of reading and this diversion helped Rose focus on getting dressed. When she was ready, I put the book away and we skipped off to our next adventure.

❤ **Shift Focus:** When you feel overwhelmed by a situation, have you ever tried switching your focus, like Rose did with me by asking another question and like I did with her by reading a book while she got ready?

Build Trust with New People and Situations

Helping the people I work with to feel safe with people and new situations can be challenging at times. One way Rose bonds with people is to give them silly nicknames. She delights in calling my husband Tom, who is over fifty years old and stands at over six feet tall, "Tommy Boy." We get a kick out of that too, so much so, we even used this nickname for his retirement party invitations. Since Rose and her family are longtime friends, we invited them all to this party at our cabin in the woods near Wolf Lake. I stayed at the cabin to give directions, coordinate food, and greet people when they arrived. When Rose arrived with her family, her dad asked me to come down the driveway to say hello. She gave me a huge bear hug and explained she had been waiting for me to come down to her because she felt nervous about joining the party. The combination of a hug and sharing her feelings helped Rose overcome her anxiety and feel comfortable walking up with me. Patti said Rose was feeling afraid to have fun at the beach, which was unlike her. Patti was relieved seeing Rose at ease after spending a little bit of time with me. I wondered why Rose was anxious at the beach and now felt relaxed after seeing me. I was grateful my presence was a comfort to her. We had quite an eclectic mix of people attending: our nuclear family, science and yoga teachers, Haitian and American people. Shad was grill master and emcee, playing dance tunes and Haitian music, kept at a lower than usual volume so people could chit chat.

Rose immediately felt comfortable, introducing herself with a handshake to all of our guests, selecting gluten-free food and most importantly, a burger for dinner. Rose got tight with Shad, and it wasn't long before she was dancing, sometimes on the picnic table, having a wonderful time. Our daughter, Anna also loves dancing and had a plan with Tom to do some twerking together, so I was called out to join them for these hip jerking, bum jiggling moves, then Rose jumped right in with us. What fun to let loose for a bit and have a silly, fun time. Patti commented about how comfortable Rose felt with our family. Rose's anxiety had gone, and she even gained access to the microphone from her buddy Shad. She was making speeches at the end of the party, sending her mom off to get her phone so she could read the poem I wrote her a couple months ago. Rose revels in being center stage when she feels comfortable and welcome.

After everyone watched fireworks at the lake, it was time for goodbyes. Rose gave me a long hug, resting her head on my shoulder and sighing, "I wish this could last forever." Oh, to be loved so very much is quite a gift. I suggested she could sleep over at the cabin sometime, and she blurted out, "Three weeks!" I said, "Oh that would be a long time. We don't usually stay here that long." Rose's mom laughed and explained Rose meant she has plans the next few weeks but would be available after three weeks. The contrast between Rose's anxiety at the beach with her frolicking fun at the party shows how Rose has come to trust not only myself, but our family and friends. She feels safe being her silly, fun self when with us. For some reason, Rose didn't feel this open, free atmosphere down at the beach.

♥ **Build Trust with New People and Situations:** What allows you to trust people in unfamiliar situations? How do you help people feel safe to express themselves freely? What helps people you work with to feel safe and comfortable? How do their needs differ from your own?

Set Clear Intentions

I took a week off working because Rose was away at camp and Tom was recovering from hernia surgery. Even though I work part time, I find distance gives me time to recharge and gain valuable perspective. Over the weekend, I attended Matt Kahn's retreat at Omega Institute in Rhinebeck, NY. He is an amazing teacher and role model for living a life powered by love; we can learn to love ourselves, the people in our lives, and every situation that arises, if we approached with joy, humor, and authenticity. One thing Matt teaches is to set intentions before situations which may be challenging. For example, Rose sometimes says things that trigger me to feel offended. Like many intuitives and caregivers, I am super sensitive. To help counteract this tendency, I decided to set this intention in my head the next time I was driving to her house:

> *I want to hear what you have to share and I do not allow you to speak to me in disrespectful ways. And so it is.*

I knocked on the door, and Rose came to greet me with a soft and mellow hug, accompanied by a gentle sigh and light caress on my back with her hands. No words of greeting were offered, nor were they needed. I could feel her express in a very real way, *I missed you and it is so comforting and wonderful to have you here today.* This is an example of appreciating the unspoken with Rose. She shifted gears and was joyfully dancing, showing me some moves from the Disney movie "Leap" she had recently watched, plus asking me how to do those big jumps. Rose was performing some wonderful spins and then morphed into doing some yoga moves like "chair," flowing into balancing on her toes, followed by "stretch of the dancer." Our time together was filled with deep, joyful connection, and I felt setting an intention before working together which stated how I did and did not want to be treated contributed to making our time together delightful for both of us.

❤ **Set Clear Intentions**: Is there an area of your life where setting an intention of what you would and would not like to happen might be worth trying?

Get to the Root of the Problem

While working with people, it can sometimes be challenging to understand the root of an issue. One day, while I was waiting for Rose to get ready, her dad, Joseph, started talking about Rose's Garden and how he used to till his gardens and water them every day. Rose got nervous hearing this discussion, as I have noticed before, saying she doesn't want to "start rumors." The language she uses doesn't always exactly make sense to me: we were openly talking about our different methods, so there were no rumors, just different philosophies. After a few moments, I noticed Rose was not with us, and I asked where she was. We found her in the TV room not looking too well. Joseph called Patti right away to check if she was struggling this morning, which Patti said she had not been. With Rose's adrenal failure episodes, there can be warning signs, so this was important for him to find out. Joseph gave Rose an ice pack for her head, she laid back for a bit and in a little while was feeling better. She got ready relatively quickly and we went off to her Community Garden plot, feeling pretty good, but the Rose with me then was not the joyfully dancing Rose who first greeted me. I wondered what caused this shift to occur.

Upon arrival, there were sparrows eating her sunflower seeds, which was sweet. We stopped to take some pictures for the cards we planned to make. Some bugs began swirling around her head. She didn't have a hat, and they were annoying her. I gave Rose my hat, which was a bit too big on her. She kept the hat for a bit, yet stopped often to scratch her head. As a remedy to Rose's hair pulling, her parents shaved her head, to see if this might be a way to shift this destructive habit. Now that she didn't have hair to pull, she started scratching her head, causing it to bleed, form scabs, and then the whole cycle continued. It is hard to know what triggers this behavior, but it seemed something had stressed her out this morning as she was scratching while we were working.

This whole scratching and picking habit was one I am quite familiar with, I do admit. Part of me wishes this weren't the case and yet, I also feel like having experience with this nervous habit helps me understand why Rose would do this. In fact, when I saw how Rose started this habit familiar to me, I vowed to work on my habit of scratching and picking scabs myself, to help her. For a long time, I had picked and scratched my head too. I would have scabs on my head, which would be annoying and to get rid of them, I would pick them. They would bleed and make it worse, creating a whole vicious cycle. Currently, I don't have any head scabs, thankfully. I've succeeded in stopping this habit but I do have bug bites and scratches on my arms and legs, which I do pick at, so I am still learning how to stop these self-harming behaviors.

Picking is a curious thing. I do believe there is an anxiety that spurs people to start looking for something to pick. I will even visit healed spots of skin which had a spot I picked for many weeks and feel disappointed to feel smooth skin. When I do find a rough patch where a scab can be picked, there is a sense of relief. It hurts to pick off the scab and when it is off, there is a sense of both accomplishment and shame, especially if the area starts bleeding. There are internal vows to be better the next time, until the next time comes and the urge to pick just becomes way too great, and this partially unconscious habit perpetuates. I can relate to Rose's challenges with changing her habits and hope we can both make progress.

I believe part of Rose's trouble this morning may have been affected by Joseph and myself discussing our different gardening philosophies. She interpreted our discussion as an argument. Maybe this is just another thing she obsesses over? I believe Jon Jon tills some of his plots because he has so much land to care for with limited help. Maybe next time we visit his place, we can discuss tilling versus not tilling, so she can hear a number of different views and realize it is okay and very healthy to have a diversity of opinions. If Joseph wanted to till her garden next year, we could try that. I wonder if what Rose perceived as an argument caused her to be upset, shut down, and then pick at her head. Since Rose isn't able to express herself, we may never know the reason. What I have come to learn about myself is if I feel anxious about a situation, I feel like I have done something wrong and will be hard on myself, or pick on myself both mentally and physically. Often, the picking starts before I am aware of the cause of the anxiety.

Get to the Root of the Problem: Are there times when you are challenged to understand why someone is acting the way they are? Taking time to review the situation from a detached perspective, to discern what might be causing a challenge may help with understanding. Asking these questions about the situation might help:

- Have you noticed this behavior in the past?

- What might you be feeling if you were in their place?
- Is the person aware of their feelings?
- How do you feel about what you are observing?

Explore Without an Agenda

Rose was tired and disoriented when I picked her up, and I told her how brave she was to go off on an adventure, even though she was not feeling especially well. I followed her lead for the pace at which she wanted to move and rest. If she seemed uncertain about where to walk, I would give her two choices, for example, I asked if she wanted to walk in the woods or along the lake, and she chose to walk near the lake. Right away, there were three dogs approaching us, and I suggested Rose ask if she could pet them, which worked out really well. All three dogs were friendly. She first pet the white dog with black spots, then when the two brown dogs came, Rose sat down on the trail to give and receive lots of love. The dogs felt like angels who swooped in to offer Rose comfort. We hadn't planned to meet them, they simply appeared when she needed them most.

Next, we walked by a cove at the end of the lake which was rich with wildlife. I pointed out the blue heron, turtles, ducks, geese, and birds that were visiting this abundant, secluded area. If Rose couldn't see an animal, I took a picture of it so she could look at it up close. After knowing what to look for, she was able to search again to see it herself. When we got to the wooded side of the lake, we sat down to observe the wildlife, hiding in a natural screen of trees. We took pictures of wildlife to share, then she showed me videos from her vacation with her mom. Rose enjoyed the peace of sitting and observing nature, and I felt like Mother Nature was holding us in her hands, healing us both. We did walk a bit further to a bench by the lake where frogs entertained us with their delightful chirping. Rose went in search of where they were and one went leaping into the water with a big splash. Rose told me even on days when she doesn't feel well, she is still happy to do things with her mentors and to have a positive attitude. On our return walk, I shared with Rose how I noticed her hands were more settled today, compared to yesterday, which means she was not scratching her head. For me this was quite a relief. It seemed as if spending time in nature, exploring without an agenda was healing for Rose.

Driving back home, she seemed to get anxious and was touching her head more. She started spinning her fidget spinner, which I believe was her strategy to keep from scratching so much. I admire her determination to continue working on changing this habit. Rose finished her lunch while I filled out paperwork for the day. She wanted to stay outside to finish her lunch, so we said our goodbyes with a hug and then I danced, skipped, galloped, and twirled my way to the car. Rose was delighted by this exiting dance and the time we spent exploring in nature, which seemed to be healing in ways I could observe and my guess is also in ways I will never know.

♥ **Explore Without an Agenda:** When is the last time you went exploring without an agenda, in nature or another place where you love to be, like an art gallery or a town you have never been to? Notice how you feel before, during and after your explorations. What shifts are you aware of?

Teach and Model Respectful Behavior

Often, I am called upon to help people learn respectful behavior. After a period of illness, Rose was feeling better, which meant her sense of humor had returned. She was laughing, telling me I was freaking her out when I danced with my shoulders in the car. We have such fun playing together! One challenge we sometimes have is with time management. As I've mentioned, she takes a long time eating. On this day, she had ordered a gluten-free carrot cake for dessert, which she loved and insisted on finishing the entire portion, designed for at least two people to share. I suggested she bring some home to her mom and she said her mom wouldn't like the shape of the cake, which cracked me up because it was such a lame excuse for eating the whole thing herself. I suggested she pack up the cake to finish at home later, but she refused. Earlier at lunch, she had a serious discussion about why using a cell phone during lunch was disrespectful. This came up because I asked to see pictures from the family wedding she attended over the weekend. She had left her cell phone in the car, and I suppose she reasoned since using a cellphone during lunch was disrespectful, she did a good thing leaving her phone in the car.

I thought about this theme of disrespect, since she had brought it up. Because her plan to devour the whole carrot cake would make us short on time for getting home so I could work with David, I explained her unwillingness to pack up some of the cake to eat later was disrespecting both David and me. I was very calm while discussing this and extremely patient, repeating the same words several times until the words sunk in. Rose learns best with calm repetition. Inside I was fuming and yet, I funneled that energy into being patient and clear about how her behavior was affecting me and other people. In order for me to teach Rose to respect David and myself, I needed to respect her, even though the way she was behaving was triggering a lot of frustration inside of me. If I chose to yell and try coercing her, I would be modeling how to disrespect her. I wanted to show Rose a better way.

After much patience on my part, Rose finally snapped into recognition and apologized. I praised her for choosing to change her behavior and pack up the cake. I told her I realized how challenging it was for her to adjust because the carrot cake seemed to have her under a spell. Just after saying this, a fun song came on and we both started singing and giggling our way out of the restaurant. I was proud of handling the situation with patient firmness and then being able to switch to a fun mood, rather than holding on to the intense frustration I had felt. Rose apologized several more times, which was another annoying habit we were working on changing. I repeated the good news about how well she respected my wishes by changing her behavior. I hope someday, she will be able to apologize one time and move on with confidence from there. With love and patience, I imagine she will be able to do this.

🖤 **Teach and Model Respectful Behavior:** Being loving, patient and compassionate when setting respectful boundaries with someone who is resistant and disrespectful is worth the effort because the person will feel your good intentions and shift more easily. You will be modeling how to be respectful, even when your feelings have been hurt, which is an important skill to develop. Sometimes, you may be too upset to speak in a kind way. Taking a few breaths, stepping away to regain your composure or even choosing not to respond until you are able to speak in a kind tone are all strategies to try when you feel angry at how you are being treated. You can honor what you are feeling by taking the time you need to process, while also being mindful to address the issue when you are ready.

Find Meaning in Every Situation

Sometimes, even in the middle of a not-so-great day, inspiration can appear. One day when working with Rose, we both weren't feeling well, so I asked if she wanted to try some yoga. We started to do a gentle yoga class together, and it was clearly too much for Rose, who struggled to balance and do anything active. I remembered Yoga Nidra, which is full body relaxation, so Rose and I decided to give this a try. We set up pillows and blankets on her living room rug, got nice and cozy, then listened to a lovely woman guide us through deep breathing and relaxing all parts of our body. We both dozed off after the deep relaxation, which helped us both. I waited until she woke up and then we colored together, had some lunch, and enjoyed a mellow day together. Rose's energy and symptoms fluctuated throughout the day–she would have energy, then crash and go on this up-and-down cycle without warning. Rose seemed stable, and I was getting a bit antsy, so I asked if she would like me to collect the recycling and garbage, then bring the cans down to the bottom of the driveway.

When I brought the large rolling cans down her long driveway, I noticed some large black and green cicadas. I even found one live cicada on its back and was able to move it over to the grass. Not long after this, a cicada landed on my shoulder and traveled down a good portion of their driveway with me. When walking back to the house, I picked up two deceased cicadas to show Rose. She was both scared and interested in these curious creatures, so we looked up information about them, watching a video that showed the cicada's life cycle from a long period of dormancy in the ground to their short lives above ground, where many different animals enjoy eating them. What fascinating creatures they are. I looked up the spiritual meaning of cicadas on Totem Wisdom.com https://totemwisdom.com/?s=cicada and found this description:

The Cicada is a symbol of rebirth and longevity. People with this totem are strong communicators and often find rewarding opportunities as the result of patience and persistence. Their callings sometimes come later in life after a period of seclusion. Cicada teaches communication through music – it's song is easily recognizable and noticed by others. Cicada also speaks of the ability to "shed one's skin" and emerge as something new and different in life. Coming out of your shell and expressing yourself authentically are themes of this totem.

Cicada remains underground for much of its life before emerging. When cicada appears to you it speaks of a need to come out of hiding, to break free of what restricts you.

While I do not know if cicada is my official totem animal, these words really speak to me during this time of life, where I am finding a new and meaningful profession mentoring young adults with special gifts. While I have not been officially in hiding, I am not out and about networking with a lot of people the way I did when I wrote my previous book. I feel like I am discovering more of my authentic self each day, which is truly liberating. This book and my experiences will be of help to people working with adults with special gifts and a way for me to reach out more. Maybe the wisdom of the cicada has meaning for Rose as well. This time of health challenges may be compared to the time cicadas spend underground, waiting to be reborn. She is being forced to slow down, to live in a more yin way, sending her roots down. I wonder how Rose will choose to come out, shed her skin, and be reborn. Maybe the symbol of the cicada was honoring the place we both were in of growing more roots, while also showing us there will be a time when we will shift to send out branches.

❤ **Find Meaning in Every Situation:** Sometimes we want to be calm when we are agitated or energized when we are sleepy. How can you acknowledge how you are feeling and work *with*, instead of *against* this emotion in your day? Honor what is happening in the moment, while choosing activities which gently shift you in the direction you prefer to go. Be open to inspiration, whether you are growing roots or branches.

Accept Disappointment

Rose had been sick for over a week now and I was hoping she would be feeling well enough to visit her community garden plot. I talked and texted with Rose's mom the night before I was due to work with Rose and it seemed like she might be okay to spend a bit of time in the garden, getting some fresh air and Maria-time in. I was excited to see her and gathered seven jars so we could collect flower arrangements with all the colors of the rainbow she had in her garden. I figured doing a quieter, more artistic project at her garden, rather than the hard weeding work we often did might be healing for Rose. I checked to make sure we had scissors and a container to collect the flowers, as well as a bowl to collect veggies. I packed a healthy lunch, clothes to change into since we got soaked on hot days with hose water fun. I packed the folder with our paperwork, along with two pens. I was excited to see Rose because I wanted to share some ideas for putting our words to music. This was a secret project we were working on together. Rose wanted to surprise our families by performing the song we wrote together. Are you noticing how much time and energy I put into planning before working with Rose, when I am not being paid? I say this because the success we have when working together on the clock, when I am getting paid has a lot to do with the love and dedication I put into reflecting on the time we have been together, plus planning our activities.

Patti called just before I was ready to leave, saying Rose was not doing well, and they were going to Urgent Care. I was worried about Rose and hoped she would be okay. Also, can you imagine after all the preparation I had done for our day together, how very disappointed I was that we would not be working together that day? Yet, this is what happens when people have health crises which need to be attended to right away. I have learned to adjust and make other plans when the schedule changes. They planned to stop by our house after the appointment because Rose wanted to see me. My hope was she would be well enough to visit our house and would not have to be put in the hospital. They were able to help Rose this time without admitting her to the hospital. I was thrilled she stopped by after visiting the doctor for a hug and quick re-connect and had found other activities to do that day. If I had depended on being paid in order to live, there would have been an added layer of distress, but since this wasn't the case for me at this time in my life, I was able to adjust to having a day off.

♥ **Accept Disappointment:** Feel what it would be like chiseling your plans for the day in stone, as opposed to writing your plans in the sand at the edge of the ocean. How would you feel about changing your plans with these two scenarios? How might you balance planning while also being adaptable?

Dance as if Nobody is Watching

Sometimes, I run into other colleagues from the support team around town. Tom and I were in the grocery store one morning, and there were hardly any people in the store. He was following behind me pushing the shopping cart when the song "Everybody dance now" came over the store speakers really loud, ba ba ba ba ba, and I started dancing in the middle of the aisle. I heard a loud voice saying, "Maria?" I turned around to see one of Rose's Circle of Support team members looking at me. I said, "Hey, now you know why Rose and I get along so well!" She replied, "It is too early to be dancing like that." I laughed at her comment and moved on. In the car on our way home, Tom shared what he observed at the dance scene. He had said quite loudly as if he didn't know me, "How'd you learn to dance like that?" while an employee looked at me with his head tilted. I hadn't realized people were watching me because I was filled with so much joy in the moment. Imagine how the world would be changed if more people expressed joy spontaneously and openly on a more regular basis.

♥ **Dance as if Nobody is Watching:** When do you allow yourself the freedom to dance and be silly, not worrying about what anyone thinks of you?

Get Organized

Rose's health had improved tremendously, for which I was extremely happy. We were back to working in her garden, a place which brought us great peace and joy. We were there one sunny September day, after it had been abandoned for over a month. Both Rose and I liked our gardens to be neat and orderly, so we were a great team, yet had different styles. There were a lot of sunflowers which were past their prime and needed to come out. Sunflowers have deep roots and strong stalks, which makes pulling them out challenging. I figured out a quick removal technique of bending the stalks back and forth, which often worked well, but sometimes the stalk would break and make a mess. The stalks had many rough branches sticking out from the main stalk, and if they touched our skin, would scratch and hurt. I was not in calm awareness when we first started this process and I overwhelmed Rose. She spoke up strongly, asking me to wait and work together. I admired how confidently she spoke her wishes out loud a couple of times and I finally slowed down to understand her methods. She asked me to strip the lower branches off so they wouldn't get in our way when pushing and pulling on the plants to get them out. Her method was really smart because it kept our arms from being scratched so much.

We were successful in pulling out all the sunflowers that day. When she got a bit tired, and I was still raring to go, I worked on a section of sunflowers in the corner, away from where she was weeding on the ground and pulled them out using my original method. My arms got all scratched up, which wouldn't have happened if I had worked slowly, stripping the leaves first, like Rose taught me. Maybe next season I will remember this lesson from Rose and my arms will be happier. Mentoring is an interesting experience because there are times when I teach Rose important lessons, and there are also many times she teaches me invaluable life lessons.

🌱 **Get Organized:** When feeling overwhelmed, taking time to organize your desk, house or garden is a great way to bring order to the space you are in, which often brings more order to your mind. How you organize is important. Rose taught me an important lesson in slowing down and considering how to get organized in the most effective way, causing the least amount of harm. Sometimes, we might feel like the mess in front of us is way too big to manage. Instead of organizing your desk, you might want to just throw the whole thing in the dumpster and the sooner the better. Slowing down and getting organized systematically is a wiser method and one Rose had to repeat several times in order to teach me. Insanity is doing the same thing over and over, expecting different results. How about opening your heart and mind to a new way of getting organized? Teachers sometimes show up in the most unexpected places.

Honor Friendships

Unfortunately, Jon Jon, the director of the Inspiration Farm, was leaving. Rose and I were invited to his going away party, which we were both excited to attend, yet we were sad about him leaving. At first, the room full of people with a variety of special gifts was overwhelming to Rose. She asked me, "Are you sure these people are okay, and we are safe?" I assured her this was a good group of people we could trust. We inched our way further into the crowd. A man was standing up front speaking into a microphone, looking intently at Jon Jon. I am sure he knew what he was saying, but the sounds coming out of his mouth were like loud moaning, with no words understandable to me. Jon Jon listened with his whole body, giving this man his full attention, as challenging as that must have been for him. After a while, the man's aide encouraged him to finish his speech, and we all clapped.

How delighted Jon Jon was to see Rose. He remembered her name, despite the number of people he works with and the fact that we have only visited a half dozen times. Jon Jon patiently opened her present of green beans, kale, and a pepper she grew from her garden. They each picked up a green bean, tapping them together as a toast before eating them. The DJ and his assistant were fantastic and played some amazing songs, while encouraging guests to request songs. They also had instruments we could play, and Rose enjoyed drumming and dancing her heart out. How wonderful it was to see her joy and exuberance for living fully, despite still wrestling with serious health challenges. The energy in the room was electric as could be with people dancing, singing, playing instruments, and enjoying the celebration. I felt great joy, but also a bit melancholic because DJ Brown, reminded me of my brother. While his skin was darker than Evan's, physically he was similar, with his curled-up hands and arms, challenges with sitting up, and drooling onto his shirt. Just like Evan, DJ Brown loved music and he was fortunate enough to have more skills than Evan. He could sing karaoke, and I could understand what he was saying, plus he played a tambourine to the beat of the music. What a lucky man he was to have these skills in order to express his joy with music. Maybe Evan was on the other side singing and keeping a beat right along with us all.

On our ride home, Rose said, "That was one heck of a party" and once again played her usual playlist. After a bit of time, she was fighting hard to stay awake and I suggested she take a short nap during the last part of our trip. She reluctantly agreed because no matter how much she longed to keep the party going, her body just needed to rest.

After arriving home, Rose shared a song for me to sing to my daughter Anna who was leaving for California the next day. The song was "Not That Far Away" by Jennette McCurdy. Rose asked what time Anna was leaving. I said "8:00 am." Rose asked, "What time are you getting up?" I replied "6:30 am." Immediately, Rose said, "Good, there is enough time." I did play this song for Anna the next morning with tears streaming from my eyes as Jennette sang about California being not that far away, the dream she is chasing, how she is writing the story of her life, and that she will call every night to say, "I love you." One cool coincidence is Jeanette looks very much like Anna's travel partner Kyla.

Rose and I showed our gratitude for the friendship Jon Jon offered us. Rose showed me friendship by sharing the song about California for me to play for Anna. Both of these experiences touch my heart deeply, especially since people with special gifts have challenges forming close relationships. Because they interact with the world a bit differently than the average person, it takes time and patience to form strong bonds, yet the efforts are beautifully and uniquely rewarded.

❤ **Honor Friendships:** How do you honor important friendships in your life?

Decide When or if to Speak

Thankfully, Rose's health improved greatly over time, and she was getting excited about the upcoming holiday season. Even before Halloween, Rose had been playing Christmas songs by her favorite acapella group, Pentatonix. The same playlist rings loudly in our ears each and every time we are in the car, so loud it is hard to hear anyone in the car talk. And you know what the worst part is? Not the repetition, nor the noise or the fake cheer — none of these is the worst. The absolute worst part is that *I was the one who introduced Rose to Pentatonix*. Augh! What was I thinking? Because she loves them so much, David, and I have to listen to these same holiday songs over and over again at high volume.

The first few times really were magical and exciting because I do so love the group's creativity and musical mastery– I even tapped to the rhythm and sang along with Rose. She would look at me with a twinkle in her eye as "Mary Did You Know" began and say with a smile, "Your favorite song." I have to say it used to be my favorite song before I listened to it over and over and over and over and over and over again! Now when we get in the car, I try to engage her and David in conversation as long as possible before the dreaded mix comes on. This day, our conversation only lasted eight minutes. Ugh! I have a once-a-year opportunity to consider cashing in on the fact that it was my fifty-fifth birthday. Would I cry if I want to? Would I ask for mercy for our ears and minds? I think turning off the music would certainly have been a relief, but if Rose wanted music, couldn't I request something different? It was my birthday, after all. Wouldn't this be okay? Well, I could have asked, and I guess it wouldn't have been terribly unethical. I wouldn't have to report on my timesheets that I couldn't muster the patience for one more blasted holiday song, most especially on my birthday, but would I be proud of myself for using my birthday to give us a break from what Rose receives such joy from? I made the decision to not play the birthday card this year. We were only in the car for an hour total. There were those eight precious minutes of conversation with blessed quiet in the background, followed by twelve minutes of loud holiday music, when, "Glory be!," the volume was turned down so Rose could tell me a story about her dad's hunting trip.

As I sit writing this now, I feel like I could have been grateful for the decreased volume, and maybe I should have been. The truth is I wasn't. While my brain debated about asking for some new tunes, I decided allowing Rose to choose the music was a spiritual practice for me. How often does she get this opportunity in her life? So, on my birthday, I gave Rose the gift of choosing what music she wanted to play. While it would be nice to write that I engaged with the music fully during the end of our trip, tapping to the rhythm and singing along, I have to admit, I didn't embrace the moment that completely. I did the best I could by driving safely and not pulling the birthday card to request different music. For a mentor, there are so many options for handling a situation. Some choices are better than others, depending on circumstances. Some days when Rose is terribly tired, the most merciful action for me is to give her space to unwind and do just what she wants. Other days, Rose is feeling ready to learn new social skills, like noticing who is in the car and considering their preferences. I will wait for a day like this to present the idea of offering listening choices to passengers every now and then. Today, the gift of my patience was given, and on my birthday no less.

♣♥ **Decide When or if to Speak:** How do you decide when to speak up about something which is bothering you and when to be patient, allowing whatever is happening to continue?

Share Thoughtful Gifts

I took a five-week vacation from mentoring in order to visit Australia and spend time with family over the holidays. Tom and I traveled to New Zealand for a week, exploring the beaches, towns, rainforests, and volcanoes. During our adventures, I thought about each of the young adults I mentor at different times and brought back carefully thought-out gifts for each person. The gifts were not necessarily something material. The intention was to bring something back which would be meaningful to them.

When visiting gardens and witnessing funny animal behavior, I thought of Rose. There were three swamp hens in a pond at the Royal Botanical Gardens that were building a nest together. One stayed at the nest site while the other two went to collect dried leaves to build the nest with and swim the leaves back to the construction site. I couldn't clearly see what was happening initially, but after quite a bit of exploration, I found the perfect filming spot to take a video of them. What I realized after viewing their activities was just how funny their antics were. At one point, there were three birds working on the nest. One would bring some new materials, handing them to the bird on the nest. The bird on the nest would take the gift and place it down where she thought it belonged. The next instant, another bird would snatch that piece up and put it in another place. When I showed this video to Rose, I acted out what the birds might be saying to each other: "This piece goes here, no there, no I don't want it there, it belongs over here. Wait, what are you doing? It goes over here." and on and on. I created a comedic, fast-moving dialogue to go with the birds' quirky actions. She just howled in laughter, asking me to play it over and over again. How wonderful it was to be together again, enjoying this slapstick type of humor. Instead of purchasing something for Rose on my vacation, I chose to find a way to have her experience the joy I felt while traveling at a time when I was thinking of her. This was a gift of pure joy to Rose and myself. Had I given this gift to another person who didn't appreciate this kind of humor with animals, there would not have been such joy and connection. Each person is unique as to what kinds of gifts are most meaningful.

❤ **Share Thoughtful Gifts:** What kinds of gifts do you give people so they know how much you care about them?

Give Yourself Credit

When the Coronavirus was spreading across the world and countries started shutting down, it all felt so surreal. How could something we couldn't see cause our lives to be turned upside down? Rose's "A Helping Hand" program had an extended Spring break while the instructional leaders figured out how to move forward, and I also took a break from working with her in-person. People around the world were trying to figure out how to adjust to this new reality and to decipher what was best for individuals and the collective. In my family, there was my mom, who was eighty-two years old, and my daughter, who was pregnant, who were at the highest risk. Rose and her mom had compromised immune systems so they also needed to be extra careful. The decision was made that I would work only remotely with Rose during this time of so much uncertainty. I wasn't sure how to work with Rose remotely when so much of our time was spent in the garden.

On the morning of the day I was scheduled to work with Rose, her mom called saying she wanted Rose and me to do some planting after her online classes, because she thinks Rose is happier outside. Also, it would be good for Rose to dig in the dirt so we could show ESS she was still gardening. I absolutely love growing plants and was excited to give this idea a try via Skype. Rose's mom set up the pots and bag of dirt near the computer so we could see each other, but right away, I could tell that Rose was not happy. She was putting dirt in the pots while saying she did not want to be doing this. I listened and encouraged her to just give it a try and after a bit of time she said, "You don't understand. I just don't want to do this. I am tired, and I didn't take my three o'clock medicine." This was a whole lot of clear communication from her in a short time, which was excellent. I asked if she could tell her mom how she felt and she looked at me, then asked, "Could you?" I suggested we speak to her mom together, which she agreed to. Patti didn't know Rose hadn't taken her medicine and did not realize just how tired Rose was. Rose completely melted down from exhaustion and after resting said to her dad that night, "I can't have too many mentors."

This was such a valuable experience for me because I understood at a deep level what not to do as a mentor. It was not my job to fill a need—either mine or a parent's—for productivity in our work together. There is no deadline with mentoring. It's about being together and noticing what is ready to emerge. Instead of consulting Rose about what she wanted and needed, I had agreed to follow her mom's plan. There was nothing wrong with the idea as it was related to Rose's interests, yet it just wasn't right for that day, especially having to coordinate it with video technology. We decided to take a break from mentoring until she finished her online schooling because after a full day of zooming, Rose was too exhausted to do anything else but relax and unwind. During this time when I wasn't mentoring Rose, I missed spending time with her because we have an unexplainably beautiful relationship. For a while, I was hard on myself, feeling like I had done something wrong because Rose did not have the energy to work with me. Over time, I was able to adjust and be kind to myself during these unusual circumstances, which were out of our control.

❤ **Give Yourself Credit:** When life throws us curveballs, sometimes things don't work out as we would like. Give yourself credit for getting through tough times and let go of over analyzing what you could have done better.

Embrace Silence

Six weeks of not seeing Rose passed and I wanted to find a way to mentor her in-person again. After extensive discussions, I felt reassured that both Tom and Rose's mom were in agreement with me going back to work with her. I found the Love Farm, just a fifteen- minute drive from Rose's house, and we made a plan to volunteer there on a sunny, clear, perfect day. Rose got in the car, and we said back and forth, "Hi! How are you?" We both replied that we were doing well. I complimented her on her hair, which was very pretty with loose curls all over, evidence of how she has healed beautifully from the self-harming hair pulling and scratching. What relief and joy I felt. After about ten minutes of awkward silence, Rose looked at me and said, "Welcome back!" Wow! This greeting felt like a blast to my heart after such a long period of silence. This was a genuine, hearty *welcome back*, spoken to me with the greatest of love and deliberation. If she had said the same words at the beginning of our trip, I am not sure if the impact would have felt so profound. This scene is a great example of what it is like to mentor. Often there are long periods of time when it seems nothing much is happening, followed by an amazing blast to my heart.

Embrace Silence: Practicing meditation cultivates patience with silence both on our own and in the company of others. Our minds much prefer to be entertained with lots of fun things to capture our attention, while our souls yearn for stillness. Cultivating the ability to be silent allows us to hear wisdom from within. My mind fights to distract me every time I sit for meditation, yet through stillness and noticing what is happening in the present moment, I am able to understand myself and others more clearly. There are many different ways to meditate. At this point in my life, I spend fifteen to thirty minutes each morning in silent meditation. I sit and observe the thoughts going through the mind and sensations going through the body. Somehow at the end of this time, I feel clearer and more settled, even though sitting still and observing may seem tortuous. Each morning, I come back to sit and practice, no destination in mind, just learning how to embrace silence whether I feel at ease or not.

Face Fears

Rose decided it was time to resume work on a song project she had been planning since before COVID. She knew she wanted to have the background music be "I Want You Back" by Michael Jackson, and I was able to find the karaoke version to the song, but I didn't know how to get the words and the music to mesh together well. I asked Rose's mom if we could have some music lessons to work on a special project or as Rose said, "a secret project." She allowed Rose two lessons, which was a bit tight because there was a lot of work to be done. I felt anxious, wondering how to help Rose with this secret project since I didn't have many musical skills. Each time worries came up, I did my best to address them right away.

We struggled with one big problem: having Rose stick with the beat of the song was just not happening, no matter how slow the music or how aligned the lyrics were. In order to see if we could find a way to get the performance coordinated, I spoke to Rose's other mentor, Kristina, who gave me valuable insights about Rose's style of singing. She explained, "Rose has a processing challenge where she waits to hear the beat and will echo the words in the song. No matter how slow you make the song, she will always be a beat or two behind. Rose knows all of the words and will have no problem learning them; the issue is the delay in processing. I suggest having Rose sing without the music and setting the lyrics to a repetitive part of the song so she can learn to keep the beat herself." This input was extremely helpful. Since our lessons were over, I asked Tom to help me with music and lyrics, since he is more musically inclined than I am. We spent many hours getting the music and lyrics in synch. Once the song was ready to practice and perform, there were angel costumes to search for and order, curtains to be set up, brochures to be made, producers, backup singers and dancers to find. "Practice, practice, practice," was in my mind–"Bigger, better, Disney-style production," was in Rose's mind. How on earth we could perform a song with all the splendor of Disney without knowing the lyrics or being able to sing with the rhythm of the music was beyond me. Dreaming and creation are wonderful things, yet I did hope the song would someday be performed. I had to set my foot down when asked to look for a producer, back-up singers, and dancers; I explained it is not part of my job as a mentor to look for these people Rose wanted to have help her. "Alright," she replied with her head hanging low. Momentarily, she was sad, but the next time we got together, she explained she had found a producer and wondered once again if I could ask my son-in-law Shad to play drums for her song.

On and on this went for months, still with minimal practice of actually singing the song. It took me a while to realize the dreaming about performing was a stronger pull than actually performing. I hoped at least by her birthday, Rose's show would be ready to go, as the costumes had arrived, and we would have time to practice over the winter. Then the coronavirus hit and as I explained earlier, we didn't get together for six weeks. Eventually, when we started gardening again, Rose regularly brought up the song and we finally set a date for her performance. The dress rehearsal would be at our cabin for my family and then the full out performance would be on her mother's birthday. I felt great relief to have a date set after all of this time both preparing and experiencing delays. Finally, when we went to our cabin for a weekend away, Rose was ready to set up the curtains, put on costumes, and practice. She was still adding extra lyrics the day before the performance. I didn't know if my nerves could take this and I set my foot down, explaining how musicians practice the same song with the same lyrics over and over again until it is perfect. I talked about how practicing may not be as exciting as creating is, but if she wanted to do a good job with the song, she needed to practice the same lyrics over and over again. "Okay," Rose relented after I explained this to her several times. I don't like being firm with her. This is my least favorite part of mentoring, but I hope my guidance supports her growth and eventual independence.

Just before the performance was to happen, Rose experienced stage fright and was even too nervous to do a dress rehearsal. She was able to share what she was feeling with Shad and myself, which allowed us to help her work through these fears and Rose finally practiced her performance, complete with costumes and dance moves. Here are the lyrics to the song she performed:

Ooooooooooooooo until now   Ooooooooo oooooo
Earth angels are here today to brighten up your day
We bring you joy to spread around
With love for you we say

Worms grow under the ground
We can leave them alone

99

To do their work

Earth Angels you are loved oh yeah
Smi-ling faces show
Love in our hearts (repeat)

We really love our earth you know,
Helping plants to grow.
Every day

We love adventures all 'cross town
sharing laughs with all
who gather 'round.

Earth Angels bring you joy to share
With love for you we say
We bring you cheer

Earth Angels you are loved oh yeah
Smi-ling faces show
Love in our hearts (repeat)

The worm lyric was one of the additions made at the last minute. It's placement still confused me but hey, this was Rose's song. The beginning lyrics and "oooohs" are all hers, and she had some fantastic moves to go with them. The curtains made of white blankets were set up and ready for the dress rehearsal with my family on the Fourth of July. Tom, Carina, Shad, and three of their friends were there for the show. Although Rose was nervous, she did a fantastic job and was absolutely beaming, announcing at the end, "My stage fright is gone now!"

The next big performance was for her mom's birthday on the fifth of July. We arrived and Rose gave her mom a huge hug and a happy birthday greeting. I started setting up curtains for the performance while Rose unpacked and prepared for the big event. I noticed her looking worried and frantically searching in her bags. She asked, "Where is the angel costume?" I said, "I don't know. What did you do with it when you took it off last night?" Rose said with shoulders drooping, "I don't know." Then standing up tall, she said, in an accusatory tone, "What did you do

100

with it?" I replied, "You packed up all of your things. I asked if you had everything before we left." "I know" she said with drooping shoulders, followed by, "I am such an idiot. My mom's birthday is completely ruined," and she started kicking her bags with frustration and anger. I had to think quickly because I didn't want her to go into full meltdown mode, so addressed her frustrations right away. Here is what I said to her several times:

- I can tell you are really frustrated and angry you don't have the angel wings costume right now.
- Everyone forgets things sometimes. I feel like you are being hard on yourself.
- Your mom's birthday is not ruined if you can open your mind to possibilities in order to find other costume ideas.

After a few repetitions with these words, the kicking slowed down, her lack of response shifted to a more open gaze, followed by the idea to use a white dress she wears to church sometimes. After a little bit of time on her own, she called me upstairs to show me the dress and sweater she would use for the performance. Whew! Disaster averted, and the show was still a go. Rose's mom loved her performance, and all was well. Rose first overcame her fear of performing, then not having the right costume. Contrast this with not being ready to jump off the high dive and we have two successes with one fear still waiting to be addressed, if Rose decides she would like to take on the high dive challenge again.

Face fears: Are there places in your life where you or someone you are working with would really love to do something, yet are paralyzed by fear? Sharing how you feel or listening to how someone feels opens a door to possibilities.

Offer, Then Let Go

Rose is a twenty-three-year-old who is eager to gain more independence. She is usually very good about remembering when to take her medicine, but sometimes forgets. Her mom asked me to make sure she takes her medications four times a day, so I set alarms for those times. This is something I have wanted Rose to do for a long time, but she has resisted for reasons she couldn't explain. Each time the alarm would go off, I would ask her if she knew what the alarm was for. If there was no response, I would ask if she had taken her medicine. She was noticeably annoyed by this reminder, asking if she could say something politely, then sharing, "You know at home, I really don't care when I take my medicine."

This statement was baffling to me and I asked her questions about why she takes medicine, if the time of day makes a difference, etc. I explained her mom asked me to make sure she took her medicine, which is why I set alarms on my phone. I suggested if Rose set her own alarms, I wouldn't need to remind her as her own phone could do that. "What a great idea!" she exclaimed, then rushed to get her phone. She put a 7:00 alarm in, asking me if this was am or pm. Whew, setting this one alarm seemed like a big task. I got my phone out and deleted the 7:00 pm alarm, since she has this one on her phone. I explained I would delete the other alarms, once Rose put each alarm on her phone. She needed a bit of help getting the times correct, but completed the other alarms relatively quickly. Rose wants to be independent and she also recognizes she still needs help with certain things. This back-and-forth struggle frustrates her, yet she keeps trying and making steps forward, with gentle and firm guidance along the way.

The next day, the last day of our Wolf Lake Cabin weekend, Rose told me she was not going to keep the alarms on her phone at home. We had a discussion going back and forth, and Rose got steeped in confusion as my frustration grew, along with the negative tone and loudness of my voice. She got overwhelmed and asked if we could talk about something else. She wanted a calm conversation. I took a few breaths, realizing I had been so excited about her independence breakthrough, I thought it was a done deal. I had forgotten what a long time it takes for Rose to learn things well, to master new skills, and to break through restrictive habits. Wanting to continue our conversation, I proceeded by sharing my thoughts and feelings with Rose in a calm manner by letting go of expectations of how she would respond. Sharing my observations about Rose being frustrated when I reminded her to take her medicine, followed by Rose's amazing breakthrough that she could set alarms on her phone had given me hope Rose could be more independent. Because Rose had taken the initiative to remind herself with her phone, I had been hopeful her parents could let go of the medicine reminders as well.

Rose respectfully listened and when I asked her thoughts, she lifted her right shoulder saying, "I don't know." I asked, "What don't you know?" Rose said with tears in her eyes, "It seems too hard." I said, "I understand this feels hard to you right now. You have shown me you can be responsible and remind yourself to take your medicine on time. Maybe when the time feels right, you might want to try this at home." Rose was quiet, then said, "Let's have some fun." She started getting ready for the beach, bringing her clothes into the bathroom to change while I washed the dishes. After about ten minutes, I heard a faraway sounding, "Mawia." I replied, "Yes Rose." Inching close to the closed door, I heard, "I think I might try that." "What might you try Rose?" I replied. "I want to try keeping track of taking my medicine at home," she whispered. "Oh Rose, this makes me so happy you are considering taking responsibility for taking your medicines. How wonderful!" I exclaimed. What a way to end our day together. Even if she did take so long getting ready that we weren't able to swim before heading to her home, this was amazing progress. Four steps forward, three steps back, then another step forward to independence and personal responsibility: Back and forth, back and forth.

While packing to leave, Rose said to me, "I get annoyed when people remind me to take medicine and sometimes, I don't listen the first time. I listen the second time." I am impressed she is being honest about the fact she does not listen the first time. What an important observation she made about herself. This leads us to a discussion about setting an alarm and back-up alarm for her medicine. My shift is coming to an end, and I sense a sort of completion in our work together. Rose will soon be starting her last year of the "A Helping Hand" program, and her family is planning to move to South Carolina after her graduation. I know I will keep in touch with Rose and her family and treasure the times we have learned together. What a ride we have taken and how much we both have to be proud of. It will be interesting to observe Rose as she slowly inches towards as much independence as will be possible for her. I know how very blessed I have been to be a part of Rose's life when our hearts were blooming in ways which were new to us both.

Offer, Then Let Go: We may offer suggestions, yet there is no guarantee of these ideas being put into action. The healthiest way to mentor is to let go of any notions about how these offerings are or are not accepted. You might be surprised by what happens next, while you are enjoying life and not stressing over the results.

Finishing Remarks

From Rose, I have learned much about how treating her with consistent kindness and patience has allowed her to confidently share what is important to her and to believe in herself more than she ever imagined possible. I learned to access my intuition for guidance when we were in situations which were filled with uncertainty. She taught me the importance of noticing and appreciating the loving, joyful connections we have experienced time after time together. Since Rose has Downs Syndrome, her achievements are more subtle and require finely honed intuitive abilities to notice. I cherish all of the experiences I have had with Rose and the incredible learning she has inspired in me. I realize the importance of slowing down, laughing, playing, speaking up and being loving with each other. What a blessing our time together has been!

Rose has graduated from "A Helping Hand", which has been an incredible confidence boost for her. Rose's parents have retired and the family is excited to be moving to the beach. Unfortunately, the mentoring support she has received in this state may not be available where she is going, which is a concern I have for her. My hope is the community they live in will embrace her loving spirit and she finds a place where she is appreciated and honored just the way she is. I will keep in touch with Rose and look forward to witnessing how she continues to bloom and inspire people she meets to open their hearts to her joyful love.

I began mentoring the following young man, B.D., who is on the autism spectrum, about six months after starting with Rose. You will notice a difference in his skills and gifts as compared with Rose. I hope you will celebrate each individuals' gifts, without judging some as better than others. Each person is unique and has amazing inspiration to offer us, through abilities which may be present or not present.

Perseverance Pays Off for B.D.

Observation

I first met B.D. at his mom's home in the early morning. We sat around the counter of the eat-in kitchen with B.D. in between us. His mom spoke most of the time, and as she spoke, she kept her hand on his forearm, tapping him when making a point or to get his attention. B.D.'s mom was clearly very anxious, and I felt nervous being around her. B.D., a twenty six-year-old man, was quiet and acted shy. As his mom shared important information about B.D., she would ask him questions, which he would take a long time to answer. It was as if the words B.D. was looking for were just out of reach. Yet I could already sense if he waited for a bit and concentrated, the words would bubble up and come out. Being rushed to answer questions during this first morning meeting seemed to prevent his words from flowing out with ease. His face was tense, as if his emotions were frozen inside. Challenges with speech, feeling and expressing emotions often occurs with people like B.D. who are on the autism spectrum. Unfortunately, part of the reason for the tension on this day may have been due to the timing of our meeting, since I learned at that time, both B.D. and his mom are night owls, and mornings are a challenge for them. I wanted to get to know B.D. better, to be alone with him and see what words, ideas, feelings, and passions he might share and possibly, discover.

B.D.'s mom told me a story about a time she was driving with B.D. in the car, when a large tree branch had fallen across the road ahead. As she was navigating around the tree, she crossed the double yellow line, and B.D. panicked because he said she was breaking the law. Repeated explanations wouldn't change his mind that what she did was wrong. I found this story interesting and asked, "How would you define autism?" She replied, "Difficulty with socialization, speaking, understanding conversations, being expressive and receptive during communication, rule followers to a fault, sometimes without using common sense." B.D.'s mom said people with autism often have trouble with grey areas, as was illustrated by her story about crossing the yellow line. I realize B.D.'s mom was helping me to understand B.D. better so I could work with him to the best of my abilities.

On that first day, I witnessed B.D.'s mom as a strong-willed advocate for her son's continued learning and independence. She loved hearing I was a math and yoga teacher. She felt he could benefit from learning math to improve his problem-solving and life skills, and she hoped I could teach B.D. yoga for stress management. I was open to working with him in both of these areas and eager to experiment to find the best way to approach these topics. This would be the first time I had worked one on one with a person on the autism spectrum.

My heart was really aching to see what I could do to help B.D. I felt excited, but also nervous, wondering how our work together might progress. I certainly couldn't guess at how effective I might be, but I had complete certainty I would do my absolute best.

B.D.'s mom loves this last sentence.

Observation: When beginning anything new, observation with all of your senses is vitally important because you gain valuable information.

Pay Negotiation

At the end of the meeting was pay negotiations. B.D.'s mom talked about disappointing experiences with previous mentors, who didn't show up or weren't reliable. She and B.D.'s father, her ex-husband discussed my hourly rate before our meeting, and she told me they would offer a small amount to start. If I proved to be trustworthy, my pay would be increased. Oh boy, was I offended! I sat up straighter right away and am proud to say I spoke up for myself, something which I would not typically do. I explained I had been a teacher for thirty years and could be counted on. Furthermore, I let her know I would be paid at least three times what they were offering me to tutor people in mathematics. B.D.'s mom said she would speak to B.D.'s father and get back to me. I could tell she really wanted me to work with B.D., and I had a feeling they would figure something out. Later I found out B.D. had some bad experiences with mentors who were not responsible. They would show up late or not at all and one mentor was writing in hours of working with B.D. when they weren't together, which is against the law. I understand their hesitancy to offer me an hourly wage which respected my education and experience based on the bad experiences they had in the past. I was especially proud of myself for speaking up right away, and strongly advocating for reasonable pay, with full confidence in my ability to be reliable and responsible.

As you have learned from Rose's stories, mentoring is challenging work which has the potential to help people grow and learn in ways nobody can even imagine. When mentoring in any type of work, you will need to be professional by showing up to work on time, following through with what you say you are going to do and showing up ready to be mentally and emotionally present for the person you are with. While parts of mentoring can be really fun and relaxing, there are other times when it can be extremely stressful. Honoring the importance of this work with respectful wages is important and it will be your responsibility to advocate for yourself. When a person feels valued in their work through proper pay and respect, they do a better job. Don't you agree?

Pay Negotiation: Know your value and speak up if you feel you are not being paid with enough money or respect. Before going to an interview, research going rates for the job you are applying to.

Start Where You Are

Although B.D. was rather shy and reserved when I first began mentoring him, he had mastered many life skills. He worked two jobs, lived on his own part-time, and had been driving for many years. B.D. wanted to become better at mathematics, especially long division. We met for the first time in the library, sitting in a quiet corner so I could assess his skills. We didn't have a book or any kind of outline to follow, so I felt my way through this beginning assessment moment by moment, making decisions based on what seemed right at the time. He had strong skills in basic math— addition, subtraction, and simple multiplication. B.D. wanted to practice long division, so I made up problems for him to work on. Following his lead, we made a plan to focus on his long-division skills and brush up on other foundational mathematics.

As I began working individually with B.D., he seemed tense and reserved, with a stoic attitude. No smiles, no excitement, just a dogged determination to give this a go and do the best he could. I asked if he wanted to talk about ways to practice relaxation. He seemed eager to learn to de-stress, even though I wasn't sure exactly how he was receiving what I was saying because his expression did not change at all. As a starting point, I decided to see how a really simple mindfulness exercise might work for him. I softly suggested to B.D.:

When you feel stressed, notice your feet, really feel your feet in your shoes. Notice how they touch the ground. Imagine tension flowing down through your shoes, into the earth below. Visualize the earth holding you up, supporting you.

B.D. looked at me, listening intently, but I wasn't sure how much he understood because I could not sense any emotions on his face. I wondered if this simple relaxation technique would have any effect at all. If it did, wonderful; if not, we could try other methods. We wrapped up by filling out the timesheet and making a plan for our next meeting. I felt uncertain about how much we had accomplished during this initial meeting. It was a beginning, and on the surface, it was a calm and seemingly uneventful encounter. What was happening underneath would be revealed at our next meeting.

We next met at B.D.'s dad's home. As we began to talk, B.D. was excited to share with me how much noticing his feet had helped him relax at work. He was animated while he explained how tension and stress just went away when he noticed his feet. In addition, because he was paying attention, B.D. had observed differences in his level of tension during the day. He realized he felt more relaxed when he was walking, especially when putting away carts at the grocery store. Oh my, I was so very excited hearing B.D. share this feedback with me! Learning how he connected with this simple exercise made me feel like we had hit a home run at the very beginning of a baseball game. Isn't it amazing how suggesting he simply notice his feet made such a huge difference in allowing him to let go of stress?

Since this basic relaxation method went so well, after we finished doing math problems, I taught B.D. a few yoga poses as another relaxation experiment. I didn't have any expectations about what he would do with the yoga or how often he would practice. I had been a passionate yoga teacher for ten years. During that time, yoga meant the world to me. I received so very much awareness, strength, and relaxation from this practice and was quite disciplined. I had been on a mission to share my commitment to yoga with as many individuals as possible. I especially wanted people to develop a home practice like I had. Despite teaching quite a bit and giving many private lessons, I don't know if any of my students developed regular home practices. During this time of my life, I was not practicing much yoga. I had no expectation for B.D. to embrace or dismiss this discipline, and, to be honest, it didn't matter either way to me. We were simply experimenting to see what B.D showed interest in. He asked me the best time to practice and if he could watch TV when doing yoga. I explained the main idea of yoga is to get in tune with your body and mind through breathing, movement, and awareness. I didn't believe watching TV while doing yoga was conducive to mindfulness. However, he could certainly experiment. I also suggested morning or evening as the best times to develop a daily yoga routine.

Start Where You Are: Especially in new situations, we all want to do our best and may feel nervous about the choices we make. We won't know how something might work out until we try it. Start with what you know, give it a go and notice what happens. Even if you can't read someone right away, it doesn't mean that nothing is happening inside them. Sometimes, you have to wait to discover how a person will connect with a lesson.

Support Growth

The next time we worked together, B.D. told me he had been practicing yoga two times a day, in the morning and evening. He described how the tightness in his head just melted away. Woohoo, a hidden passion was revealed! I was surprised and delighted to witness how B.D. embraced yoga and dedicated time twice a day to practice. I was eager to help him explore how he could continue his interest in yoga. We researched and attended a few different styles of classes so he might discover which would be the best fit. B.D. is such a natural, with great balance, strength, and focus. He was a yoga star in his very first yoga classes, which was really cool to witness. He enjoys learning new poses from YouTube and sometimes posts videos of himself doing yoga on his social media pages. I hope someday he will take yoga teacher training, not so much to become a teacher, because he says that doesn't interest him, but for deepening his practice and understanding of yoga. This first hidden passion of B.D.'s surfaced so effortlessly, requiring just a little bit of encouragement and attention from me. He continues to practice regularly on his own, which is wonderful. Since I was not in the position of being B.D.'s dedicated yoga teacher, I transitioned from teaching him a little bit to taking him to experience a few different styles of yoga. Finally, this evolved into checking in occasionally on his practice, which has been just the right amount of mentoring he needs.

If I had only been a yoga teacher for B.D., I might have been disappointed because I wasn't needed anymore. As his mentor, however, when he doesn't need my guidance in one area, this signals a job well done and opens more space and time for other explorations.

Support Growth: Once a flower has bloomed, it withers, leaving space for something new. Seeds form, which have the potential to grow lots more plants and many more flowers. Mentoring is like this. Once a project has been seen to completion, there is space for something new to happen, potentially something that could sprout from seeds formed from a previous learning or heart blooming.

Have Fun with Learning

B.D. is interested in improving his math skills. He was especially intrigued by long division, which involves a lot of steps to complete. I sang a fun little division song for him one day, which I used to sing for my Foundations of Elementary School Math Classes: "Divide, multiply, subtract, bring down." I sang it over and over. Oh yes, this funny little sing-song is childish and playful, and while I felt a bit self-conscious singing it, I know learning through fun and silliness works. And yes, indeed, I did witness a smile from B.D. with this quirky creative outburst. Oh my goodness! Was being silly ever worth it when I got to witness B.D.'s glorious smile—and even a bit of a giggle. Early on in our work, B.D. excitedly described to me how he had found the perfect program to learn long division. The program was wonderful because it coached the student on each of the four steps of long division. B.D. practiced with this program regularly and he enjoyed showing me how his skills were steadily improving.

🌱 **Have Fun with Learning:** There is a small part of our brain, the size of an almond, called the amygdala which plays a role in memory. When something can be learned in a fun, exciting way, the amygdala records this emotional memory, making learning more deeply connected and easeful. When you think of it this way, it makes a lot of sense to have fun when learning new things and isn't it wonderful to know joyous learning works better?

Switch Your Focus

As time passed, we got to a point in our work when math was not so interesting to B.D. and neither one of us was engaged. I was getting sleepy. B.D. was getting sleepy. I asked myself: *Why do we keep working on these skills if neither one of us is engaged?* In response, I heard the echoes of former math colleagues arguing the importance of mathematics. With full confidence, I gently said to them: *Don't worry. I've got this.*

I began to consider the possibility of working on leadership and social skills instead of math. After confronting the voices in my head successfully, I decided to seek other viewpoints. B.D's mom and dad, despite being divorced and living in different households, were united when advocating for their son. Typically, I would send email questions to both of them and all replies would be shared amongst the three of us. B.D.'s mom was so adamant about him learning math, I was afraid to broach the subject with her, so I decided to speak to his dad first. He agreed this was a good idea. Whew. What a relief. For the moment, we set math aside to explore some other arenas. I didn't discuss stepping away from math work with mom at this time, bypassing input from her because I was worried she might object.

B.D.'s mom had a heart condition which caused her anxiety. Once she was properly diagnosed and had medication to regulate her heart rate, she became a different person who was much easier for me to talk with and be around. She has been a huge supporter of this book and the work I do with her son. To be honest, she has become my biggest fan. She recently invited me over to her home to discuss the book, help me correct some details, and include her view in certain sections. We laughed about how I didn't initially discuss with her the idea of switching our focus away from math when B.D. was losing interest and spoke to his dad first instead. She emphasized how she had wanted B.D. to have good math skills because she knows they will help him with life, but when this area wasn't holding his attention, switching away from this focus made sense.

♥ **Switch your Focus:** Is there something you are working on which is just flat out boring you to pieces? Why do you keep doing it? Of course, some things just have to be done like paying bills, but often there can be even a change in focus for your work which can offer more interest and possibility for joyful engagement. It could be this is just not the right time to work on something and there might be a time in the future where this work might make sense. Have you ever eaten fruit before it is ripe when it is hard and bitter? Not very good, is it? If you wait until the fruit is ripe, like when the banana turns from green to yellow or you can just push down the top of a pear, then you will experience a soft, sweet, juicy fruit and have an unforgettably wonderful gustatory experience. If we can shift our focus to the ripe fruits in life and be patient with the ones which need a little more time to be ready, consider how much more inspiring and pleasurable our lives would be.

Ask for Help

While B.D. has achieved many successes along the way, much of our time together calls for a lot of patience from me. I must calmly pay attention, sometimes without a lot of feedback from B.D.. I ask question after question after question to tap into what he might like to work on next and receive one-word answer after one-word answer—or often these three-word answers: *I don't know* or *I'm not sure*. This is a common challenge when working with people who have special gifts. Generate faith that together you will discover passions hiding inside, waiting to feel safe enough to peek out for a try.

When an area of interest is discovered and we start working in a new, exciting direction, time flies by so quickly for both of us because we are excited and engaged. Until this breakthrough comes along, however, I deeply feel a lack of stimulation—sometimes even boredom. When the rate of our conversations is slower than I am accustomed to, I have to hone my intuitive skills by slowing myself down so I can pay attention to what is brewing under the surface. I get sleepy when I slow down. This has been a problem with me when I meditate and even when doing energy healing for people. I get so relaxed; I have trouble staying awake and alert. The same issue happens when mentoring. At times, I feel stuck and am not sure what to work on. Acknowledging feeling stuck is a very important first step and alerts us it is time to open our minds to other options.

I was feeling unsure of what direction to go in with B.D. and made an appointment to see what suggestions my teacher Dechen had, asking if she could look at B.D.'s energy and share suggestions about how to help him open up. She told me because B.D. was quite reserved, it would take some time and trust for him to feel safe enough to open up more. Dechen suggested exploring art with him. I appreciated hearing Dechen confirm my feeling about how closed B.D. was and agreed to discuss art with him at our next meeting.

When we talked, I learned B.D. does in fact enjoy creating art. He showed me some fine portraits of famous actors he had drawn. How interesting it is to learn more about his hobbies and talents. I asked if he would like to take some art classes and he said he prefers to draw on his own. Even though it felt like this road didn't go very far initially, it was good to give it a try. In the near future, we would return to art and creativity and explore these topics through different means.

♥ **Ask for Help:** When you feel stuck, first of all, acknowledge what is happening, ask questions, listen for answers and consider seeking ideas from other resources like a teacher, book or even an internet search. Being willing and open to help allows new opportunities to start rolling in.

Set Boundaries

I have never been given any guidance about what I may and may not discuss while mentoring young adults, so I rely on my best judgement. I once had a conversation with B.D. about movies and Peewee Herman came up. B.D. felt strongly that Peewee shouldn't have been arrested for masturbating in a movie theater. I didn't know B.D. well at this point. I listened to what he said and asked some questions. As I reflected about this conversation after we finished working together, I knew I wanted to make sure he understood there is no problem masturbating in private, as this is healthy and natural, but there are laws against masturbating in public. The next time we met, I explained to him, when people purchase a movie ticket, they pay to see the movie. Even when people are passionately kissing in the movie theater near other viewers, this can feel uncomfortable and is better done in private. My face probably turned red during this conversation as I get embarrassed talking about sex-related things, but I felt this distinction was important to have. B.D. listened and yet was still upset Peewee was arrested. I'm not sure why this bothered him so much, and I don't believe I need to know any more. To me, this conversation was an important one for B.D. It helped him recognize I am open to different topics of discussion and he could feel safe expressing himself with me.

Looking back now, I think this conversation helped lay a foundation of trust early in our work together. This subject never came up again, except when we were discussing the book with his family. I was wondering about including this story in the book and B.D. decided to include the story just as it was.

B.D.'s mom spoke to him about Peewee and shared with me in an email what transpired:

B.D.: I find it offensive doing it in public, but I still don't think he should have been arrested.

I wrote back, B.D. is firm on his viewpoint!

She wrote back, Yup.

I wrote, I am actually cracking up laughing now. 😃

She responded, Me too. 😈

118

B.D.'s dad also said he would talk to him. I can't imagine at this point B.D. changing his position at all, but we will see... For me, it felt good bringing this discussion out in the open with his family, if only to show that it is okay to talk openly about a topic which might be considered taboo. We shared some laughs along the way, which helped me bond with his mom. Respecting B.D.'s right to take a firm stand on a topic he feels strongly about and to listen to his opinion builds trust and could allow for deeper discussions in other areas in the future. In this work, we may not know concretely how discussions lead to openings in the future. I have learned to follow my instincts and trust we are being guided to spend our time wisely.

♥ **Set Boundaries:** When someone feels strongly about a topic, often there is important information to be gleaned from asking questions and listening to their responses. If a boundary is crossed and the person seems to close up as if a door is closing, then stop and explore a different direction. If a boundary is crossed and you can feel the person opening up, as if a door is opening, keep going and see what happens in this new territory.

Be a Detective

When driving to attend different yoga classes, we had the opportunity to talk casually in the car. I asked B.D. open-ended questions, and he shared more of himself as time went on. I learned how proud he is of the work he does as a cart pusher at the local supermarket. He is strong and can push many carts in a row to do his job efficiently. I also learned about the few things that really annoy him. He particularly dislikes when people leave garbage in their shopping carts. Another frustration is witnessing people with special gifts not being treated with respect. Note: I am explaining his frustrations in my own words. What I actually heard from B.D. initially was, "People are slobs. Nobody cares anymore. People with disabilities are never treated right. They are treated like "animals"."

In the car, I listened to what he said, asking a few follow-up questions for clarity and made a mental note to further discuss these topics at our next meeting.

🖤 **Be a Detective:** Do you ever notice the thoughts which repeat in your head throughout the day? Take some time to jot them down and consider where these thoughts might have come from. Keeping track of things people say when you are working with them can be important leads for investigation. You can be a detective for yourself as well. I sometimes repeat the same complaints in my head over and over again without stopping to pay attention. Once I recognize there are feelings fueling these thoughts, which are not being expressed out loud, I can ask what I am frustrated about, fully listen to the complaints, address the issue out in the open and take action to work through the challenge.

120

Dig Deeper

I noticed in our conversations over time that while B.D. was a devoted employee for both of his jobs, there was not much passion there and quite frankly a lot of dissatisfaction. Wherever strong feelings abide, there is material of substance to explore, so we began discussions. B.D. spoke while I wrote his words on paper. I asked lots of questions, definitely a specialty of mine. With each question and reply, we were digging deeper and deeper into what the core issue was.

Exploring his comment about people being slobs, I asked questions like, "Are all people at the grocery store slobs? Do you ever see anyone who puts their garbage in a can or makes the effort to return their cart back to the store?" He replied, "They don't have garbage cans in the parking lot."

I asked why there were no garbage cans and decided this was something B.D. might be able to address, with my help. At work, could he suggest adding garbage cans would be an improvement to the grocery store parking lot? This seemed like a good opportunity for him to express his feelings and then consider possible solutions.

B.D. spoke while I listened and recorded what he said. We then crafted his suggestion for installing garbage cans into a letter to his boss as practice for approaching his boss verbally. Even without going to speak to his boss, this process allowed him to share his feelings in a productive way. This was the beginning of a series of sessions designed to offer B.D. opportunities to express himself freely through speaking and writing. He approached his boss and, unfortunately, garbage cans were not installed, which was disappointing, yet the whole experience gave B.D. great opportunities for learning and practicing communication skills.

🌱 **Dig deeper:** Asking questions about repetitive thoughts is like digging for treasure in the ground. It is a very helpful tool for uncovering hidden emotions. You might discover some cool things and you might not. No matter what the results, the exploration is worthwhile because you will learn something in the process.

Compliment Sandwiches

B.D. and I continued exploring new and better ways of communicating with family. B.D. sometimes expressed a desire for more freedom. For example, he told me he wanted to be responsible for his appointments without reminders from his parents. I shared a technique my daughter Anna used with her cheer team: *compliment sandwiches.* This is a great tool to use when you want to share a request for change in a nice way. The discussion starts and ends with an expression of gratitude, with a request sandwiched in the middle. In this case, we worked on letters to his parents. B.D. would share how he wanted to be treated differently, and he would start and end the letters with an expression of appreciation.

This process was quick for the beginning and ending of each letter, the positive sections. Writing the middle section, which requests a change, took much longer. This was completely understandable, as it is not easy to ask people to treat us differently, especially parents who have been *the boss* for a long time. The letter to his mom took us a few weeks to complete. I coached B.D. to express himself even though he might feel afraid.

After writing a beautiful letter to his mom, he started the letter to his dad. B.D.'s letter to his dad was written with more ease and speed, yet his language was much angrier and stronger than he had used with his mom. I asked him how he thought his dad would feel reading this letter and B.D. said in a harsh tone, "He is going to understand what I am saying." No matter how I asked, B.D. wasn't feeling the impact his words could have on his dad. It was time for a change in tactics. I acted out the words he used in the letter with strong language and pointing my finger angrily at B.D. as I read: **"You really need to stop reminding me about appointments."** B.D. burst out laughing, quickly covered his mouth, and turned his head away from me abruptly. I laughed with him, letting him know it was okay to find this funny. B.D. said he really got my point and understood why changing the feeling in the delivery of the request to his dad would be wise. Once the wording was softened, I read it to him again and the letter was ready to share.

It took a couple of months for B.D. to build up the courage to read these letters to his parents. He wanted to share the letter with his dad first, after he recovered his strength from having hip replacement surgery. I asked B.D. week after week when he would read the letter to his dad, but he was steadfast in his decision to wait. I have learned much from B.D., as I have from all the other people I have worked with. He was thoughtful and wise to wait for when his dad was stronger, while I was a bit impatient. I am a force to be reckoned with when I want a project to move forward and do not always take time to pause and consider how moving forward will affect the people involved. Through this experience, I realized just how tuned in B.D. is to his dad. On the surface, B.D. doesn't often show strong emotions, but this is an example of just how much empathy he has and how he shows he loves his dad.

Once B.D. decided the time was right, scheduling a meeting with the three of us was challenging. Finally, we found a day when we could all get together. I arrived a few minutes early because I was so excited this day had finally arrived. B.D. let me in the door as we shared our usual greeting:

B.D.: Hello, how are you?

Maria: I am fine, how are you?

B.D.: Doing well, thanks. Would you like something to drink?

Maria: I appreciate your drink offer. I am going to pass today.

B.D. Okay then.

I put my sandals on the shoe mat in the kitchen and we were done with this ritual. Since socialization is challenging for many people on the autism spectrum, simple routines like this are comforting because each person knows what to say and there is no dreaded "awkward silence".

I said hello to his dad, noting how well he was walking after his hip surgery. B.D. left the room, quickly heading upstairs to get the notebook he writes in. We sat on high seats at their dining room table while B.D. read this letter, his dad smiling at B.D. all the while.

Dear Dad,
I really appreciate you taking my Volvo to New Jersey to get it fixed when any messages come that need to be dealt with. I would really appreciate you to stop reminding me that its that person's birthday because you write

it on the calendar and I get birthday notifications on facebook. I appreciate you letting me be independent.

Love, B.D.

Afterwards, his dad thanked B.D. for expressing himself and said he will stop reminding him about relative's birthdays. He said, "This is really a great method and would help B.D. talk to his mom about going to Rhode Island with the family." I was proud of B.D. and how he was able to express his feelings to his dad in this constructive way. He has come a long way. His dad was truly appreciative of the work we have done together, saying, "B.D. never would have done this six months ago." What wonderful feedback for us! My most valued payment, however, was the huge smile on B.D.'s face when he shared his feelings and his dad listened with love and openness, respecting his requests.

Week after week, I asked B.D. if he scheduled a time for us to meet with his mom and finally, the moment we had been working toward arrived. I walked into his mom's house five minutes before our meeting was scheduled to begin. When B.D. arrived, our attention turned to him. He began by asking what he had written in his notebook was called. I explained they are compliment sandwiches and showed how they were designed:

This is why I am grateful for you.
This is what I would like to be done differently.
This is why I appreciate you.

B.D.'s mom listened as he began reading his letter, watching as B.D. looked up at her to connect and guage her reaction. I could feel the nervousness in his voice and demeanor when he asked his mom to stop reminding him about appointments and the triumph at the end of the letter when he assured his mom she can relax and trust him to take care of himself. Oh, how wonderful was the huge smile on his face when he received his mom's reassurance that she would honor his request. I shared how I had also learned not to remind B.D. about things. For example, I thought of reminding him to bring his notebook to this meeting about five times beforehand and did not, in order to honor B.D.'s request, not spoken directly to me, but understood by the letters to his parents. With that success under his belt, B.D. also read a second letter to his mom:

Dear Mom,

I would like to take you out to lunch, your choice of place. I do not want to go to Rhode Island. I would like to travel to Alabama to visit our family there.
Love, B.D.

His mom asked why he did not want to go to Rhode Island and he struggled to find an answer. When she said it was okay for him not to join them, she shared that she is considering moving to Rhode Island and asked if he would visit if she moved there. B.D. reassured her he would visit if she moved to Rhode Island and offered to take care of her dog Misty while she was away this summer. He shared his success with watching Misty recently, when he helped her lose weight and trained her to walk. His mom was so appreciative and excited because Misty was now able to go walking with her, rather than pulling to go home the way she used to. B.D. knew to his core he did not want to go to Rhode Island this summer and lightened her disappointment by telling her the places he *would* like to go with her. His mom also let him know she doesn't need the compliments. She likes discussing things straight out, having a back and forth conversation. I shared how proud I was of B.D. for expressing himself and got teary when marveling at the love between mother and son.

When I was leaving, I gave B.D.'s mom a big hug and then I asked if B.D. gives hugs. I was quickly surrounded by a big bear hug, even rocking back and forth a bit, followed by B.D. exclaiming, "Now that's communication." Oh, this most fantastic and rewarding job I have! What a lucky person I am. The first hug I received from B.D. was an explosively wonderful gift. If he were always outwardly expressive like this, it wouldn't mean nearly as much to me. Remember how I described B.D.'s often stoic expression? The contrast made this moment extra magical.

❤ **Compliment sandwiches:** Is there someone in your life you would like to share feedback and you would like to do this in the gentlest way possible. Try writing and sharing a compliment sandwich which is:

> ➤ Something you appreciate about the person
> ➤ Something you would like this person to do differently
> ➤ Something you appreciate about the person

Learning Opportunities

When B.D. made comments like, "People with disabilities are never treated right. They are treated like "animals"," I wanted to understand where these ideas came from. You must guess what came next—lots of questions from me about why he feels this way. Had he been treated unfairly? I was surprised B.D. did not have any stories of being treated badly during his school years and wanted to dig deeper. Since B.D. has been treated really well by his family and friends throughout his schooling, where had these strong feelings come from about people with disabilities? As far as I have been able to discover, these feelings have come from hearing and reading stories on social media. B.D. speaks proudly about being on the autism spectrum and being a high functioning individual. He says, "I don't need a lot of assistance, that is for sure. I feel great to be honest because it shows I can be independent."

I heard about an autism conference which was being offered at a university an hour from us, so asked B.D. if he wanted to attend this conference with me and he immediately said, "Yes." I hadn't been to a conference in several years and was excited to learn more about how to help young adults on the autism spectrum, and to witness how B.D. interacts with people at the conference. His parents were enthusiastic about this adventure too. We registered and made a plan to meet there as B.D. wanted to try driving there himself. He met me on time in the lobby, where we signed in and found a seat.

I suggested B.D. bring some paper and a pen to write notes and he chose not to do this, so he listened to the introductions and keynote speaker while I took notes—not only to remember what I was learning but also to stay awake. I tend to get sleepy when listening without being active for too long. I noticed B.D. getting a bit sleepy as well, as the keynote speaker talked quite a lot and did not involve the audience much. However, B.D. perked up when this quote was displayed on the screen and he took a picture with his cellphone.

I was

> The dignity of risk is the right to take risks when engaging in life experiences, and the right to fail in those activities.
>
> ~ Janet Shouse, parent of a child with autism.

intrigued by his strong interest and curious to explore why. Since B.D.

feels so strongly about this quote, I ask myself, "Do I give B.D. the dignity of risk? How might I and everyone who supports B.D. give him more opportunities to take risks, knowing he may succeed or fail, both options giving him experiences to learn from?"

We had the choice of several workshops and attended two together. I was impressed with B.D.'s confidence in answering questions and participating in this small group setting. I was also surprised the conference did not include a speaker who was on the autism spectrum. B.D. and I talked to one of the organizers and asked if they might consider inviting B.D. to speak at a future conference. He had never done this before, although he has participated in many high school theater performances in front of large groups of people. Sharing his perspective in the workshops at the conference had made him open to this idea of being a speaker. I was thrilled to see him want to become more involved with the Autism Community in a professional way. I absolutely love giving presentations, so this new area of interest that was opening up for B.D. was particularly exciting for me.

🖤 **Learning opportunities:** Are there topics you or a person you are working with are especially interested in? Maybe there is a conference, gathering, class, books, documentaries or other ways to learn more.

Create an Inspirational Quote

We set to work on sharing B.D.'s story and wisdom through a PowerPoint presentation. At first, I, of course, asked lots of questions, then wrote down his responses. I explained this as the brainstorming stage of the process, where all information is welcome and there is no editing or comments. Simply sharing ideas at first without analyzing how they will be used or organized is the best way to be thorough and allow creativity to flow through. After this brainstorming process, we looked over B.D.'s ideas and considered how they might be organized in a logical way. I made suggestions, he made suggestions, and together, a cohesive outline was created through his slides, awaiting B.D.'s storytelling to expand on these topics. He included the slide about the dignity of risk from the conference.

B.D. quickly learn how to create slides using PowerPoint, so I asked if he wanted to create his own quote for one of the slides. Right away, he shared ideas for a quote, which I wrote down and we refined together. What a fun process this was for both of us. It seemed to flow forward with little effort. Here is his quote:

> # Let me make my own mistakes because I actually learn from my mistakes.
>
> # B.D.

B.D. was eager to get lots of likes and comments on his social media pages when he posted this quote. For this project, B.D. used his artistic abilities to write inspiring quotes and put them on exciting backgrounds, which don't show up here because the book is printed in black and white. I remembered Dechen's suggestion to explore art with B.D. and realized his creativity was coming through in a different format than I originally imagined, which was very cool.

♥ **Create an Inspirational Quote:** Each of us has gained wisdom in our lives. Consider writing an inspirational quote and sharing it with friends and family. Some interesting discussions may arise.

Evaluate Messages Shared

B.D. was ready to run with these new skills and much to my surprise, when we looked at his Facebook page the following week, he had created two more posts completely on his own. I was thrilled to witness him embracing this new method of expressing himself. However, I was also concerned about the content of the posts. Instead of being inspirational, they had more of a venting feeling, of sharing frustrations in a way that made me as a reader feel hopeless. We discussed his role as a leader at this point and I talked with him about how it is important to be careful about what messages are shared with people. While venting is important to get feelings and frustrations expressed, it may be best not to share with the public until the inspirational message waiting to emerge from those feelings is discovered. I gave him numerous examples to consider. B.D. listened to me and over time came to understand what I was saying. This was a lesson in patience for me, because as his mentor, I can make suggestions, but I cannot make him do anything unless he wants to. B.D. chose to keep the two posts he created on his social media page. I shared with his parents these posts were not created with me or endorsed by me and described how we are working on sharing inspirational messages. Learning takes time and sometimes people just want to do what they want to do. As a mentor, I sometimes need to accept this and move forward with my process, which at this time meant returning to the PowerPoint presentation.

♣ **Evaluate Messages Shared:** What kinds of social media posts do you share or someone you work with share? Are they inspirational, educational, funny, sad, confusing, clarifying? What message do you most want to share with the world? Maybe you are in alignment with what is important to you and maybe some changes could be made.

Circle of Support

We showed B.D.'s dad the PowerPoint he had created, and even from the first introductory slide, he was impressed. He liked the layout and encouraged B.D. to include the reasons why he likes living alone, which led to one particularly funny story he tells which I will share later. I told B.D.'s dad how quickly he had been learning these skills and said I would help him practice and go with him the first few times he spoke in public. After that, I felt quite sure B.D. would be giving presentations on his own. We showed the presentation to his mom and she had several helpful suggestions to bring more depth to what he was sharing with his audience. Next, B.D. showed the PowerPoint to his Circle of Support team.

B.D.'s Circle of Support meetings are usually scheduled every three months. I brought my laptop to this one so he could briefly show everyone his presentation. The meeting went well as B.D. expressed himself confidently and everyone enjoyed having a sneak preview of his presentation. The group suggested other places where B.D. might speak, which was wonderful. His team was excited to witness his steady progress toward working full time at a supermarket, instead of working part time at two different places.

There is always some business to address at these meetings, many regulations to understand and much paperwork to fill out so B.D. can receive the support he is so fortunate to receive. I like the way his dad is always thinking about what support B.D. would need if he or B.D.'s mom were not around. One question he had at this meeting was who would help B.D. fill out the medical insurance updates every five years, as those forms were very complicated and they had to be filled out on time. One possible benefit of B.D. landing a full-time job would be that he would be covered for medical insurance through his work and wouldn't have to worry about applying through the government for benefits.

❤ **Circle of support:** Who is on your circle of support team? Have you ever gathered them all together when you were wanting some encouragement?

Dream Reflections

The night before this meeting, I had this dream:

I was late getting to a court appearance for B.D. and was searching all over for the courthouse. Even the cab driver had trouble finding it. When I finally arrived, a big group of his family was at the court and they were all waiting for B.D.'s turn. They were a lively group, having a lot of fun. The judge told us all to take a break before he continued. We all jumped into the ocean and played, which was awesome. It felt like a celebration.

While we didn't take a break to swim and frolic in the ocean together during the Circle of Support meeting, this gathering felt like a wonderful celebration of the progress B.D. has made, which felt like the celebration in the dream. Filled with joy when walking home after the meeting, I am thrilled B.D. has the skills and strength to work full time. I think about the many other young adults with special gifts who will never be able to work full time because of their skill level or health. Don't all people deserve meaningful work and health insurance which is easy to obtain? Someone who is unwell and has mental or emotional challenges on top of this needs coverage which is easy to manage. Not all people with special gifts have a loving support system like B.D.. I know I can only do so much and am grateful for the incredible support he receives from his family and Circle of Support Team.

❤ **Dream reflections:** How do your dreams relate to what is happening in your life? Is there wisdom to be gleaned from your dreams?

Be Vulnerable

I enjoy helping B.D. learn how to express himself. When he experiences situations in his life which trigger strong emotions, I give him the opportunity to share these things in a safe way. Sometimes we use these opportunities to jump into an inspiring creation or an unexpected surprise. Other times, just speaking about what is on his mind may be enough. I create an open, safe atmosphere so he feels comfortable risking opening up.

For example, we had one such moment about B.D.'s dad who lived in Florida part of the year, especially when it was cold, and would move back during the Spring. When his dad was going to be moving back soon, I asked B.D. how it would be having his dad living with him again. B.D. started laughing and holding his hand in front of his mouth in an attempt to keep his laughter inside. This was new behavior for me to witness, and I wasn't quite sure how to handle the situation, so I walked out of the room to give him privacy. When I came back, I couldn't believe he was still laughing. I asked what was so funny and he said it was inappropriate to share. I dropped the subject, and he worked his giggles out before it was time for me to leave. I was really curious about what was so funny, while at the same time, I realized everyone deserves to have their own secret laughs. It was both intriguing and fun to see B.D. laughing like this.

Another day, when we were working on his PowerPoint presentation, I asked what he liked about living by himself. He got the giggles again, putting his hand on his mouth and said what he was thinking wasn't appropriate. I assured him this wasn't a problem and suggested we work on something else. Finally, he blurted out, "I like walking around butt-naked!" Laughter ensued from both of us, and I assured B.D. this was not inappropriate to say and in fact, would be great fun to share when he is presenting. Specifically, he likes not having to put clothes on when walking to the shower, and I assured him this was appropriate, honest, and fun to say even in front of a group of people.

As I considered our conversation later, I realized Tom and I had not been able to walk around our house without clothes for several years because at different times, we have had various family members living with us. I smiled as I remembered B.D.'s giggling admission and I thought how well I understood how he felt. I was looking forward to a time when Tom and I could walk to the bathroom on a warm summer night "butt-naked" as well!

133

Be vulnerable: How often do we think we are the only one who does something and we are not sure if there is something wrong about the way we live our life? Often in these circumstances, when we share something vulnerable with a trusted person, commonalities can be found and it feels good to have the "secret" or what we thought should be private out in the open.

Expand Social Circles

B.D.'s social circle is really tight. His parents and brother are at the center and it expands out to a large, loving, extended family on both his mom and dad's sides. The next ring of social connection is with friends from high school, many of them are thanks to B.D.'s older brother, who introduced B.D. to his big group of friends. B.D. is also involved with a welcoming and accepting group of friends from the arts through the chorus and musicals he participated in. As his mom shares, "These friends made B.D.'s high school experience phenomenal."

His social circle continues out to the people B.D. has met in his adult life through an autism spectrum social group his parents started, plus mentors he has worked with and co-workers from his two jobs. Another group of people are those he sees when he performs karaoke at a local bar a few times a month. B.D.'s social activity could be quite extensive if he were to reach out to any of these groups of people on a regular basis, but he does not. He does go to all of his family celebrations as long as he isn't working. He attends his social group meetings once a month, yet doesn't reach out to friends much to talk or get together. While B.D. has very good social skills for meeting people initially and connecting with people he knows, there are still many skills to learn.

B.D.'s dad told us about a Self-Advocacy Picnic, which was an opportunity to socialize and meet new people. This picnic happened to be at a park near David and Rose's houses. You know Rose well and David just a little bit. David is also on the autism spectrum, and just like everyone on the spectrum, he is his own, unique, spectacular self. I shared information about the picnic with both David and Rose. We all signed up for the picnic, which was thrilling for me because socializing and meeting new people are important skills for people with special gifts to practice. The day turned out to be full of learning and positive experiences for all of us—it was a real blessing, and it never would have happened if we had not sought out new connections and joined each other at the picnic.

❤ **Expand Social Circles:** Seeking opportunities to meet new people expands our horizons and provides opportunities to create new, possibly meaningful connections with people.

Reduce Stress as Much as Possible

B.D. drove both David and myself to the picnic. This was a great opportunity for David to experience B.D. driving, as he is a role model for David who wasn't driving, yet wants to learn. We were half an hour early for the picnic, which was completely acceptable as many other people were early. This is a commonality between B.D. and David because they both like to arrive early for events to reduce anxiety. In previous years, I remember one of Tom's colleagues, a chemistry teacher at the high school where he worked, who would always arrive early for parties we hosted. As a mother of two young girls, I remember being annoyed because we weren't ready and instead of helping, he wanted to chat, requiring lots of attention. I now realize this man may have been on the autism spectrum or perhaps was just lonely. I now have an *aha* realization and softness with this memory. The experiences I have with the people I work with help me to understand things which have happened in my own past. Maybe I should have been more patient toward Tom's colleague, as there might be aspects to his story I didn't know back then.

♥ **Reduce Stress as Much as Possible:** Arriving early helped B.D. and David feel more comfortable with large gatherings. In the section with Rose, I shared how my family's accepting attitude helped Rose feel safe with a group of people she did not know. How might situations be made less stressful for yourself or the people you work with? Are there any tricks or changes which could be made which might turn a seemingly impossible situation into a manageable one?

Network

We were greeted right away by Mark, who told us all about the event and immediately started introducing us to people who were wonderful connections for B.D.'s speaking endeavors. Contrary to what many people might expect from a person on the spectrum, Mark excels in people connection skills, which shows how each person is unique with their own valuable gifts. Mark is proud of knowing everyone at the picnic and each person's role in the self-advocacy community. He introduced us to Bonnie, who was very excited about the idea of B.D. presenting to professionals in the field. Mark also suggested we speak with someone else named Cynthia and brought us over to her at the other end of the park for an introduction. His ability to remember names and roles, plus keep track of people's locations, is a real gift. The people I work with often experience challenges making connections with new people, yet having ties to the community and with peers can make a big difference in both social and professional settings. These connections would prove invaluable as B.D. set up his speaking gigs and began his efforts at being a self-advocate.

❦ **Network:** When is the last time you attended an event where you didn't know most of the people attending? Meeting new people often leads to interesting connections and new possibilities. Which events and people might help with finding networking opportunities? How can you help facilitate those connections?

Be Open to Differences

The people we work with can be very different, even if they have similar diagnoses. For example, B.D. and David are both on the spectrum, and both have been diagnosed with OCD. These differences became really apparent when we were playing cards at the picnic. After B.D. and I spent some time networking, David, B.D. and I decided to play UNO, so we headed over to the shelter where there were games set up. I have only played UNO a few times and needed help with the rules, which both guys were happy to teach me. B.D. shuffled and dealt first and the game was quite smooth, until I forgot to say UNO. I realized this pretty quickly and said "UNO" just as B.D. was pointing out my omission. David was going to let me off the hook since I was a beginner, but I decided to follow the rules and pull two more cards. B.D. won this round, then David and I duked it out for second place. When David had one card left, he said, "UNO!" too late, then put down his other card right away in a flurry of fun and laughter between us. "Oh, I see who I am dealing with now," I jokingly said to David.

What fun and levity there was between David and myself. B.D. was very serious and focused throughout the game. I didn't notice how B.D. responded to our kidding around—I worried he might feel left out because we were having so much fun, while he wasn't participating in our jokes. More likely, our jokes just were not funny to B.D., which is completely okay. I have different relationships with each person I mentor and it was interesting to notice this when they were both with me at the same time.

When David shuffled, he had a unique style of dealing. He would drop extra cards, then count to see how many we each had, adding extras where needed until each person had the proper total of seven cards. This was an insight into his challenges with understanding numbers and was the most creative way of dealing cards I have ever witnessed. David was also unique in the way he put out cards, often sending them sliding off the pile, which was immediately followed by B.D. putting the card back on top of the pile. After doing this a bunch of times, B.D. explained, "It's my OCD." Whereas David would let the cards fall where they may, B.D. had to tidy up the pile. David shared that he has OCD also, which made me chuckle inside because their types of OCD are really different. I realized how I really like having things in order and maybe I have a touch of OCD as well. Hey, being orderly is a good quality, isn't it? So many insights to people's personalities can be gleaned just from playing a game together.

♣ **Be Open to Differences:** How does the person you work with express their unique needs or challenges? Which coping mechanisms do they use? Even among people with similar issues, what do their different ways of coping help us to learn about them? How do we cope with our own special issues?

Let Someone Else Be In Charge

Another important phenomenon we witnessed at the picnic was how displays of leadership from one attendee inspired more actions of leadership from others. This became a great learning and confidence building experience as people passed an invisible leadership baton from one person to another. B.D. held the baton first when he drove David and me to picnic.

Later in the day, David in turn took the baton when he suggested B.D. and I go on a hike, guiding us to a path he selected. David was our leader in the beginning as he guided us up and down some small hills. When we came to a long, steep hill B.D. grabbed the baton as he moved out in front for the rest of the hike. B.D. passed the baton to me when he asked what poison ivy looks like. I was able to show both of them what was and wasn't poison ivy out of the plants with three leaves. David and B.D. didn't need me to be leader of the entire hike and it was fun to witness how we shared the invisible leadership baton seamlessly. We were all pleasantly wiped out after this long hike on a hot day.

This notion of sharing the leadership baton continued through the picnic. I had been thinking how Rose would have enjoyed hiking and was happy to see her at the picnic with her mentor Kristina when we returned. Kristina said Rose had been missing us, but they met two nice people while we were hiking: Jason and Roger. Having Kristina with us was really lovely as she engaged both B.D. and David in some wonderful conversations and I was most grateful she took the leadership baton with them as this was a pleasant change. There are times when I just don't know how to get a conversation going with these lovely young men and so I am quiet. Allowing Kristina to take the lead not only provided me with a break, but it allowed B.D. and David to have interesting discussions with a new person.

Yet another important mentorship opportunity emerged at the picnic. Allowing David and B.D. to be a leader, inspired more acts of leadership. Rose couldn't open her can of soda, which David noticed and asked if he could help. This act, which showed David's gentleness and respect toward Rose, was heartbreakingly beautiful. Rose was really grateful. Both Kristina and I let David know what a wonderfully patient teacher he is. Rose was catching me up on her news and then bounced over to her new friends, Jason and Roger, inviting them to join us for lunch. I noticed Jason struggling to open his chip bag with his teeth and suggested he get some help. Roger started to help out, until Rose asked if she could open the bag for Jason. Right away Roger handed the bag to Rose. She carefully puffed out the bag at the top so she could grab it on either side, then opened it with ease. We talked about how David helped Rose open her soda and she now helped Jason open his chips. Clearly, she was inspired by David's kind and respectful offer to help, and wanted to contribute her own kind and respectful service as well. How wonderful it is noticing this circle of kindness!

Let Someone Else Be in Charge: How can you facilitate this kind of respectful leadership opportunities with the people you work with? What about in your own life? Are there specific areas in which people are experts? Which areas might be improved with some help from another leader? Is there anyone you could turn to who might have the kind of knowledge which could support you?

Celebrate

After dropping David off at home, B.D. took me to his house where we filled out paperwork together before I walked to my home a few blocks away. What a successful day of learning on many different levels. I felt blessed as a mentor witnessing these amazing young people interacting in their own unique ways. This day made me realize my work as a mentor was meaningful and was creating positive change in these three magnificent young adults. I was inspired to keep finding new activities and experiences to help each of them thrive. When I told B.D.'s parents about all the wonderful connections B.D. made at the picnic, his mom sent me this email:

OMG, this is wonderful on so many levels...what a beautiful day all around!!!! I love the idea with the conference, would love to see you both in action B.D. My heart is full of gratitude Maria for what you bring to our lives.
XOX,
B.D.'s mom

How fun celebrating both through my own reflections and also B.D.'s mom. You already know compliments are often the best kind of pay for me.

♥ **Celebrate:** How do you celebrate your successes and have them live on, through sharing stories, creating a scrapbook with pictures, writing a poem or drawing a painting to express your excitement? Putting energy into celebrations in different formats elevates your energy and expresses clearly what you would like to have more of in your life.

Practice In Order to Succeed

I worked with B.D. as he practiced his PowerPoint presentation, giving him a few pointers, as we added a few new things to his slides. I couldn't wait to see B.D. present in front of an audience, and I felt like this could bring him many wonderful opportunities. During his presentation, he mentioned the *Autism Spectrum Disorder Conference: Support through Transitions* that we attended in New Paltz, which was perfect because that is where this idea came from initially. How proud I felt of B.D. for embracing his upcoming speaking career with great gusto. B.D. told me he was also rehearsing what he would say on his own. He wanted his speaking to be lively and interesting. I felt excited for his debut performance. I knew B.D. would have support from family and friends cheering him on, and imagined people with special gifts benefitting from his story and wisdom.

❤ **Practice in Order to Succeed:** When preparing for an event which is important to you, how do you practice and prepare yourself? If something seems very challenging, is there a way to break it down into smaller, more manageable pieces? Is there some way to feel fear or anxiety when they arise, yet still continue forward with plans?

Recognize Lessons Learned

On his own, B.D. realized the importance of promoting his presentation in order to have an audience to hear him speak. When checking his page on Facebook, I was pleasantly surprised to see B.D. had tagged me in a post about his upcoming presentation. Here is what he wrote:

I shoulda post this earlier. On September 26, at the Self Advocacy of New York State (SANYS) meeting, ill be doing my presentation there. My presentation is called "Successful Living with the Autism Spectrum." On that day, I'm gonna be talking about growing up with the Autism spectrum, my challenges and advices. If guys are interested, you are welcomed. It's free and free admission. It will take place at Middletown thrall library at 6pm-7:30pm. When you guys enter the library, it's upstairs and make a right. I've been working on my presentation for months with the help my mentor Maria Blon. Can't wait to share it with you guys 💯 🙏 🧩

As I wrote about earlier in this book, B.D. has also been practicing expressing his feelings in appropriate ways. He told me about helping a co-worker whose father had passed. Later that day, I found this thoughtful, supportive post B.D. had put up:

Today at Shoprite, I found out that my fellow cart pusher Derek's father passed away. His father suffered a stroke months ago and lived in a nursing home since. But his health was just not getting any better. Because of this, Derek has been calling out of work and I'm the one who's been covering his shifts most of the time. Derek is one hell of a cart pusher. Derek is a great guy and I was happy to cover his shift so he can be with His father. Derek, I promise you this, you and your family will get through this tough time. Shoprite gives u our condolences 🙏 ♡

How pleased I am to witness B.D. expressing himself in effective ways and inspiring people with his kindness. Although I was initially apprehensive about some of his social media outreach, I actually look

144

forward to his Facebook posts now as they are introspective and I get a feel for what is truly important to B.D. When I first started working with him, he acted more robotically, as is typical of people with autism. I wasn't sure what made B.D. tick or how I could learn what was important to him. Interacting with B.D. has taught me so much and there is pride when I notice him mastering lessons I've shared with him, like these examples of communicating with people in positive ways. This evidence of his eagerness to be an uplifting role model within the Autism community is inspiring. Here are a few more bits of inspiration from B.D.'s Facebook page:

I finally got done with this amazing book, "Black Profiles in Courage" by Kareem Abdul-Jabar, 1996. Even though there's still racism in this world, it's not as bad [as] back then.

You don't find your worth in a man or woman, you find it in yourself – and then you attract those who are worthy.

I used to think I was introverted because I really liked being alone, but it turns out that I just like being at peace, and I am very extroverted around people who bring me peace.

There is a boy with autism who has taught me more about life than anything else in this world ever will. by Walk Down Autism Lane

❦ **Recognize Lessons Learned:** When working on different skill sets, do you notice when you or someone you are working with really gets a lesson and is competent now to navigate this area of their life on their own? I love receiving inspiration from a person who at one time, I offered inspiration to. This feels like what I give, eventually I receive in return, either from the same or different source. Since there is often a gap in time between the giving and receiving, making an effort to recognize lessons learned is of great value, with many rewards.

145

Allow People to Make their Own Decisions

I was wondering if introducing B.D. would make sense or if he would prefer to get up there and start presenting right away. I asked B.D. and said he would like to speak on his own, but appreciated me being there as a backup in case he wasn't sure of how to answer a question. I was so glad I asked B.D. what he wanted, because now I knew how I could be of greatest service to him.

After much preparation, the big day finally arrived for B.D.'s first presentation, "Successful Living within the Autism Spectrum." We met in the presentation room fifteen minutes early to set up. The SANYS meeting organizer, Andy, was there with his projector ready to go, only it was an old projector, and unfortunately, the connections didn't fit either B.D's or my laptop. I explained the library had a cart with projector, which I used in the past. Andy left to inquire and found out the AV person was gone for the day and the equipment needed to be reserved ahead of time. I could have run home to get my projector, but didn't because B.D. was content using what was available to him. Since there was no way to connect to the projector, there would be no pictures or video to enhance his presentation. B.D. set up his PowerPoint on Andy's laptop as it had a bigger screen than mine. He handled these technological challenges like a champ, staying calm and trusting all would be fine, which it was. B.D.'s slides were mostly used as prompts for his talking points, so this set up was adequate for his needs. I tend to want things to be perfect and get very stressed when making a presentation, so I prefer to double-check everything is exactly according to plan. However, B.D. really dislikes being reminded about things, so I didn't remind him to double-check these things. I chose to respect his wishes, even though it might mean facing challenges before his presentation. B.D. was thrilled to be there, giving his presentation for the first time and he didn't care about the tech problems. He just wanted to enjoy the moment without having to worry about issues which turned out to be irrelevant to him. It was a learning moment for me observing how he was able to simply be present and not stressed. I am glad I respected his wishes and was able to learn so much from him.

♥ **Allow People to Make Their Own Decisions:** When do you try to make decisions for people based on your own fears? How can you allow them to take actions according to their values? What might happen if you let someone follow their own path instead of trying to lead them down yours? Is it possible another path might be helpful for you? What can you learn from seeing others choose a different way?

Support the People You Work With

Do you remember Mark from the picnic? He was co-leader of the SANYS meeting, with Andy functioning as the other leader. They started the meeting with a couple of quick items and then B.D. was invited to take the floor. The room was full of friends, family, and SANYS members, people who made up a supportive, interested audience. B.D. was confident, practiced, spontaneous, and funny. He did an amazing job adapting to people interrupting his presentation, politely reminding them he would take questions at the end. I loved the confidence he exuded as he spoke about the importance of taking risks. He explained how challenging it was pushing carts at the grocery store where he works. Sometimes cars don't pay attention to him and there is always the possibility of getting hit by a car. Employees are only supposed to push a few carts at a time when putting them away, but this is not time efficient method, as B.D. explained to us. He uses his strength and focus to push five or more carts at a time, saving time and developing his cart pushing skills. I just love how he is proud of his work and when he shares his ingenuity to do his best. This example of taking risks when at work was actually another example of his willingness to take on the challenge of public speaking, which was a different kind of risk, yet he was definitely embraced in this supportive environment for his debut performance. When B.D. said, "What I value most about living on my own is privacy. Privacy is so important to me. I like walking around butt naked," everyone cracked up, and B.D. had a huge smile on his face.

B.D.'s friends shared their excitement for him to give more presentations, along with the desire to share their stories and present with him in the future. The hugs, congratulations and excitement for B.D.'s first successful presentation were heartwarming and inspiring. People were already asking him to speak at other venues. The next morning, I received this lovely message from B.D.'s mom who could not attend the event since she was out of town.

You should be a proud mama, I heard B.D. did great! I can't wait to see the video. When I spoke to him, he was so pleased with himself, and thankful for you. I can't even express my gratitude for what you have brought to his life on so many levels!!! You're an angel!

How lucky I feel to have been one of B.D.'s supporters and to witness him shining so brightly, seeming to feel completely at ease in the spotlight.

♥ **Support the People You Work With:** How can you create a positive environment to help someone or yourself try new opportunities? What is needed to create a supportive environment? Where might you find a safe place to test your own new ideas?

Share Appreciation

It's absolutely important to let people know when they have made a positive difference in your life. Simply acknowledging those gifts can make a huge difference for another person. For example, during his presentation B.D. explained how he learned to read at the movie store FYE (For Your Entertainment). Because he loved movies, his mom would take him to FYE where he would read the backs of movies for two or three hours each visit. B.D. acted out his mom waiting patiently for him on a bench outside with her chin in her hand, to everyone's amusement. Throughout his presentation, B.D. thanked the people who have helped him be successful in his life—his mom, dad, brother, speech therapists, teachers, and mentors. B.D. thanked me for teaching him yoga and even introduced me to the crowd, which was a surprise, as he had never thanked me personally before. I was deeply touched.

At the end of the presentation, I met his older brother for the first time. I shared how much B.D. appreciated him, especially for introducing B.D. to his friends at school. His brother said, in a hurt voice, "He has never told me that." Oh, how my heart went out to him at that moment, as I know how painful it is when we don't hear love and gratitude directly from people in our life. I told him B.D. had shared his appreciation with me many times and reiterated what a great brother he has been. His brother minimized the important role he had, saying B.D. already knew his friends. I emphasized how many older brothers would not want their younger brother, most especially one with special gifts, hanging around their friends and how important this was for B.D. Telling the people in our lives how much we love and appreciate them is a hard thing for many people to do. I made a mental note to begin working on this skill more with B.D. Imagine how healing this would be for B.D. and his family to speak appreciations out loud more often.

❤ **Share Appreciation:** How could you show gratitude for people in your life? Especially in situations where a person is doing heroic things and not being noticed, a kind word with acknowledgement of their impact on your life can make a real difference. Have you acknowledged and appreciated your own contributions?

Respect and Hear People's Stories

After his presentation, B.D. opened the floor up to questions, answering them with ease and grace. This new role I was watching him take on as he attentively listened to each person's story was amazing to witness as a new aspect of B.D.'s personality was shining through quite strongly. An eight year old boy, who is also on the autism spectrum asked some great questions. Then people started sharing their stories of living successfully with not only autism but also other special gifts. Some of these stories were long and could be quite sad, but B.D. was empathetic and patient with each person, allowing them to fully express themselves. After many questions were answered and stories were shared, a parent of a young boy with autism actually went up to stand with B.D. and began sharing many challenges he has faced when searching for support to help his son. I felt annoyed with this adult who had taken over B.D.'s stage, instead of waiting until after B.D. had finished. When I couldn't stand it any longer, I walked over to Andy to ask about what would come next, hoping he would ask this man to step down, but Andy didn't do that. I guess their policy is to let every person speak as much as they like, whenever they like. Judging by the way audience members rolled their eyes, I could tell lots of people were annoyed with this anxious parent who was going on and on, taking the attention away from B.D.. And yet, when I spoke to B.D.'s dad at the end, he was proud of how B.D. listened to each and every person as they spoke, even this parent who I viewed as being intrusive. B.D.'s poise in front of the crowd reminded his dad of when he was a member of the school board and used to give community members the opportunity to be heard. My perspective about how a meeting ought to be run was different, and this was another learning experience for me. Since adults with special gifts may take more time to express themselves and parents are not always given a place to share their challenges, the SANYS meetings are a forum where everyone may speak freely. B.D. seemed to intuitively understand this, which will make him an excellent advocate for others. This is just the beginning of a wonderful career for B.D. and it is exciting to be part of his journey, witnessing where he will go from here.

Since B.D. has been showing an interest in advocating for people on the spectrum, I felt he could benefit from learning about the challenges other people on the spectrum face through reading books which share their stories. I asked B.D. what he thought of this idea and he was very interested. I leant him the novel, "The Rosie Project," written by Graeme Simsion, published in 2014, which is a sweet novel about a young man on the spectrum who is determined to find the perfect girlfriend. I also suggested he read John Elder Robinson's memoir, "Look Me in the Eye", published in 2008. When I notice skills and see potential areas of growth for a person, I enjoy finding ways to encourage expansion, building on skills already apparent.

Respect and Hear People's Stories: What can you learn from hearing people's experiences? When can you be of service by simply listening to someone share their stories?

Don't Give Up if You Believe in Something

At his Circle of Support meeting, I explained B.D. and I had applied to speak at the SANYS State Conference. They were a bit shocked we applied to speak at this conference and asked what the title of the presentation was, as well as the dates. I couldn't remember the title, but did know the dates. As soon as I got home, I sent them an email with this proposal:

> *Name: Maria Blon*
> *I will be presenting with self-advocate B.D.*
>
> *Title of Workshop:*
> *Blooming: Guiding self-advocates to reach their full potential*
>
> *Description:*
> *Relish in the joy of mentoring adults with special gifts who are soaring to great heights in the life they are designing for themselves. Interactive speaker, author, and mentor Maria Blon will share heart opening stories from her upcoming book and engage participants in activities. Actor and self-advocate extraordinaire B.D. will share the successful life he has made for himself, while encouraging all people to be treated with dignity.*
>
> *Please note your experience presenting to self-advocates and/or at conferences:*
> *I have presented at a number of different conferences over many years and am a mentor to self-advocates. This will be B.D.'s first time presenting at a conference.*

I was terribly anxious to hear whether B.D. and I would be invited to speak at the SANYS Statewide Conference in October, believe it or not, I was checking my email every day, several times a day for a response. Well, we finally got the disappointing news that our proposal was not accepted. We were told to speak at regional meetings first before applying for the statewide conference. I wish we had known this ahead of time, and I also wish I hadn't allowed myself to get so worked up over hearing whether we were accepted or not. We were planning to speak at local and regional meetings anyway, so were doing what they asked of us. This setback showed me how much I have missed giving presentations and was a wake up call to make efforts for myself to search out speaking opportunities.

♥ **Don't Give Up if You Believe in Something:** When feeling disappointed, this is a sign of something worth putting more effort into. Be flexible and refocus your efforts. What could you do to make this happen? How could you improve your materials? Are there any other pathways you might try? Who might be a helpful ally to refocus your efforts?

Admit What You Don't Know

B.D. was determined to continue speaking about self-advocacy, and we in his circle of support were eager to help him achieve this goal. Not long after this, B.D.'s dad made a speaking connection for him at a local university for an education class. B.D.'s presentation was wonderful and it was fantastic having his mom there because she was able to answer a lot of questions about his early schooling. If there was a question he didn't know the answer to, mom was there as a backup. B.D. didn't get flustered by not being able to answer a question—I know I would have. Since learning is not always easy for him, he has had lots of practice calmly saying, "I don't know" and being okay with that. The students were very impressed with his confidence while presenting and asked some thoughtful questions. What a boost this was for B.D., speaking to a college class. The professor even asked him to come back the next semester.

❤ **Admit What You Don't Know:** How hard or easy is it for you to say, "I don't know."? What can you learn from not knowing information? How will being honest about what you don't know help you be a better mentor, presenter or person? It really is okay to not know everything and to ask someone who does know to help out. The person who helps out will feel valuable because you asked for their assistance.

Know When to Step In and Out

Sometimes, I am not sure of the best way for B.D. and I to spend our time together. Mother's Day was coming up and I asked B.D. if he would like to work on a project together to honor his mom, which he agreed was a good idea. I asked him what he appreciates and loves about his mother and wrote down what he said. Then we looked at what he had come up with, created a quote from his words, went to the computer so he could look for pictures which might work well with his quote and he picked one out. I showed him how to add text to the picture and the options which were available for fonts. B.D. makes decisions quickly when doing creative projects like this. He is very focused and once he makes a decision, he sticks with it. I admire his decisiveness and focus, which are gifts many people on the autism spectrum have.

B.D and I also talked about what he might write to go with this beautiful post written in his mom's honor and this is what he created:

If you care that much about someone, do what's best for him or her.

B.D. Anthony

My mom is a perfect example of this person. Because of my autism, she put me through school at the Orange-Ulster BOCES. I was in the BOCES program until I was 15 yrs old. After that, she sent me to Pine Bush High School in IEP (Individualized Education Program) class. Because of this, I made a lot of friends there (which I still keep in touch with) because of mom and also my brother. Also because of going there, I graduated in 2011. Before going to PBHS (Pine Bush High School), I knew people from Pine Bush because of Wallkill fire soccer that dad use to do yrs ago. If my mom didnt do this, I've woulda been non verbal autistic and not social for the rest of my life. Happy Mother's Day mom, love you.

Oh my, hearing B.D. share how much love and appreciation he has for his mom opened my heart and eyes in new ways. I hadn't witnessed him speaking a lot about his mom, much less sharing his feelings with such thoughtfulness. What an absolutely amazing Mother's Day gift.

The following year when Mother's Day rolled around again, I asked B.D. what he planned to do for his mom this year. He said, "I don't know, to be honest."I started asking questions about what his mom likes and there was silence for a long time, followed by, "I'm not sure." I kept asking questions with little response or excitement and at the end of our work, I was feeling defeated as if I had somehow failed this year, when the previous year had felt like such a success. What I came to realize is B.D. didn't want or need my help to honor his mother. He knew how to do this on his own and wanted take care of this himself. Upon further reflection, I realized we never worked on a Father's Day project together. B.D. was quite capable of appreciating and celebrating his dad and mom. This was my cue to step out and let B.D. honor his parents in the way he chooses.

🖤 **Know When to Step In and Out:** There are times when our guidance is welcome, then after skills are learned and confidence gained, our guidance is no longer needed. Recognizing when to step in and out takes awareness of both your motivations and the needs of the person you are working with. How do you discern when your input is valuable or a distraction to the well being of the person you are with? Do you speak up if someone is offering their guidance when you would prefer to work on something on your own?

Balance Silence With Talking

Do you know people who, even before they set their foot into a room, seek to be the center of attention? All conversations, regardless of how captivating they are, come to a halt as this person begins to chatter loudly about whatever is on their mind. Every single person in the room is forced to listen as the blabber recounts dramas occurring in their life. Even happy celebrations like weddings can be taken over and twisted as the person takes over the agenda with their personal problems and opinions. I don't ever want to be that person. It is my intention to listen first and then respond. I like some silence and pauses in conversations, and this serves me well when mentoring because I have the opportunity to settle, feeling into the surrounding energy. Being a person who likes to be productive and moving forward on something all the time, I also have an urge to know where our work is heading. I am forever asking questions in order to discover what might be ready to emerge. For that reason, since B.D. doesn't typically initiate projects on his own, I become the instigator of the next project by being—yes, you guessed it—the noisiest, most talkative person in the room or in the Zoom room, if we are virtual. It feels necessary in this case, but I am not blabbing just to blab about myself. I am presenting possibilities and asking questions until B.D. shows interest and we begin to move forward.

Let's consider the opposite of the blabber in the room, the person who stands in the corner, not approaching anyone, looking like they are afraid someone might approach and they won't know what in the world to say. While B.D. can be outgoing and sociable with people he knows well, he does experience awkward moments when he just doesn't know what to say or how to connect with people. When there is a purpose, conversation can flow with greater ease. When there is simply chatting, this is even more challenging for B.D. and many people on the autism spectrum. I believe this is because they are often very focused on a few interest areas, areas in which they may be exceptionally knowledgeable. B.D. has a deep interest in and factual information about movies and actors. His ability to remember the history of movies and the people who played in them is amazing. He remembers every movie he has watched, as well as what was happening at the time, plus what other movies the lead actors have been in. While most people enjoy movies, not everyone wants to spend a lot of time delving into all these details.

I experienced this same intensity growing up because my father had a limited number of interests which he was extremely passionate about: fishing, exercising, practicing golf, and playing tennis. He was a great model for me of going all in when doing what I loved and maintaining focus to do my best. All of our vacations revolved around Dad's passion for fishing. When he went into a tackle shop, he reveled in chatting with the shop owner and other fishermen, while being careful not to share too much information about his secret spots. Time just melted away for Dad during these conversations, while we melted away in the hot car waiting for him to finish chatting. Yet, when hosting or attending a social gathering with family, Dad really struggled to simply hang out with us, chill, and enjoy being together.

Looking back, I suspect Dad may have been on the autism spectrum, with his intense interests and challenges with socialization, as well as some other clues I'd noticed over the years. I spoke with him one time about the math students I had who were very smart, but were challenged in social situations. He immediately said, "Sounds like me." I smiled in recognition inside, yet didn't reply.

I do find I need to lean toward talking a bit more than I might in conversations with other people. At times, I consciously attempt to model casual chatting with him in the hope this will foster more social skills. Not that he doesn't already have lots of wonderful conversations to model: he has a big, loving family who embrace him with open arms. B.D. often tells me how funny his family is and how he enjoys hearing the funny stories they share. Our one-on-one meetings are different than interactions with family. I have time to ask questions and listen deeply to what he is ready to move forward on, without the emotional entanglements family members tend to develop over time due to shared experiences and history. In other words, I can be objective. Regarding conversation then, the questions I am always asking myself in this work are, "To blab or not to blab?" These are the questions I ask as I attempt to find the right balance as B.D. and I explore social skills and discover the next creation waiting to grow.

❤ **Balance Silence with Talking:** How do you decide when to speak and when to be silent in different situations? Do you appreciate the power of silence? Of a well-designed question? Are you able to notice when the people around you need one or the other?

Get In Synch

Being aware of your energy level and the energy level of the person you are with can be very important. I have witnessed my friend Sapphire working in synch with a young lady named Aurora. Aurora works very fast, quickly buzzing from one activity to another, with Sapphire doing a great job keeping up with her pace. Watching them, I realized I would need to rest before spending time with her and learn to speed up my tempo if I were to mentor Aurora. I function better in calm and peace, rather than rapid movement all the time. Yet, I also feel challenged when I need to slow down from my typical pace. Some days I will make sure to exercise before spending time with B.D. in order to release some excess energy so I can be more patient.

With B.D., I have learned to come into synch with his rhythm so I can discern what is important to him. His speaking and movements are slower than my typical movements an speaking. I may feel antsy and impatient at times, but when I notice these feelings, I purposely slow down to his speed and get to the point where I feel more relaxed and engaged in the moment. I listen closely with all of my senses, asking what does B.D.'s face look and feel like? Is he moving around more or less than usual? What is the tone of his voice? Each time we are together is different. When there is a project we are working on, the time goes quickly as we are immersed in the flow of creativity. When there is no project being worked on and no clear focus, we sit with not knowing, with uncertainty, which compared with today's fast-paced society may feel quite uncomfortable.

♥ **Get In Synch:** Whether working with or simply being with another person, notice their energy level in comparison to yours. Consider and maybe even experiment with how you might find a way to become in-synch with their energy level. Imagine your body is a car which you are driving and you can shift your energy up and down. How might you do this?

Value Incubation Time

Despite feeling discomfort during times of uncertainty, where there is no clear direction in our work, I have come to value this time as extremely important and have learned to find ways to be more comfortable in this space. I notice myself observing B.D.'s body language and asking lots of questions, testing out what might ignite a spark of interest in his eyes. The way this happens continues to be quite mysterious to me. Where do the questions come from which lead us forward together? My guess is spirit is with us guiding the way.

Interestingly enough, while writing this, our entire world is sitting right smack dab in the middle of uncertainty, as scientists and medical professionals seek to understand this coronavirus pandemic, we all find ourselves in. No plans can be made until more is understood, so while we wait, we live one day at a time, with uncertainty as our companion, sitting beside each and every one of us. There is a time before creativity emerges when ideas are brewing in the unconscious, and we wait to feel what is wanting to show up. Finding ways to be comfortable during this incubation time is what I am learning to do.

❤ **Value Incubation Time:** Waiting for something exciting to come forth can be really challenging. There are times to act and times to stop, plan or reflect. Just because you are not acting doesn't mean you aren't doing anything. A tremendous amount can be occur beneath the surface which we are not aware of. Have you ever found a butterfly chrysalis and brought it inside to observe it hatch? This incubation time before birthing seems to take forever. For monarch butterflies, gestation takes eight to fifteen days; human babies take nine months; elephants are pregnant six hundred-eighty days, over twenty-two months or almost two years. Waiting for something new to be born may seem challenging and yet, this incubation time is vital when bringing new life forward. How might you befriend incubation time in your life? What blessings have you noticed coming from the pause?

161

Set Boundaries with Family Members

I found a flier at our local Shop Rite grocery store about free one-on-one consultations with a dietician. I shared this flier with B.D. and his mom to see if this might be of interest. B.D. was intrigued by this opportunity, so I gave him the flier to look at. Since this idea appealed to him, I told B.D. and mom about a talk entitled "Eating Healthy on a Budget" which the dietician was offering at our local Thrall Library. While the three of us were sitting together at a table, B.D.'s mom slid the flier away from him and placed it in front of her. She used my pencil to write down the details of time, date, and location. Part of me wanted to suggest B.D. write this information down himself and another part of me wanted to simply observe and not say anything. I wonder if I held back due to fear of her taking offense to my suggestion or due to wisdom of knowing it is not easy having people outside of your family coming into your life, making recommendations for change. Nobody likes to be called out. Did I do a disservice to B.D. or was I wise to lay low on this issue for now? I can't go back in time, so the best I can do is recognize I responded to the situation with the utmost of respect. I must admit there have been many times I have really wanted to remind B.D. of something and it was challenging not to. For example, since B.D. wants to be more independent, I choose not to remind him about appointments or meetings.

My primary focus is always the person I am mentoring. I was not there to mentor B.D.'s mom, just B.D. However, this process can't proceed in a vacuum. To provide the most benefit for B.D., we must work as a team. Communicating with B.D.'s family is a necessary part of the work, but it needs to be done with sensitivity and wisdom. When to talk? When to listen? It is a balancing act which I feel my way through each and every time we are together.

❤ **Set Boundaries with Family Members:** Family members may be in the habit of doing things their loved one may be able to do for themself. How do you remind them of that and set healthy boundaries with people? How do you involve parents in the growth process without hurting anyone's feelings? Is there a sensitive way to approach the situation? Are there additional things the person you work with can do for themself?

Encourage Leadership Skills with Compassion

B.D. sends me an email each week with his work schedule. From the beginning, it has been my job to look at my schedule and suggest a few good times for us to work together. This was an effective system in the beginning, and, yet over time, I started feeling annoyed to be doing all the work scheduling our meetings. I spoke to B.D. about being the leader to coordinate our meetings and suggested verbally that he take the initiative to figure out the best day and time for us to meet. He agreed to do this for the next week. The following week, he sent me his schedule with no correspondence from him suggesting when we might get together. The next time we met, I again spoke to him about how to coordinate scheduling our meeting. Once again, he agreed this was a good idea and said he would do this. The following week, I once again received his schedule with no correspondence from him. At our next meeting, we went through this exact same routine, plus I asked if he wanted me to show him an example in writing of what I wanted him to do. He said, "No, I can handle this."

So, what do you think I received in the next email from B.D.? You guessed it, his schedule with no correspondence. The next time we met, I again asked if B.D. would like to see in writing what I was asking him to do and he said, "Yes." I felt relieved he was open to looking at this new skill from a different perspective because he was just not comprehending how to schedule our meeting time. He brought down his notebook, in which we do writing projects, and together, we worked on a sample email. Here is the next email correspondence between B.D. and myself:

B.D.:   *Hey*   *Maria,*
Would you be able to work with me on Tuesday at 1:30pm? If not I can do Wednesday as well. B.D.

Maria: Tuesday 1:30 is good for me B.D.
        Great job! Maria

Now, we are having productive, clear scheduling conversations through our emails, like this one:

Hey   *Maria,*
Are you available to work with me on Tuesday at 1:30pm?
   B.D.

Yes B.D.!
I look forward to seeing you Tuesday :)
   Maria

B.D.: Me too

I am excited B.D. learned how to schedule appointments with me via email and am also thrilled to read his words saying he too is looking forward to seeing me, because I am not sure how much B.D. looks forward to seeing me. He, like many people on the autism spectrum, is not always open or expressive with emotions, so I am excited when I receive concrete proof of how he feels connected with me and appreciates our time together.

The new skills B.D. has learned by being the leader in scheduling our time together, as well as carrying on the related meaningful exchanges, have the potential to improve all of his relationships. This project challenged my patience, but I am happy to have persevered week after week until he was able to make this breakthrough. In fact, these skills were used just a few months later when B.D. was selected to be featured in Apple Magazine. He was contacted by the editor, who asked if he could come in for a photoshoot for their upcoming publication. B.D. could not meet with them during the days they first suggested and offered two other alternatives, using his new scheduling skills beautifully! I talked to him about how it felt doing this scheduling on his own. He said, "Really good." I asked him who usually scheduled appointments for him and he said, "Usually my dad or mom." I feel excited for B.D. as he learns leadership skills by scheduling his own appointments. Each of these successes gives him, and me, more confidence in his growing independence.

♥ **Encourage Leadership Skills with Compassion:** Sometimes when we have skills which come naturally to us, we may not recognize how doing this task might be challenging to another person. Taking time to break down the skill into concrete, simple steps helps people understand what we would like them to do. Learning may take a lot of repetition and guidance until there is full understanding of what is expected. Be patient with yourself and the people you work with during transition times.

Lean into Trust

Sometimes, I only notice progress when looking back in time. Leaning into trust while waiting for change is often necessary. I only just recognized B.D. was getting closer to his employment goal when I started writing this chapter. I have realized the importance of reflection more than ever in my work as a mentor. Even though I only work an hour a week through video chat with B.D., a lot happens during the time we talk together. It doesn't feel like a lot is happening because, as I explained before, our conversations are relatively slow. I ask many more questions than B.D. and often receive one-word responses, after which I might ask for more details. As I reflect back on the hour we were together, I notice we talked about many important topics. I can tell from the occasional smiles which appear on his face that the time we spend together is treasured. And yet sometimes, there are no smiles or feedback, and I wonder if the time spent with B.D. is having any impact at all.

Mom's comment after reading this section, "The struggle to have to ask so many questions to get very little feedback is real."

When reading this comment from B.D.'s mom, I felt immediate relief, knowing I am not the only person spending time with B.D. who is not sure how to handle asking lots of questions and receiving very little feedback.

❤ **Lean into Trust**: When it seems like you are working really hard and not seeing many results, sometimes having faith all will be well and moving forward will happen when the time is right is necessary. What areas of your life might benefit from leaning into trust more?

Be Persistent, Yet Flexible

There is a worldwide pandemic happening now and B.D. knows the precautions he needs to take at work. He wears a mask and gloves, stays at least six feet away from people, and when he gets home, puts his clothes in the laundry and showers. His dad is living in Florida during this time, and B.D. is feeling frustrated by his dad's anxiety and constant text messages about being safe. I asked B.D if he talked with his dad about how he was feeling. He liked this idea of talking with his dad and said he would try this.

The next week, I asked B.D. if he had spoken with his dad, and he replied, "Yes, I asked him to stop texting so much and Dad said he never will because he loves his kids." I asked B.D. how he responded, and he said he didn't reply. B.D. then said to me emphatically, "Dad is nagging me and it doesn't feel good." I would like the reader to keep in mind B.D.'s typical demeanor is calm with not a lot of emotion. These strong feelings being expressed are out of the ordinary and signal something is genuinely bothering him. I pondered this for a bit, and an idea appeared: Could you try going on offense with your dad, instead of defense? Just like in soccer. There is an offense and defense. Right now, you are playing defense by receiving your dad's texts. If you go on offense and send your dad texts about how you are staying safe, even sending him pictures of wearing a mask and gloves, maybe he would feel more confident that you are following all recommended precautions and he might nag you less. B.D. smiled at this analogy and said he would give this strategy a try.

The following week, I asked how going on offense with his dad had worked. B.D. explained he sent his dad a picture of a big box of gloves he just bought and his dad had texted back with another question about the gloves, so B.D. didn't feel like this method worked too well. I gather from his response, B.D. would like to have less questions to answer, which means going on offense didn't work from this perspective.

He tried going on offense through Facebook posts, but the nagging continued from his dad, increasing B.D.'s stress. So we referred back to a skill used in the past and worked on writing a compliment sandwich he could read to his dad. Here is what he came up with:

Dad, I really appreciate you looking out for me and making sure I have everything I need for this difficult time. But you really need

167

to stop overdoing this. I get the feeling you don't think I can take care of myself when you keep texting me to ask if I have everything I need. I am aware of this difficult time. I am aware of the coronavirus and have been thinking of it more than anything else. I am taking good care of myself. But again, I really appreciate you caring about me and Matt as well.

The next week, I asked if he shared his compliment sandwich with his dad, and B.D. replied, "Yes, I texted him the letter and nothing changed. He said he is not going to stop texting me and Matt because he loves us, and this is what he needs to do as a father. I talked to Matt and he said Dad does the same thing with him. Dad is just a germophobe."

We talked about the importance of expressing himself, even if he did not get the result he had hoped for. We also discussed how his dad would be moving back in a few weeks and might feel more relaxed when he is able to see B.D. in-person. B.D. also had a sudden realization, saying, "You know I really notice how relaxed my mom is now and what great work she has done to help her heart heal." Wow! I asked him if he might consider sharing this with his mom and he thought this was a great idea.

Week after week after week, we discussed B.D's feelings about being nagged by his dad. We spent a lot of time on this, and several different strategies were tried without much resolution. Yet, who knows what might happen when his dad returns. And what an amazing insight he'd had about his mom (which he did share with her). B.D. is continuing to develop his ability to express a variety of feelings. He is practicing several communication skills which we have worked on in the past, reinforcing his learning.

These experiences have also taught me a lot. I learned the benefits of persistence, along with recognizing when to move on. To keep the ball rolling, it is necessary to ask follow-up questions of B.D. each week, in this case about how communication went since the last time we spoke. I usually write myself reminders about what to follow up on. Listening, as always, is of paramount importance during these weekly conversations. Each week I ask questions about how B.D. is feeling and closely listen to what he says, offering suggestions to address the need at the time or simply letting him know I feel the pain he is experiencing.

After working on a common theme for a number of weeks and noticing a lack of resolution, it is sometimes wise to let an issue go for a bit and accept what is happening. As I write this now, I realize other skillsets for us to work on are acceptance and choosing how to react to situations. For example, when feeling annoyed by his dad's frequent texts, which seem like nagging, B.D. could acknowledge his feelings, but make the choice to recognize the deep love his dad has for him and send a message back like, "Thanks for the love-nag Dad!" Something like this, which is funny and loving, as well as being true to B.D.'s feelings, might work. This is a tactic to suggest next time.

Hindsight is 20/20, they say. Writing these stories and reflecting on how I handle different situations gives me fresh insights to try in the future. Even if I hadn't been planning to publish a book, I would still use writing to brainstorm ideas about next steps.

Interestingly enough, B.D.'s dad was interviewed by a local magazine to talk about his anxieties about his sons during this time of coronavirus. I was going to include the article here in the book and even got permission from the magazine to use the full article. When a wise friend was sharing her perspective of the book during its early stages, she suggested not including the article within B.D.'s stories because what matters most is how B.D. feels. He was feeling his dad didn't trust him and was able to express this with confidence directly to his dad. B.D. was not able to change his dad's love-nag texts, yet succeeded in speaking up for himself, which takes a lot of courage. I also realize, I want B.D.'s dad to trust him, but teaching parents to trust their children is not part of my job as a mentor. I have let this go.

Ultimately, B.D. inspired me when he came to accept his dad was a germophobe and wasn't going to change. B.D. learned to focus on how much he loved his dad and recognized in most instances he was calm, rational and supportive. What a wonderful example B.D. modeled to me of how to let go.

❤ **Be Persistent, Yet Flexible:** How do you know when to push forward and when it is time to ease up?

Acknowledge Your Own Needs

In the spring of 2020, when the coronavirus was rapidly spreading in New York, the situation was extremely confusing because so much was rapidly changing. Schools were closed down, and there was no precedent as to how these kinds of situations should be handled by mentors. Just at this time, B.D.'s Circle of Support meeting was scheduled for a Monday. I had been looking forward to it for many months.

When Tom, my mother, daughter, and son-in-law met for our regular Sunday evening dinner, each person discussed what they would and would not continue to do this upcoming week. My daughter, son-in-law, and Tom were all educators and their schools made the decision for them that they would not be working for the next two weeks. My mom was planning to attend her regular classes at the YMCA because she planned to keep her routines as long as she could. I said I would attend B.D.'s meeting on Monday. I don't watch much news as I find it to be skewed towards negative thoughts, but I do belong to some inspiring groups on Facebook. On Monday morning, a friend shared this poem. There was no author acknowledged, just a message that someone in Italy wrote it:

"We come to understand that this is a struggle against our habits and not against a virus. This is an opportunity to turn an emergency into an opportunity of solidarity and unity. Let's change the way we see and think. I will no longer say "I'm afraid of this contagion" or "I don't care about this contagion," but it is I who will sacrifice for you.
I worry about you.
I keep a distance for you.
I wash my hands for you.
I give up that trip for you.
I'm not going to the concert for you.
I'm not going to the mall for you.
For you!
For you who are inside an ICU room.
For you who are old and frail, but whose life has value as much as mine.
For you who are struggling with cancer and can't fight this too.
Please, let's rise to this challenge!
Come together...nothing else matters."
Thank you

After reading more, I started to reconsider B.D.'s Circle of Support meeting. My mind was whirring in circles because I had promised to attend, I really wanted to be there, and I did not want to scare or disappoint B.D. whose dad had just flown in from Florida where he was exposed to a lot of people in the airport as well as when he was sitting on a plane for over two hours with the same air recirculating. I wasn't sure it was safe to attend the meeting in-person. My concern was not so much for my health, but for the health of my 82-year-old mom and daughter, who was carrying a baby at the time. I talked the situation over with Tom and we both agreed it would be best if I did not attend. Oh how my heart was hurting so badly having to go back on my word! Just ten minutes before the meeting was to begin, I called B.D.'s mom to explain my decision and to ask her the best way to handle this and not scare B.D.. She thanked me for calling her and said they would call me so I could join the meeting by phone. I felt incredibly relieved she wasn't mad at me and on top of that, was willing to help me attend the meeting. Whew! I felt so jangled and confused that I got mixed up answering the phone when they called. The second time, I answered the phone with no problem, and was part of B.D.'s Circle of Support meeting and able to share the progress he had made over the last four months, which was absolutely wonderful.

🖤 **Acknowledge Your Own Needs**: Speaking up for what is best for you and your family is so important. When the choices you make affect other people, it may seem scary to speak up. Reasonable people will understand if you explain what you need with confidence and compassion. Often, there are ways to accommodate special circumstances which honor everyone's needs. How can you advocate for yourself and still fulfill your responsibilities?

Manage Your Emotions

Being a mentor under personally stressful times can be tricky. Mentoring involves so much of myself and requires me to invest my full attention and emotional energy into working on another person's issues. It isn't easy, especially during stressful times. When my own energy is low and moving towards depression, I must build it back up in order to be effective. When my emotional state is unsteady, I must take time to give extra care to myself. Writing and meditating are tools which help me tremendously. I also feel better when I can get back to activities I love like gardening, spending time with family, writing, and other creative projects.

When walking and thinking on my own today, I remembered B.D has told me he suffers from depression at times. Since I am struggling so much myself during these times, he probably may be as well. With that in mind, I made a list of things for us to talk about when we next meet:

- Listening to how B.D. experiences depression and what strategies he uses
- Talking to B.D. about exploring different hiking trails in the area
- Discussing his dad's article in Orange Magazine

My job as a mentor is highly personal. I listen to what is going on for B.D. and share insights I have gained through my life. Ideas come to me at all different times. I may only work with B.D. for an hour a week, typically, yet he is on my mind and in my heart for many more hours.

♥ **Manage Your Emotions:** What helps you feel your best, so much that even thinking about doing these things brings a big smile to your face and an extra bounce to your step? Have you scheduled time on your calendar to do what you love? This can really help you do your best. Taking time to do what you love and paying attention to what is going on will help you be the best you can be not only for yourself, but also for the people you work with.

Design Your Own Definition of Mentoring

When beginning to work with B.D., I wasn't sure what mentoring him would be like. As I wrote in the beginning of this chapter, "I certainly couldn't guess at how effective I might be, but I had complete certainty I would do my absolute best."

I feel like I have done my best, and am continuing to do my best mentoring B.D., but I still don't know if I can come up with a concise definition of what mentoring is, yet let's give this a try. When she hired me to be a mentor, I know B.D.'s mother had particular things in mind. She wanted me to help him continue learning, foster his independence, and assist him with stress-management. Over time, however, I think B.D. and I actually defined for ourselves what this mentorship meant. People have different perspectives on mentorship. Peggy, one of our editors, encouraged me to ask B.D. what his definition of mentoring is. I asked B.D. in a text message one morning asking how mentoring helps him be more independent. I was surprised when he wrote back right away,

Mentoring helps me be more independent by teaching me something and eventually doing it on my own. If it weren't for mentors, I've would still struggled with my financials and not understanding my paystubs.

I seized this opportunity and responded, Wow B.D., thanks for getting back to me right away with this thoughtful response! Are there any other ways in which mentoring has helped you?

B.D. responded, mentoring has helped me be more opened up.

Oh do I ever have a big smile on my face receiving his reply right away.

I wrote back to him, Awesome. Thanks so much B.D.. I can tell how you have opened up by how quickly and clearly you are expressing yourself. Have a great day!!!

For me, mentoring B.D. has been about slowing down and listening to him with all of my senses and intuition. Having bonded with him on many levels, I then follow his lead and try different things out. Some ideas

173

seem to guide us in a direction which are fun and exciting for both of us, like our yoga and speaking adventures. Yoga seems to be a golden thread following us through our work together. Some ideas are followed for a bit and then are set aside, like our math studies. While we have not written any compliment sandwiches in some time, it feels like the effects of these conversations live on through B.D.'s continued striving for independence, while mom and dad learn to trust he can really care for himself in more ways than they could even imagine.

After reading these stories and witnessing how our work together has helped him, his mom wrote the following to me:

Your mentoring styles I appreciate:

1. *Great guidelines—with examples—of all experiences, and honest evaluations of the process*
2. *Discussing verbal and nonverbal responses to questions, situations, tasks and how you navigate through them both. Love that you express uncertainty at times with the process and how evaluating it all often takes time and presents itself in interesting ways*
3. *You stress the need for repetition and working in stages, which is so important*
4. *No engagement for yourself or client? Need to move on to something more captivating. Yes!*
5. *Acknowledging when you are "stuck," and problem solving that goes into being more productive*
6. *Varied things you do to tap into interests, goals, direction...*
7. *Your acceptance of everyone being unique and celebrating that individuality*
8. *I like that you stress when your guidance is no longer needed for a task—it should be cause for celebration and then on to the next goal/passion*
9. *The feeling of no longer being needed addressed, because parents too feel this*
10. *I like to hear your honest feelings about what you're experiencing throughout—*

examples: frustration, excitement, uncertainty, thrills, disappointment, aha moments, warmth, etc.—very heartwarming.

11. *I like that you are never stagnant, always assessing and evaluating whether to jump ship or stay the course.*

She added this request: Please don't hold back with me for fear of "stepping on toes"...I may need to have things brought to my attention whether I want you to or not. I do know that you have always had all of our best interests at heart, so I would hope I would respond in kind.

❦
Design Your Own Definition of Mentoring: Who has been the best mentor in your life? What qualities of that mentor would you like to bring into your life as you mentor yourself and maybe others to be their best selves? Are you the mentor to yourself that you are to the people you work with? Are you as patient, encouraging, and loving toward yourself as you are to them?

Manage Finances

Before I started working with B.D., Mary-Jo, a retired high school business teacher and administrator, was mentoring B.D. with his finances and budgeting money. Here is Mary-Jo's fascinating story of working with B.D.:

I knew the family because B.D.'s brother was in the Academy of Finance at the high school where I worked. B.D.'s dad was my boss since he was President of the School Board. I appreciated how B.D.'s dad was a very big champion of the Academy, its philosophy and goals. When B.D. was a senior, his father reached out to me to see if I had any contacts in the business world for B.D.'s special gifts and also his accomplishments and skills. This led to an opportunity for B.D.. I reached out and opened the door for B.D. and he was ready to consistently do all the hard work I suggested for him. B.D. met with me every single day during his lunch to work on resume writing, plus interviewing techniques and skills. B.D. is very responsible and goal oriented. He had to take an online test for job opportunities and was interviewed like everyone else, with no direct support from myself or his parents. B.D. has been able to interview well, get hired, work to support himself and succeed as an employee in several retail businesses. The greatest celebration for a teacher is to work with a student who is hungry to learn and thrives because of their hard work and application of what we teach them. B.D. is a remarkable young man and an example for all young adults today, with and without issues to overcome. I could not be prouder of B.D. if he were my own son. Let me share how I taught B.D. to manage his finances.

Well, it is important to start slowly. I began with the concept of money going out and money coming in. Then I shared an example of money coming in and wrote it down. Next, I shared an example of money going out or being spent and wrote that down. I went to Staples and bought B.D. a very simple green ledger with just a few columns. One Column was for his explanation of the money coming in, which included deposits and reimbursements. The other column was for the money going out which was his spending. For a month I had B.D. keep a diary of his money coming in and going out, starting on the first of the month and ending on the last day of the month. I had him catalog every black and red cent!

In the beginning, this work was hard for B.D.. I worried he was feeling as if the process was a punishment. But once he started to recognize that he was making money and that money was his reward, he really took off with the entire process.

We took an inventory at the end of each month, totaling the in's and out's, then subtracting these totals from each other. There was either a minus (red in the finance world) or a positive (black in the finance world). In the beginning, B.D. was usually in the red. Our goal was to get his end of the month inventory in the black on a regular basis.

To do this, we discussed needs, wants and the difference between them. We went through each and every entry in his monthly diary and categorized each item as a need or a want. From there, we came up with a budget, which needs to be fluid, constantly attended to and re-evaluated. For example, when B.D. started working full time, he had a longer commute than at his previous job, so we increased his gas money. Also, before Covid, we upped his monthly allowance for recreation, fun and eating out.

The biggest challenge with helping B.D. was getting him out of the habit of buying junk food. He hadn't realized how much money he spent on junk food until he created the finance diary and we discussed it together. It took us months to get him out of the habit of purchasing so much junk food. Not only was this good for his finances, I imagine this was a bonus for his health as well.

Repetitive activities are the best way for B.D. to learn and he is really excellent at keeping financial records. At the end of every month, we always tally the reds and blacks, subtract those totals and he is almost always in the black with a big plus. This is a reward for him. I can tell B.D. is very happy because of the big smile on his face. His smile is contagious and I am pleased to notice a huge smile spreading on my face, filled with pride for his accomplishments.

I learned a tremendous amount from reading how Mary-Jo taught B.D. to manage his finances. The patience she showed by breaking down each step of the process over a long period of time is remarkable. I realize creating a budget like this is something my husband Tom and I may benefit from doing. Accounting is not my forte, so I am hoping Tom will take the lead on this project. Maybe we can ask B.D. to help us. What a tribute this would be to Mary-Jo's inspiring teaching and B.D.'s commitment to learning.

♥ **Manage Finances:** Recording money in, money out, plus looking at wants and needs seems like good ideas for all people to invest time in. What are your thoughts on going through this process to create a budget?

Go With the Flow

Mentorship often involves spending time without a specific agenda. We spend time together, and situations arise which may become teachable moments, opportunities for support and counsel, practicing communication, or problem-solving – and simply bonding over sharing an enjoyable day. This walk B.D. and I took is an example of going for a walk with no agenda, yet we discovered important insights during our time together. Since this was still during coronavirus times, we were only meeting outside and not traveling in a car together. One day we decided to meet at some new trails which go through the land around our city's reservoirs. We hadn't worked together for three weeks, and I was looking forward to the outing.

I asked B.D., Do you want to follow me to the trailhead or meet there?

He replied, Meet there.

I sent him the Google Maps location since there were four different trailhead parking options. I was right on time and was surprised to see he had not arrived yet—typically, B.D. arrives early. A couple of minutes later, he pulled in to the parking lot from a different direction than I had come. We discussed where to walk and decided to head across the street to a trail that went to the lowest reservoir. This trail begins as an old dirt road and becomes a narrow, rocky trail closer to the reservoir.

B.D. talked the whole entire walk, which was absolutely fantastic and very refreshing. At this point, he was working more than full-time. We talked about his work, and he complained about a fellow employee who did not pull his weight and how he felt overwhelmed by the number of hours he was working. We discussed his options with regard to both of these topics. As I've said before, I often help him think up strategies to solve problems, which is sometimes very challenging. For the fellow employee, I asked if B.D. had talked to him. He didn't believe talking to him would do much good as his manager had spoken to the employee many times. Since this person also has special gifts, I asked if B.D. thinks the person is just not able to pull his own weight. B.D. said he has seen him pull his weight when he had a job coach, so now, he was just being lazy. I asked again if B.D. might consider speaking to this employee in a kind way to see if this might make a difference and he said he did not want to. (This is an example of where complaining and discussion leads to a dead end for the moment.)

We talked about his being overwhelmed by working a lot of hours and I asked if he could ask for fewer hours at one of his jobs. B.D. stood up a bit taller and said with enthusiasm, "The good thing about working a lot of hours is I can pay all of my bills and stay within my budget." (Here is an example of where complaining plus discussion leads to an inspiring realization.)

One more work topic came up during our walk, when B.D. complained again about people being lazy slobs. As we've discussed, it bothers him when customers don't return their carts or throw away their garbage. I asked if he thought most people or some people were lazy slobs, to which he replied, "Most people." Just to clarify, I explained if there were about a hundred people, "most" people would be about eighty people and "some" people would be about twenty people. B.D. affirmed most people don't put their carts away.

I asked if I could meet at his work one evening to do a scientific study. We would observe and write down how many people did and didn't put their carts away. I explained this is doing research to determine what actually happens which may be the same or different from what it feels like happens. B.D. agreed this was a good idea and we decided to find an evening for us to do this observation. (Here is an example of where complaining leads to a new activity and opportunity to compare feelings with observation.)

When the road dipped to a low point, it became very muddy. While we were able to go from rock to rock for a bit, then walk in the grass to the side for a bit longer, we eventually came to a spot where every step forward was directly into mud. B.D. stopped to assess the situation while I waited behind him. After some time of silence, he said, "Hold on, I am thinking…," then paused and said, "We need something to put down here." I found a log, which B.D. put down into the mud so we could cross the area without getting our shoes muddy. (This was a natural opportunity to practice problem-solving skills.) Later on the walk came another of these natural problem-solving opportunities. We came to a gate at the reservoir which appeared to be locked. B.D. took his time considering all of our options. He couldn't fit through the side of the gate, so going over carefully was our only option. I figured since I was smaller, I would go over first. He was worried about me getting hurt—which was sweet. When I got over to the other side, I was delighted to discover the lock was not engaged, and I was able to let him through with ease, which was humorous after all the time we had taken to assess the situation.

After this adventure, we talked about end-of-life issues, since B.D.'s mom told me B.D. enjoys going to wakes and is good at comforting his cousins during times of grieving. B.D. shared how he likes seeing his family at wakes, even though it is a sad circumstance. I love deep conversations like these we were having. We talked about how people die and the choices they make at the end of their life. We agreed we wouldn't get chemotherapy late in life and would prefer to die in our sleep after a long, happy life. This led us into a discussion about what we can do to stay healthy—like eating well, exercising, de-stressing with Yoga or Qigong, and enjoying time with friends and family.

B.D.'s story will go on long after this book is printed. How much B.D. has grown, learned, and transformed in less than two years! I imagine as he grows in his role as self-advocate, this insightful, intelligent young man might eventually publish a book of his own.

♥ **Go With the Flow:** When is the last time you spent time with someone without having an expectation of what would and would not happen? How comfortable are you with flowing, rather than planning what will happen ahead of time? It is exciting to witness lessons and opportunities which emerge when you allow yourself to go with the flow while being present to what is happening in the moment.

Focus on Strengths

After that most glorious walk, I was feeling stuck again in my work with B.D., wondering what we should be working on together. We were having challenges scheduling meetings because of his work schedule as well as my uncertainty about the next step of our work together. I attended his Circle of Support meeting and when I heard the other members congratulating B.D., I asked him what had happened, and he said, "I got the full-time job at Price Chopper." I replied, "Congratulations, B.D. how fantastic!"

How fantastic indeed. His work goal had been achieved, thanks to perseverence on B.D.'s part along with help from his family and Circle of Support team members. B.D. had attended one and a half years of unpaid training to be a stocker in a grocery store at night. This was his mom's idea of the perfect job for B.D. who is a night owl and enjoys putting things into order. His dad, mom, and each member of the Circle of Support team had played an important role in helping B.D., but it was B.D. whose dedication allowed his dream come to fruition.

B.D.'s Self Direction Broker is the person who creates and manages B.D.'s budget. She negotiates with the funding sources so B.D. may receive the support he wants and needs to be independent. While reviewing B.D.'s goals, his Self-Direction Broker asked why B.D. was not using many of his allowed mentoring hours. After some discussion, she said, "You know, there may come a day when you do reach your goals of independence and won't need to receive extra help. We certainly want to support you as long as you need this assistance and yet also want to acknowledge achieving independence is your ultimate goal and a cause for celebration."

What wise insights B.D.'s Self Direction Broker has. I do hope B.D. may be fully independent and self-sufficient. Dad brought up the fact that while B.D. does live on his own a good portion of the year, he doesn't coordinate regular maintenance on the house or pay taxes and other bills. It seems like there will be more skills to learn. I felt recharged and suggested working on some social skills with B.D. after this meeting. When we met for a walk the following week, I was excited and had ideas to encourage B.D. to ask me open-ended questions so our discussions could go deeper into a topic. Unfortunately, B.D. said, "I am sorry. I don't want to work on this." Mom later sent me an app which teaches social skills. I said I would look it over with B.D. since the method I tried wasn't appealing to him.

The question I have right now is: If B.D. doesn't want to work on social skills, does he really need to? Just because mom, dad, and I would feel more comfortable if B.D. conversed and showed more interest in conversations, does this mean B.D. needs to work on these skills? I am not so sure and decided to let go of exploring social skills for now and move onto another activity.

I have been taking a class called "Be Your Own Hero" by Hannah Braime. One of the exercises we've done is a *strengths survey*. One day, I described it to B.D. and asked him if he would like to take the strengths survey himself. Right away, he said, "Sure." I gave him the website for the VIA Character Strengths Survey. Each question asks for a response from these five choices: *very much like me, like me, neutral, unlike me, very much unlike me*. He completed the survey and B.D.'s number one character strength was *perseverance*. Here is the description they give:

> *Perseverance means you put forth effort over a long period of time. You finish what you start and overcome obstacles. People see you as a hard worker and you regularly reach your goals.*

This is absolutely spot on for B.D as he has been demonstrating perseverance his whole life. What an honor it is to witness B.D. blooming in so many ways through our work together. I imagine after this pandemic is over, and it is safe to be out and about in the world, B.D. will be able to get back to karaoke nights and probably do more public speaking gigs. I continue mentoring him every other week, which is what he has asked for. My greatest wish is for B.D. to have the courage to follow whatever his heart is calling him to explore.

Focus on Strengths: When we utilize our strengths, our life is filled with more ease and joy. What are your strengths? Consider taking the VIA Character Strengths Survey when you have 10 minutes to invest in yourself.

Celebrate Blooming

I just have to add one more story before this book goes to the publisher. B.D. told me one of his friends has organized a group of young men on the autism spectrum to speak during April 2021 Autism Awareness Month. His friend reserved a community meeting room, plus is setting the event up to be broadcast via Zoom and Facebook live. Since the country is still in a pandemic, offering a virtual option is wise. B.D. has been asked to draw a picture representing what autism means to him. B.D. proudly showed me his drawing of two forearms with hands clasped together and asked where would be the best place to put either the autism ribbon or blue puzzle piece. I felt so very honored to have him ask my opinion. Even better than this, he was going to wait to meet with his friends to also ask their opinion. Normally, B.D. does what he does quite independently, but here I witness him involving other people and working collaboratively on a complex project which he feels passionate about. I didn't help him at all with this project. I am inspired by the initiative he and his friends have taken and am excited to hear about how the event goes at our next meeting. What a wonderful celebration of his growth! There will be more celebrations to come, but alas they will occur after the printing is complete and books are in the hands of readers like you.

❦ **Celebrate Blooming:** Mentoring a person is about planting seeds, then noticing which ones grow and flourish. Have you noticed seeds of new ideas planted in yourself or others growing, maybe even blooming? How will you celebrate this positive growth?

David: King of Books and Humor

Find a Good Fit

In September of 2018, Rose's mom let me know that David, a twenty-four-year-old man on the autism spectrum, who was carpooling to school with Rose, was in need of a mentor. At this time, I had just interviewed to work with B.D., my mom was scheduled to have knee replacement surgery soon, and she would be living with us during her recovery. For many reasons, this did not feel like the right time to take on a new person to mentor; yet, something told me to go ahead and schedule an interview.

Well let me tell you, I am very glad I did. I feel lucky working with David and his family. David is such a funny guy and a real joy to spend time with. His family is nurturing and encouraging, and they sit down to eat meals together, while having interesting discussions about books, movies, current events and, most importantly, each person's experiences of the day. David's oldest brother, Jack, lives in California working and living on his own, whereas his youngest brother, Peter, is on the autism spectrum and has more challenges with communication than David does. Peter darted in and out of the room, playing something on an electronic device and making noises I did not understand. Since I was there to discuss David, I kept my focus on him and his parents. David is a handsome young man, with dark hair, blue eyes, and a slim build. David blends into the average crowd of young people, which his mom explained makes his life more challenging because people don't suspect he has special gifts. When David struggles finding the right words to express himself or moves in unique ways, this is confusing for strangers. I would come to witness some unique behaviors from David over our time

185

working together. David's mother said she felt strong commonalities between me and her own mother—David was really close to this grandmother, who was a writer and gardener, plus also loved spiritual learning. Interestingly, this is a good description of me in a few short words. I felt a close bond with David and his family from the beginning and I agreed to mentor him. We worked out a schedule with the understanding that there might be times I would have to reschedule meetings because of my mom's surgery. They understood completely as they were caretakers for David's grandmother for several years.

Find a Good Fit: How can you tell if a situation is a good fit for you and something worth exploring, even if some conditions don't seem ideal at first?

Get to Know Each Person and Their Goals

Early in our mentoring adventures, David and I were sitting on stools at a high counter on a dark winter night while he ate a slice of pizza and drank soda before his martial arts class. We were chit-chatting a little bit, which is not an easy skill for people on the autism spectrum, for whom one-word answers are more the norm. At one point, David looked at me, his fingers resting on his chin, his eyes appearing a bit lost and said, "Now I don't know what to say." Divine inspiration flowed through me at this point as I have never received training on how to teach conversation skills. I suggested we ask each other questions to get to know each other, then request more details. While we did this, I took notes and diagrammed our conversation, which looked like this for one topic:

Where would you like to travel?	*Hawaii*
Ooooooh, why would you like to go there?	*I would like to see volcanos. It is warm there. I don't like cold weather.*
Do you like swimming in the ocean?	*Yes, I do. We used to visit my grandmother on Block Island every summer.*

Wow! This was lots of information in a short, lively conversation, which was great fun for both of us. David asked if he could take the outline of our whole conversation to show his social skills teacher. I was quite thrilled to hear he felt what we spontaneously created was worthy to share with his teachers. When I dropped David at home that evening, he said, "Thank you for this evening. I especially enjoyed our conversation about Hawaii." I was surprised by David's expressiveness. What an honor to have glimpsed a bit more of his interests. It felt like for a brief time, a curtain was drawn back, and I could peek into his soul. Since we wouldn't be able to travel to Hawaii anytime soon, I asked if he would like to make a model volcano, and he liked that idea. I also asked if he wanted to go to a spa I belonged to that had indoor pools and waterfalls, which might remind him of Hawaii. Again, David liked this idea. We already had some interesting projects and adventures to explore together.

Working with special gifts adults is like being a detective. For instance, I do my best to figure out what they really love. The people I work with can speak and express themselves to a certain degree, and their parents who know them well often share insights with me about their likes and dislikes. Yet, there are hidden passions in everyone which are waiting to emerge. These passions may feel sacred and tender, and don't feel safe to share with just anyone. Patience, kindness, gentle probing questions, and attentive listening with all my senses are my sleuthing tools.

❦
♥ **Get to Know Each Person and Their Goals:** When there is a desire to do something extravagant, like traveling to Hawaii, there may be more manageable ways to touch upon the same interests. These achievable activities help keep a dream alive with possibility in the imagination until it can happen in reality. What big dreams do you have which can be experienced here and now?

Apply Learning with One Person to Another Person

David is quite a good conversationalist, I imagine partially due to the loving attention his family gives him during fun family meals. They discuss many topics, including books and movies, sharing interesting viewpoints. It didn't take long before David trusted me enough to have these kinds of discussions with me. One game I discovered we both enjoy is *Vertellis: Mindful Questions for More Togetherness.* When we started our work in 2019, I brought this game to play during his evening meals. I asked David how he wanted to play the game and he suggested we take turns asking each other questions. I was happy to hear this as it is important to build skills for answering and asking questions, learning how to request details for more interesting conversation. I learned a lot about David during these conversations, about both his learning from last year and his hopes and dreams for this coming year. He wanted to know what career he would pursue by the end of 2019. We decided to keep a list of his goals in the box to refer to when we review this year in anticipation of 2020.

Interestingly enough, when I played this game with B.D., it was a completely different experience. B.D. didn't want to ask me questions— he only wanted to answer questions. While I did learn more about B.D., the one-way conversation felt flat and not as engaging. It isn't that I need people to know more about me, but showing interest and asking engaging questions of other people is an important part of learning to manage social situations. Using David's example, the next time B.D. and I played Vertellis together, I said we would use this as a listening game, where we both listen to each other and ask questions to get more details. What I discovered is when asked to participate like this, B.D. was very good at listening, which made me really happy. In a sense, David taught me how to work with B.D. in a different way. Isn't this cool?

❦ **Apply Learning with One Person to Another Person:** When have you learned something in one area of your life and have then applied this learning to another aspect of your life? How did they work in the same or different ways? What did you learn from those observations?

Commit to Passions

David loves books, so we visit bookstores and libraries whenever possible. He is intelligent, funny, meticulous, quiet, and caring. Doesn't it sound like David would be the perfect person to work in a library? For the first six months I was with David, whenever I asked him what kind of job he would really love, he would say loudly, emphatically, sounding discouraged, "I have no idea." I mentioned the idea of working at a library, but that didn't create any spark of interest which I could detect. Not easily deterred, I asked if he might be interested in volunteering at a library or bookstore and he said, "I would consider doing that." Clearly, persistence and perseverance are often necessary after we identify these kinds of possibilities and try making them a reality. We continued to pursue different options which involved visiting libraries and bookstores. Have you ever noticed when something is meant to happen and the time is right, doors will magically open? Let me explain: David and I had done research and studied at the Montgomery Free Library, which is in his town. We inquired about volunteering and despite getting the phone number of the director and calling her, no volunteering opportunities had come to fruition. Seemingly, it wasn't meant to be at this place, but we didn't despair and continued to look for other bookstores or libraries where he might volunteer in order to gain experience in a field he might be interested in.

One evening, while waiting for David as he took his martial arts class, I was surrounded in a big bear hug by a dear friend. One thing led to another as we are catching up and I learn Sapphire is mentoring a young lady on the autism spectrum and they volunteer at a number of different places, including a bookstore. David agreed it would be interesting to watch Sapphire and Aurora volunteer at the Book Exchange in Montgomery. The day we went to observe, we walked into this little used bookstore, which just had enough room for us four volunteers and an employee. There were so many books, stacks were erected on the floor in front of the book cases, which were labeled with categories. The woman working there was very sweet. She explained what she wanted us to do, and with her help, as well as the support of Sapphire and Aurora, it wasn't long before David was pitching in to price and shelve books. A great beginning! We contacted the owner to see if we could come back to volunteer other days, but never heard back from him, despite an in-person visit to check on the best days and times to help out. No sense wallowing in worry and wondering…onward we search.

In the hopes of finding David some type of work with books, I visited the Middletown Thrall Library to see if David could shadow a *shelver*, also known as a *page*. I was sent from one person to another, being bounced around attempting to get an answer, and finally one person gave me a day, time, and person David could shadow in order to learn more about this work. Whew! I felt relieved to finally receive an answer, but I was not terribly thrilled or excited. It had been a struggle, but more than this, there was a lack of ease about the experience and something there did not feel quite right, despite the fact that it is the library near where I live and take out many books each year.

One challenge of working with young adults who have special gifts is that both of us may sometimes feel "homeless" during our time together. At twenty-four, David does not want to spend our time together at his house, because he is aiming for independence. Sometimes we meet at my home, but that, too, is not quite right, partially due to our dogs with special gifts. We often need a place which has internet access for studying. David's martial arts class was in the Walden area, and I wanted to find a good place to study before his class in the evening. I texted Sapphire, who is familiar with the Walden area, and she suggested the Walden Library. How perfect! We headed to the library, intending to study, when who did we see volunteering but Aurora, the young lady Sapphire mentors. We met Aurora's mom, who swept us upstairs and introduced us to the director, so David could inquire about volunteering.

As I followed Aurora's mom and David upstairs, I felt a strong swirl of energy surrounding my heart in the front and back. It seemed like I was being filled with so much love I could fly away as a happy free bird! I kept my feet on the ground, offering a bit of guidance to David as he filled out the application for a volunteer position at the library. There was not a second of hesitation on David's part as he completed this application. A few moments after handing the director his application, she told David he had been accepted for this volunteer position. You know when you are happy and you feel like you need to keep your smile contained because your face might blow up from the excitement? That was the kind of smile on David's face: extreme pride, joy, and excitement for this new adventure. He was scheduled to volunteer the following Wednesday and I couldn't wait for him to begin this new opportunity.

Fast forward to the next week…David and I got to the Walden Library twenty minutes early. He read for a bit and then we started reviewing the stacks to see where things were located. The director saw us and started explaining key features of the library's organization. She told us she would only be asking David to do what the other staff members do. For example, anytime we see a book out of place, we return it to the correct spot. We were in the fiction section, where books are organized by the author's last name. Some of the fiction books had subcategories like in the extensive mystery section they have. "Oh yes, that is the book's genre," David said quite casually. I was doing flips inside because *genre* is not a word I have ever used. Doesn't it sound like the kind of word a librarian would use quite often? Is David destined to work at a library or what? This was our first day, and I managed to hold onto my hat for a bit, yet each moment seemed to bring more and more excitement because it felt like I was observing David in an environment where he belonged. We met a young high school student, Sook, who had been volunteering there since he was young. Sook asked if I was David's mom. I looked at David and he took over confidently saying, "This is Maria Blon, who is my mentor. I am David Lee and am on the autism spectrum." Later Sook asked me some questions about my work and said he was impressed with David's intelligence. I heartily agreed.

Roz, the librarian who is the volunteer coordinator, came in at 4:00 pm. What a bundle of joy and love she is, giving the group of four volunteers important jobs to do in the library. She supervises each person with a firm yet gentle touch, making sure there is mastery and accountability. David fit right in, alphabetizing a stack of books with no problem and performing all of the tasks Roz gave him with ease and engagement. One time, a few DVDs tipped over, making a little bit of noise. Roz assured David she had done much worse and not to worry about it. I witnessed the tension in his shoulders just melt away with these kind words. She also said, "We are in no hurry here at the library, so take your time." How often do you hear someone say "We are in no hurry," in this fast-paced culture? What a breath of fresh air. I felt very comfortable knowing David would be working under Roz's gentle guidance. Later, a young woman who went to David's high school came in to volunteer, and they took some time to catch up. Roz winked at me and whispered, "socialization is so important." Once again, such wisdom. She arranged for Aurora, Diane, and David to sit together to clean DVDs. I thoroughly enjoyed observing them interact, while occasionally also engaging them in conversation.

Time flew by this afternoon and I was able to send David's mom a picture of him working, along with this message describing my utter excitement at how amazingly well David was fitting in to this volunteer library position:

> *Hello!*
> *I am so excited for David's first day volunteering at the Walden Library. He is a natural with his love of books, gentle manner, intelligence, and attention to detail. He really does not need me here, even on his very first day. The librarian is impressed as is a young man who volunteers regularly. David is eager, engaged and doing great. The staff here are so welcoming and encouraging.*
> *David can walk to dinner and Korean MMA (Mixed Martial Arts) from here, so maybe when he is ready, I can bring him here after "A Helping Hand" and you could pick him up at 8:15 from Korean MMA. Just an idea to consider.*
> *I hope you are having a great day!*
>   *Maria*
>
> *David's mom wrote back right away: So now I'm crying. This is fantastic. And absolutely dropping him off and the evening progressing to dinner and Korean MMA , and of course I can pick him up!*

Typically, David is concerned about the time, wanting to get to our scheduled appointments early. This day however, David was not chomping at the bit to leave. He waited until the very last minute before we headed on to dinner, followed by his martial arts class at Korean MMA. I recognize this is a journey in which one step at a time must be taken, yet I was thrilled at how quickly these puzzle pieces were falling into place. On David's second day of volunteering, I stayed with him and then we walked together to Korean MMA for practice. I realized the road is quite dark. On one stretch of his journey there is snow piled by the side, which might make it hard for cars to see him. I suggested purchasing a safety vest, which both David and his mom agreed was a good idea.

Wednesdays became David's library volunteering day. The following week, I dropped David off at the library at 4:00 pm so he could volunteer then walk to dinner and his martial arts class. I could tell how proud David was by the huge smile on his face, which made me happy. At the same time, I felt terribly sad as we have had a lot of fun adventures on Wednesday evenings. I went through a grieving process for a few Wednesdays when I dropped him off, a reaction I was not expecting at all. I learned to plan special events on my drive home, like going shopping at my favorite health food store or taking a hike when the weather was warm. Part of me wants to be present for each step on David's journey, and the other part of me wants to fast forward and see him happily working at a library, to witness him living and supporting himself independently. I must admit, I am sometimes impatient. I even get impatient with books and will read the ending to make sure everything turns out okay! The problem is the book loses its fun when I cheat like that. I don't want a crystal ball to see into David's future, yet I do visualize him being happy and successful in life.

Commit to Passions: Sometimes it feels like progress is slow, yet often when we look back, we recognize how one step forward leads to another step forward. Even if there are some backwards steps in the process, as long as we keep our focus on passions, eventually progress is made. Keeping hope and faith strong while in the process, based on inspiring stories like David's and past experiences you may have had, makes a huge difference.

Joyfully Connect Through Humor

David left his ski mask in my car one day. I texted him: "Hey David, I found your black ski mask in the car. I can leave it on our porch for you to pick up or give it to you on Monday. You will just have to hold off on robbing a bank until you get it. (laughing until I am crying emoji)" I was a little nervous sending this joke as a text as I wasn't positive David would understand the humor intended. No need to worry—David totally got the joke, which we continue to play back and forth between us. I even told David I want a cut of his profits when he robs a bank. Such fun to share humor as life is so much brighter with laughter.

❦ **Joyfully Connect Through Humor:** Where can you bring humor into your relationships?

Manage Unexpected Events

David and I have experienced some scary situations in our work together. On the day before Thanksgiving, David and I made plans to go to the spa with heated indoor and outdoor pools, plus waterfalls, with the hope of receiving at least a little bit of Hawaii vibes. It would be our first big adventure. The day before, I went to our mechanic to get my Prius serviced and to inquire if snow tires would be a good idea since I am now driving people in my car for work. I was also inspired to ask because there had been a huge unexpected snowstorm a few weeks earlier, which was so bad, Patti (Rose's mom) stayed at our house overnight when she could not drive twelve miles to her house in her all-wheel drive car. What would happen if I was mentoring and got caught in a snowstorm in our Prius, which doesn't drive well in snow? Instead of snow tires, my mechanic suggested looking for another car with all-wheel drive. This was a reasonable suggestion, but I was resistant to the idea. I had no intention of trading my beloved, ecofriendly hatchback hybrid car for a gas guzzling all wheel drive car. Can you tell how attached I am to this car, to the point of being unreasonable?

The next day, David's mom and step-dad dropped him off at my house, and we were excited for this adventure. We had invited Rose, but she was not feeling well, so she didn't join us, which turned out to be a blessing. When we were about a mile from my house, on a two-lane road with a lot of traffic, there was a big bag of garbage in the middle of our lane, which I carefully steered around. Unfortunately, my attention was so focused on the huge garbage bag, I did not see the car stopped in front of me, waiting to make a left turn. When I did see the car I slammed on the brakes too late and we crashed into the car. All the air bags went off, which surprisingly felt like soft pillows easing the impact. David said, "Shit!" and then, "Sorry for the language." I replied, "That is alright. Your response is appropriate." After checking to see if David was okay, which thankfully he was, I said, "Dammit David, we had such a great day planned." He said, "Yes we did and now you really need to go to the spa."

Wow! He was making jokes right after this horrible accident. He was shaken up, of course, as was I, yet we both stayed calm and did everything we needed to. I hadn't spent a whole lot of time with David before this happened, and I wasn't sure if physical contact was okay with him. I wanted to touch him and make sure he was really okay and kept stopping myself. I dejectedly told the State Trooper, part of my job with David is to encourage him to drive, and she said, "You are doing a great job by staying calm and explaining how to handle an accident well." Her encouragement was greatly appreciated. I did not call Tom because I worried if he came, I would burst into tears, and I wanted to stay strong for David. I called the calmest, strongest, toughest, most supportive person I knew: my mom. She recently had knee replacement surgery and just got clearance to drive. Mom brought her car right over and let me use her car with David for the rest of the day. Her confidence in me being able to drive after totaling a car gave me the strength to keep going. I didn't hide the fact I was shaken up from David because I felt it was important for us to process our feelings together. We put our hands out to see how much we were shaking. I asked David how he had felt during the accident and he said, "My heart was pounding fast, and I felt shocked and stunned. It took me a few seconds before I could move."

Once we got back to my home and I figured out the system to report this to ESS, we called David's mom who was still shopping a few miles away. She could hear in David's voice he was okay and said she was fine with us continuing our day together as long as I was okay with doing that. This felt like a time when I really would have rather rested, but also a time when we both had to get back on the horse after being thrown off. We went to my house in order to settle down a bit and started making a model volcano together. This activity helped our nerves settle by keeping our hands busy as we did something creative. We enjoyed a delicious Indian lunch at Saffron, went Christmas shopping, and then met with Rose to make pumpkin pies together. When I took David home at 5:30 pm, we talked with his mom and step-dad. They were so very loving and understanding. I was in tears because of the way they trusted me with David and his mom was in tears right along with me. We all hugged. Even David gave me a hug, which was such a huge relief.

Over the Thanksgiving holiday, I felt like I was recovering from the flu as I processed and healed from the accident emotionally. Physically, I had no aches and pains, but I just felt like lead was flowing through my veins, keeping me grounded and off the roads to recover. When I meditated on the accident, I saw angel wings coming out with the airbags to soften the impact. Every time I thought back on the accident, I couldn't understand how I missed the car stopped in front of me. David even noted he didn't see the car either until it was too late. I scheduled a healing session with my teacher Dechen, who really helped me energetically and explained the spiritual reasons why the accident happened. (More would be revealed in a future reading. I will share these stories a bit later.)

The next time I was scheduled to work with David, I borrowed Tom's car, which had a loose heat flap which rattled and made noise. The "inflate your tire" light was also going on and off. His car had a lot of quirks, but was sturdy. However, the car's rattling noises and jittery tire lights matched my unhinged nerves. I left my house in just enough time to get to David at the scheduled time, but not enough time to allow for me taking a wrong turn, getting a bit lost and panicking as I wondered if I was really cut out for this work. I stopped and did some deep breathing, then found my way to David's house about ten minutes late, which was most unusual for me. We made it through the evening with no problems and after that night, I decided to rent a car, which my insurance paid for one hundred percent. The car they gave me was a Mitsubishi Outlander. It was fancy, which surprisingly enough I kind of liked. Up to this point in my life, the simpler the car, the better. My beloved Prius ended up being totaled, so Tom and I started to search for what we wanted next. Since Tom would be retiring soon, we might end up sharing this car, if one car would be enough for us. Tom likes a car which can carry building supplies for his construction projects. We both wanted an eco-friendly vehicle and were curious about trying an electric hybrid. Wouldn't you know, the Mitsubishi Outlander came in an electric hybrid with all-wheel drive. Isn't this an interesting synchronicity? We found a 2018 model with only 2000 miles on it and were able to purchase the car before the rental time ended. This whole experience felt surprisingly easy, as one challenge after another was quickly resolved. It seemed like everything we had been through was meant to be. My resistance to getting rid of the beloved Prius was shattered with the accident, which felt like these events were divinely guided.

♥ **Manage Unexpected Events:** During challenging situations, doing our best, while accepting help from others is most important. Sharing our worries openly and being honest about what is happening allows every person involved to face the challenges at hand head on, instead of pretending all is well. When reviewing an upsetting event, can you notice how you might be in an even better situation than you were beforehand?

Remain Calm

David was nervous in the car before this accident, so I wondered how he would feel after the accident. I asked him and he said, "I want to do things, so I need to ride in cars." And that was that.

We had some more car adventures over the next few months. We went to the spa over his spring break with no problem; however, driving with David in the car was always an extra anxious experience, both before and especially after the accident. I seemed to feel his anxiety in my body, which was unnerving. A few weeks into owning our new car, there was a loud bang reverberating inside the cabin after a small rock hit the left side of the windshield in front of my face. It was startling to say the least. We both remained calm and the rock did not leave a big mark. In fact, we could barely see where it had hit the windshield. Another night when I drove David to the bookstore, I forgot to turn on my headlights in addition to my day lights and got pulled over by a state trooper. Oh man. What on earth would I do next? I didn't get a ticket, the trooper just asked me to turn on the headlights. It just seemed like one thing after another was happening when working with David and my nerves were jangled. On another dark winter evening, I was driving David home from his martial arts class, when we came around the bend on the windy farm road near his house, and my headlights, which were thankfully on, shone onto a herd of Texas Longhorn cows blocking our way! Oh, my goodness, I have never seen such long pointy horns this close, much less close to our shiny brand-new car. David was nervous and didn't want me honking the horn. We waited until there was an opening, but just as I was inching forward, a calf walked in front of the car. Finally, the calf went across the road, and we were able to deliver David home safely. Whew! Disaster averted. What on earth might happen next? Nothing I hoped. These challenges were more than enough excitement for some time.

As I was reflecting on the evening, I remembered watching David learn Hapkido wrestling moves in his martial arts class. Thinking of ways to lessen the trauma of this latest driving event, I suggested we tell his instructor about how David practiced his wrestling moves on the long-horned cows which had blocked our path on our drive home the other night. We were laughing up a storm as we planned how we could tell this story in the funniest way. His instructor Bruce was a real character. He loved the story David and I told together, reveling with us in the power of imagination to transform scary events into exciting adventures.

♥ **Remain Calm:** Creating stories can transform how you feel about scary events and also can be shared to uplift people. We can use the experiences in our lives to become more bitter or more enlightened. Is there an event which happened in your life which you could use your imagination to create a funny or inspiring story to help the situation seem more manageable?

Create Adventures

I enjoy traveling and exploring while mentoring, and we take time to discuss areas of interest before planning a trip. David was auditing a Modern Asian History class at the Community College, which really fascinated him. Since he is intrigued by beautiful art and delicious food, I asked if he would like to plan a trip to New York City over his spring break from college and the "A Helping Hand" program. We had great fun looking up options to explore and asking David's professor for ideas. David planned our activities, plus looked up directions using Google maps. He decided we would visit the Japan and Asia Society Museums, the Metropolitan Museum of Art, and go to a Vietnamese restaurant for lunch.

The night before our trip to New York City, which we'd had a wonderful time planning, I was nervous. I woke up at 4 am, meditated, and imagined an energetic protective bubble around David and myself, as well as the car, for all of our travels. We drove to Beacon, where we saw an electric vehicle charging station was open. We couldn't get the car set up to charge for some reason, but since this was the only spot open in the entire lot and our electric hybrid qualified us to park there, I felt really lucky. We were excited to purchase our tickets for the train and boarded with plenty of time to spare. The ride along the Hudson River was breathtaking.

As I was reading this section to David, he asked to add the following details about our trip. David spoke while I typed his words. In half an hour, I had filled three pages with his detailed accounting of our trip. There are two places where I remembered differently from David, and we decided to use these differences as discussion points. I sent David a copy of his story, placing asterisks and question marks where I wanted to discuss what I remembered happening. I include my viewpoints in plain text in the story, while David's words are in italics.

David: We arrived at Grand Central Station and it was almost like a mini-mall with different stores like bagel shops, stores with different merchandise and a food court. Then we walked around for a while, looking at the streets and buildings. We went to the Japan Society Museum. We were early and it seemed new because there were not a lot of items to look at. There was a nice waterfall that almost looked like a pond. There were many statues of caricatures. The floor had a great carpet and the stairs had plastic wood with a light cover on it. Very Japanese which makes sense since Japan is in the name of the museum.

I went upstairs and there was more of the tiny statues of caricatures and some things in Japanese writing. There was also a poster of exhibits that would happen later in the afternoon or evening which we wouldn't have more time for. I wanted to attend the other events, like a movie about a tragic love story which would be playing in the evening. I was interested in attending this, but didn't have enough time. And so, Maria had a small talk with the woman looking after the museum. I don't remember what exactly they were talking about. I do remember when we were ready to go, we said our goodbyes and moved on to the next museum.

We went to a Vietnamese Restaurant, which I researched ahead of time at the college during our planning meetings. Since our trip was Asian themed, we chose this restaurant. I don't remember the name of the restaurant. Inside the restaurant, it was a combination of a fancy restaurant and a casual place, if that makes any sense. I ordered a boneless spare rib with rice. It was delicious but it tasted like spare ribs I would have at any Chinese Restaurant. I felt like if I traveled to Vietnam, I would have a different experience. The food might not be as healthy, since we are more health conscious in the US. I was disappointed to not have a different experience than I would have at another restaurant in the US.

After our lunch, we walked to the Asian History Museum and it did have a different vibe to it. Some of it was a more experimental art and some traditional. Upstairs, there were different writings and items from the 1400s and it showed its origins from where it came from. And there was one room, a specific room where taking pictures were not allowed. Up to that point, I was taking different pictures of the trip. And inside was a slightly lit room and it had a circle of different wax sculptures of the head of each soldier who died in a specific war. I wanted to take a picture of them, but I wanted to respect the older gentleman who was pretty much looking after the items. It fascinated me. It was sad and also disturbing. After Maria and I left the room, we continued to look *around. On the first and bottom level, because there are three levels of floors. Downstairs, there was experimental art of different people's tongues. I forgot what they symbolized. I like to think I was open enough to examine what they meant, but I also thought they were kind of gross. The room was kind of psychedelic. The walls in the room were a mixture of white and red and also mixed colors from a stage light.*

And after that we looked at the merchandise store. I wanted to buy some souvenirs but they were way too expensive and I didn't have enough money for it. And once I was ready to leave, Maria and I left that building and so we headed to the Metropolitan Museum which was a place we planned to visit.

We came across Central Park. We passed a zoo and then we passed a pond, which was in a park. We then crossed a street and then after taking some turns, we went near the museum. We went past a man playing a saxophone for money and then we walked up the big stairs and through the main entrance doors. The building was massive and the crowds were huge. And so, we didn't know this but we had to wait on line to get a visitor's pass and ticket for a specific area of the museum to visit. I gave the woman at the counter my ID card and I gave her money and got a wrist band, a visitor pass. I was confused as to why I had to show my ID because everything seemed to be happening so fast.

Maria's view:

At the Museum of Natural History where we visited, New York residents could show their identification and give a donation for admission, rather than paying the full admission price. I showed them my New York Driver's License and asked David to show his New York Identification Card. This way we could each donate to the museum and save a bit of money. I realize hearing David's story, he thought I was not following the rules of the museum, which means I did not explain what we were doing in a way he could understand. I am grateful we cleared up this misunderstanding through writing and reading this story.

David: We walked up other big stairs. It is a big building. I believe I saw a massive portrait or tablet with historical figures and text. I felt like I was on a movie set. Then we walked around more. We

203

saw every day uses, ancient weapons, small statues of dragons, and I believe we saw small statues of dragons. And then at some point, we headed into a garden with a pond, benches, and a mini stream of specific fish swimming. It felt relaxing. So then after a while, I decided that I wanted to leave. And then after walking back again, I noticed earlier that there were different sections, for example a massive painting of Rome in the 1700s. It made me want to visit those areas more but the evening was hitting so then we left the building.

I forgot to mention earlier, after visiting the museums, we went to one part of Times Square. And it was big. There were lots of electronic flashy advertisements. There was a McDonald's, which was nothing new because I see McDonald's everywhere. There were diners and a red stairway, which made me think of the Amazing Spiderman 2. Most of the landmarks I recognized because of watching a lot of Spiderman Cartoons and Comics. That character is set in a real city, which is how I knew some of the landscapes. And then I decided to record some videos on my experience. After looking at advertisements of "Shazam" and "The Missing Link", I actually felt closed in because it is a big city with a lot of cars and noises. I wanted to go to the Japan Society.

Going forward in time again, we walked in a lot of streets and we passed a lot of diners and one of them reminded me of Seinfeld and I even felt as if I was in Seinfeld for a second and I even heard the theme song in my head. Maria showed me a famous library in the city. I was impressed and we passed through Radio City where a lot of talk shows take place.

And then finally, we headed back to the Grand Central Building and we actually got tickets for the train back. Since we still had some time to kill, we went to some of the food courts and I went to a pizza court. It wasn't a traditional long slice of pizza; it was square shape. It might have been because I was hungry, but I thought it was delicious. And since we would get back after midnight, I wanted to eat something. With my dinner and pizza, I also had a root beer. And Maria got a bagel because she wanted to bring one home for her husband and from what I remember, she was also hungry so she killed two birds with one stone.

Maria's Comments:

There were so many places I would have loved to check out which I did not when David and I were in the city together. This was not a trip for me; it was a trip for David. I did make an exception at the end of the trip when I stopped at a bakery in Grand Central Station to purchase a loaf of multigrain sourdough bread to bring home for Tom and myself. Then when David and I went down to the food court, he purchased his dinner and I got a Greek assortment of falafel, hummus, salad, pita, and beets. Delicious!

David: When it was time to go, we got to the train earlier than expected and then it was a little awkward because I collected fliers for each of the museums we visited and I was finishing my dinner on the go. Slowly but surely, more people came and I finished my food and the train began to move. I was taking pictures of some areas we were passing and then by the time we got back to the station we started our day with, it was dusk. Then it was close to being midnight when Maria dropped me off home. I told my parents about my day trip. And they were thrilled. And my step-father asked me about the streets I saw. He asked me which area I walked towards and wanted to guess what street that was because he used to live in the city. They were thrilled and proud I was able to have this adventure. This year, it won't be the last time I visit the city, but that is another story. And it was March 2019 that this happened.

This is the most David has ever spoken to me at one time. I was thrilled to hear him express how important this trip was for him, and I am delighted to be able to share our experiences with you, the reader, as well. Clearly, our trip to the city made a big impression on him and inspired a lot of thought. As you can imagine, I was contemplating how I might encourage David to express himself like this in his daily life.

Our entire trip to New York City was magical. On our drive back home in the evening, David and I marveled at how wonderful the day was and recognized that nothing went wrong—for which we were exceptionally grateful. As I write this story now, I realize how much courage we both have shown each time we got in a car together. I also notice that without the traumatic experiences we shared in the past, this amazing day would not have meant nearly as much. Sometimes contrast is necessary in order to recognize what to be grateful for.

♥ **Create Adventures:** Going on adventures near and far is life changing, as you can tell from this trip David and I took to New York City. We were able to glimpse cultures both from around the world and around the corner. Where would you like to go on your next adventure? Consider planning an adventure somewhere close-by once a week, a little further once a month and a bit further once a season. Sometimes, like during global pandemics, you may need to be creative with the kinds of adventures you can safely take.

Respond in a Positive Way

A few weeks later, I was driving David to have dinner before taking him to a Circle of Support meeting at his home, which I was not invited to. Despite having a good relationship with David's family in the beginning of our work together, I was not invited to the meetings he had with his Circle of Support Group. With each family I mentor, there is a different protocol for meetings. With Rose, her meetings are a celebration of her blossoming independence and an opportunity for her to voice her desires. I wasn't invited to B.D.'s meetings initially, but now my presence is most welcome and treasured. With David's family, I often have a sinking feeling when hearing about meetings where I seemed to have been the only uninvited member of the team. I didn't know why, and still don't know why I was not invited to so many meetings over many months, which doesn't feel good.

While driving, we saw a middle-school-aged boy walking down a steep bank of a bridge which went over the road. I worried he might cross in front of us, but he simply walked on the sidewalk. A moment later, there was a shattering bang reverberating throughout the car. Some young boys up on the bridge had thrown a huge rock at my windshield, which hit on the left side of the car. "Dammit!" was the first word out of my mouth. It's not a word I use often, but I have used it twice now in front of David. I looked over at David to make sure he was okay and then started talking through what to do next. I saw the kids on top of the bridge looking at us and not running. There was a car behind me, and nowhere to pull over safely. I had stopped the car, but I did not want to get the kids in trouble, and David was nervous about getting to his meeting on time. I decided to leave the scene of the crime and simply get David something to eat, then bring him home safely.

I called my car insurance company when he was ordering his food, then joined him while he ate his dinner, explaining how the accident needed to be reported to the insurance company so they can help us replace the windshield. I was getting yet more practice coping with a traumatic event. This seemed a too-familiar lesson by now, which showed up time after time when working with David. We got home safely with no further incidents and in plenty of time for his meeting.

On my drive home, I called my daughter Carina who has been doing mentoring work with children and families for many years. I said to her, "What is wrong with me that I worried about the kids who damaged our car and scared us?" She said, "Some people would have gotten out of the car, chased the kids down, yelling at them, and possibly trying to hurt them. Your reaction, which was to not do anything was a better example for David as it showed self-control and compassion." Well, having her view of my reaction from that perspective made me feel a lot better. David was my priority and his safety came first.

Unfortunately, when I called the police, they were not so thrilled. They were angry I waited so long to call them because it diminished their chances of catching the kids who did this. I agreed to drive to the police station and fill out a report. As I was pulling into the parking lot across from the police station, Tom was driving out of the lot. He looked at me with questioning eyes, and a worried look on his face, which was interesting because he did not notice the huge spider web shaped crackling on the windshield. I motioned for him to join me in the parking lot, as I didn't want to cause an accident stopping there to talk with him. When he saw the windshield after parking, he was concerned about my well-being, grateful the rock did not go through, and angry with the kids who did this. I was genuinely more concerned about the kids getting help and not getting in trouble. I worried about them having trouble sleeping at night. The police officer had a dim view of the kids and said they probably don't care at all. His viewpoint was even more disturbing to me than the kid's behavior.

❤ **Respond in a Positive Way:** Depending on our personality and life experience, we each have different ways to respond in difficult situations. What is your typical response style? Are you happy with how you handle yourself or would you like to be more or less assertive?

Seek Spiritual Guidance

A few days after the incident, I scheduled a session with my spiritual teacher, Dechen. I wasn't sure if this was necessary since I was feeling better after a few days of processing. I was getting lots of self-healing practice lately. I felt extravagant spending this money because I already treat myself to massages and trips for yoga and spa swimming on a regular basis. I also remembered an insight I received recently when hiking with my two little dogs in a nearby park. In my mind, I was debating about whether or not to make an appointment with Dechen. Right then, our eight-pound Yorkie, Coco, was stressed out because he couldn't find a way to cross the creek safely, even though our ten-pound Pomchi, Lacey, and I had just crossed. I showed him where we crossed and he joined us easily. I heard this message in my head, "We all need help finding our way at different times in our lives." I decided to make an appointment with Dechen and ask her why David and I have experienced so many traumatic events together. She shared some helpful insights, cleared out negative energy from my head, aura and meridians, plus helped me write this prayer for protection.

> *May a bubble of healing protective light surround us and the car on all of our adventures. We are yours, you are ours, we are one, all is well.*

I used this prayer for the next few car rides. Thankfully, I am no longer afraid when driving in the car with David as the passenger. He still gets anxious when a car approaches us from a side street or driveway, fearful they will not stop, but I don't feel his anxiety as strongly in my body as I used to. I am as confident and relaxed driving with him in the car or not, which is an enormous relief. I am grateful I was open to hearing encouragement to seek guidance and to have followed through with this suggestion by scheduling a session with Dechen.

♥ **Seek Spiritual Guidance:** What kind of spiritual guidance helps you most when you are trying to understand what is happening in your life?

Discuss Emotions

When I was driving in the car with David and Rose one day, there were men working on a bridge at the side of the road. I asked Rose what they were doing and she said very confidently, "Welding." I was curious about how she knew they were welding. She told a story of a young man, her speech teacher's son, who didn't treat Rose nicely in school. Her speech teacher believed Rose when she told her about how her son treated her, apologized and let Rose know her son has matured since those days and he is now a welder. Rose said she did not want to talk more about that young man because she likes to be joyful, not angry or disgusted. We talked about the difference between anger and disgust. I shared how feeling those emotions sometimes is normal and also said it is not okay to act these emotions out in a hurtful way. I asked if it was okay to throw rocks in a river when angry and while she agreed that is fine to do if nobody is in front of you, then shared a story of when she hit her brother with a rock accidentally and felt badly about doing this.

Rose asked me, "Does David have feelings?" Rose sometimes showed interest in David and seemed unsure how to balance her eagerness to get to know him with not being annoying. I suggested Rose ask David directly, as he was in the car listening to our conversation. David replied to Rose's question by saying, "I have the full range of feelings just like other people. Some people who act happy all the time are repressing other emotions." Rose talked about their classmate Xander, who she thinks represses emotions. David described him as being tall with hair sticking out to the side of his head and hair coming out of his nostrils. Even with that clear description, I said, "I can't place him," and David repeated his description and added, "He always looks worried." Now I knew who he was talking about. Sharing the emotion we all felt from this classmate helped me know who he is. We then discussed emotions we see most often with different people. Rose and I had watched the Disney movie "Inside Out," which has an interesting way of explaining emotions. The language in this movie has been very helpful for our discussions. David added:

"Xander talks about cars the exact same way every day. He is more severely autistic and is more limited in language skills and conversation. He is smart. Having a casual conversation with someone is something he is always struggling with."

♥ **Discuss Emotions**: How comfortable are you with talking about emotions? We all feel and respond to emotions in unique ways. Taking time to notice similarities and differences can be fascinating.

Delve into Stories Shared

David's animated stories about the college program he attends reveal interesting examples of his insights and viewpoints. One day, David joined me in the car, and I asked him what his plan was for the afternoon. He was ready to go, saying he wanted to visit the frozen yogurt place before the library, then walk to Korean MMA. I told him this is a great plan and asked if he had directions. David got his phone out to search for directions, asking the name of the yogurt place we often visit. He realized there are two locations of Sweet Frog. We got started and then as we approached the stop sign, he got flustered. I pulled over and he explained ads were popping up and he couldn't see the directions. Once he and his phone calmed down, David directed me where to drive and all went well.

Typically, other than discussing what he wants to do and going over directions, our time is filled with a lot of silence. Quite unexpectedly on this day, David talked to me with great expression about events which occurred that day and I was thrilled to listen with my utmost attention. His expressiveness let me know these events were very important to David. First was the movie, *Biz Kidz*, they'd had to watch about managing money. David found it insulting. There were corny cartoon characters and way too much noise from annoying "boing" sounds like you hear in kids' animation. The show was made for teenagers, and he was insulted to to be forced to watch this childish video as a twenty-five-year-old man. He told me he went for a walk after the movie. I asked if this was to destress from the childish video and David explained it was a nice day. He ate his lunch outside and enjoyed walking. David also told me about a classmate, let's call him Ben, who'd had a meltdown that day. Ben was waiting to meet a friend, but when the friend didn't show up at the agreed upon time, instead of waiting for a few minutes, he left right away and got upset with the teacher who was trying to help him. David said, "Ben uses his autism to get away with things and it looks bad for us. I do not like him." I asked David whether he thought Ben could control his emotions and he said he thinks he can. As I reflect now, I recalled David being flustered at times, and wondered if he was too hard on himself when his emotions make him feel out of control. Maybe this would be something to discuss further. I also want to have David take on more of a leadership role in our work and on our trips.

♥ **Delve Into Stories Shared:** Often the greatest gift we can give each other is to deeply listen to our stories and ask questions which help the story teller share their experiences more completely.

Slow Down

People with special gifts often move through life at a slower pace, as I have mentioned in Rose and B.D.'s stories many times. Their mental processing may take a bit longer than mine does, so in order to flow in harmony with people, I do my best to match their energy level or get on the same wavelength as them. It's like when singers harmonize. They sing at sound waves which complement each other and create beautiful songs. I often bustle about doing several different things one right after another, and slowing my pace is sometimes hard to do. "Downshifting" from being busy, I transition to breathing more deeply, listening more closely, observing finer details, and feeling more relaxed. Slowing down actually opens up awareness of so much more than I ever imagined possible. I notice beauty all around me, which wasn't apparent when I was bustling about.

Our society values work—hard work, fast work, nonstop work, unceasing work—even in the evening, on weekends, and holidays. Work, work, working, being productive and efficient and doing more each day than we did the day before, lest we be labeled a "lazy" person. What is the purpose of working so hard? So we can relax someday, take a break and not have to work again? Yet what happens when that day comes? We can't relax, much less sleep well because we haven't practiced taking a break, even on days off. Even though I am not required to work at a frenetic pace, this work ethic infused in me by society runs deep within, reinforced by repeating patterns, not only in my conscious, but most likely also my subconscious mind. Isn't it cool this work which chose me is requiring me to have a more relaxed work ethic?

One way I encourage people to set the pace when we are together is to walk behind them. Letting the Divine take the lead is a spiritual practice I am learning from author Tosha Silver. Instead of allowing my ego and mind to run my life, I sit back, breathe deeply and feel the inspiration from my soul shining through. When I walk behind, I often hear in my head, "Let the Divine take the lead." I do believe every single person is Divine, with a brightly shining spark glowing inside, radiating outwards, offering guidance and direction. This guidance can be heard most clearly when moving at a relaxed pace. I see other mentors charging ahead, with the person they are working with lagging behind, doing their best to keep up. How does this make them feel? Is walking behind a position of power or submission? I want the people I work with to feel empowered and in charge of their life as much as possible.

I first learned this from my friend Peggy. Tom and I were on vacation with Peggy and her husband, plus all four of our young children, ages three, four, five, and six. Walking on a trail in the Adirondacks, the pace was quite slow as the children explored along the way. I was feeling especially impatient and was doing my best to hustle Peggy's youngest son along. Peggy looked at me and asked, "Are you in a hurry?" This question gave me pause to consider why I was hustling little kids along on a walk in the woods. What was my hurry? Then Peggy suggested we ask her son to be our leader as usually kids will be proud being in the front and actually move along at a quicker pace.

Another story my mother shares about me when I was little comes to mind. My parents were hustling me along when we were walking in the woods and I said, "I like to observe nature." Mom laughs when I as an adult often lag behind her, while observing and collecting treasures. Isn't this interesting how I had forgotten the importance of slow exploratory walks as a young mom? These days, I allow myself time to meander when walking in the woods, often bringing my camera to take pictures and a bag to collect treasures, like mushrooms which I am learning which ones can be eaten and which ones can not. When my eighty-one-year-old mom comes along, she would still rather keep marching along, rather than dawdling. After all these years, some things change and some remain the same.

In some cultures, women are supposed to walk behind their husband. For example, in traditional Japanese marriages, the woman was instructed to walk three steps behind their husband. Women are expected to walk behind their husbands in the Muslim tradition as well, as a sign of respect for the man of the house. In my work, perhaps when I walk behind, I am showing a sign of respect and empowerment by honoring their desire to be independent leaders.

David and I have a kind of dance we do when walking together. I keep reminding myself to allow him to take the lead, which works great until we get to a door, where he, being the polite gentleman who he is, holds the door for me. Now I am in front. What do I do from here? Take a deep breath and remind myself having him walk in front is metaphorical. He is taking the lead by holding the door for me as a man does for a woman, showing what a gentleman he is. I thank him each time and then if there is a second door, I hold it for him, and we are even. David enjoys being leader when crossing streets because he is careful to look both ways and will put his arm out if he sees danger to protect me from harm. When he has determined it is safe to cross, I follow him as leader of his adventure. I wrote this poem to describe what this feels like.

Getting out of the Race
A simple gesture
A symbol divine
Walking behind
Honoring the pace
Of a life of grace
A different way
To remind us all
There is another way
To get out of the race
Which everyone is running
Yet nobody is winning
The faster we go
The more miserable we feel
Slowing down feels wrong.....
Until it feels right
And we wonder
Why we were racing at all....

❤ **Slow Down:** Are there areas of your life in which you would like to experiment with slowing down?

Be Your Own Support System

Understanding the structure of ESS and the dynamics of each family has been tricky for me to navigate as you learned in Rose's story, especially in the beginning. Although we as mentors must be nurturing and flexible, the company I work for is not nurturing to me at all. They handle the money, processing the paperwork as if unfeeling robots were doing this work. Since I am so passionate about mentoring each person to the best of my abilities, I want to share my excitement and feel like the people I am working for also care, but unfortunately, this was often not the case with the bureaucracy of the organization. They describe themselves as a fiscal intermediary and are in charge of making sure we get paid by teaching us to fill out the required paperwork correctly, plus providing the state mandated training we do once a year. After I figured out how to complete all of the forms properly, they stopped hassling me, and everything went smoothly. I surrendered to how the system worked and learned to provide my own emotional support. I nurture myself by writing these stories, sharing the excitement of each discovery made not only in this book, but also with family members at evening meals.

❧ **Be Your Own Support System:** Knowing what your support systems are and how to navigate them is so important. We need support in different areas: physical, emotional, financial and spiritual. Do you feel supported in all aspects of your life? Where might you benefit from receiving more support? How might you learn to take care of yourself in nurturing ways?

Seek Training

ESS is fairly new, having only been in existence for eighteen years. The training we are required to do is online through PowerPoint and YouTube presentations. We are required to sit through two hours and fifteen minutes of mostly the exact same training each year. The first year of watching the training provided me with some good examples of how to do this work with creativity and compassion. They showed examples of how to ask questions which offer some guidance, while also giving people a voice in what they want to do. For nonverbal people, this involves watching body language to understand their desires. Having to watch these same videos each year feels insulting and a waste of time for me. I am grateful to be paid for the time I spend doing the training, but at home I rant and rave at the ridiculousness of it all. After calming down a bit, I eventually shared my feelings in productive ways with the company. Wouldn't you know, in a few months, changes started to happen both on the inside of me and within the company. With my background in teaching, I often think of ways in which mentor training could be offered in more inspiring ways, and I feel excited about the possibility of this book being instrumental in those trainings or this might even be a new career path for me. Offering adults with special gifts the power to create the kind of life they and their families dream of is a relatively new concept with great potential, but much fine tuning is still needed. I am in a wonderful position to make a positive impact on how this can be done with integrity. How lucky I feel to be a part of this change.

I like to keep learning all the time. I was never trained to work with people who have special gifts through my formal education, yet I am self-educated in many ways through my own reading and experiences. In fact, one of the project options in the Foundations of Elementary School Math class, which I developed and taught at the State University of New York Orange (SUNY Orange) was to read *The Curious Incident of the Dog in the Nighttime*, published in 2003. This book, by Mark Haddon, is about Christopher, a young boy living in England, who is on the autism spectrum and is especially good at "maths" (In the United States we say "math," instead of "maths"). He is afraid of lots of things, yet he chooses to investigate who killed his neighbor's dog, Wellington. I asked my students to write about how they would teach Christopher if he were in their future classroom.

I kept my eyes open for training in my area to help me work with people in ever expanding ways. I attended a class on Socialization Skills at "A Helping Hand". David and his mom attended with me, which was really wonderful. B.D. and I attended the autism Conference at SUNY New Paltz, which you read about earlier, if you have read these stories in order. I envision both David and B.D. becoming leaders in the autism community in their own unique way.

♥ **Seek Training:** Continuing to learn is extremely important to keep us inspired and open to new ideas. What kinds of training or learning are you interested to participate in?

Find Space to Work Together

David wants to be independent from his family, so we look for places other than his home to work with me. The challenges are, he wants to learn to cook and sometimes there are movies which I would like him to see for education and inspiration purposes. So, where do we go? Fortunately, I have a home with lots of extra space. We can watch a movie in a room separate from the rest of the house. Cooking is a bit trickier since we have two little dogs, one of whom only likes five people in the world, and she attacks the ankles of any intruders not on her list. For adults with special gifts, this is not a good match. If I put her away in another room, she gets offended, barking like crazy and sometimes showing her disgust by peeing because she is "pissed off" when people dare step into our home. I would love to create an apartment in our home which has a small, safe kitchen, a bathroom, and a hang-out room so people with their mentors could use the space when they wanted to learn to cook or do relaxing activities. Until then, we have a room in the basement with an outside entrance and bathroom. This is the perfect room for mentoring work as we can go in and out of the house without having to deal with our ferocious furry friends.

♥ **Find Space to Work Together:** When communities are planned well, there are different public spaces for citizens to interact and learn in. Libraries are an amazing place to find books, read, and research, plus many libraries have meeting rooms for tutoring and for people to get together. What other kinds of spaces would benefit people with special gifts who want to learn skills to gain independence? Are there any spaces in your community which might work for your educational plans?

Eat Healthy Food

Part of my job is to encourage people to eat healthy food. The question is: who defines healthy food? For me, eating healthy food means eating a lot of vegetables, fruits, nuts, whole grains, along with some cheese and fish. While I absolutely love sweets, I don't eat white sugar, instead using a bit of honey occasionally. I make healthy versions of favorites, like chocolate banana ice cream made with frozen bananas, cocoa, and nut butter, with crunchy nuts on top. I have plenty of time to grow, shop for, and cook nutritious food, for which I am extremely grateful. I am fortunate to have been raised eating healthy food, refining my food choices even further after getting food-sensitivity testing done. By eating foods best suited for my body, I have noticed my painful knee and neck arthritis healing, while my digestion is better than at any time in my life. Best of all, my brain is clearer and more focused than ever before. My food choices have enabled me to feel better and be more supportive toward the other people in my life. This is one way in which I nurture myself.

I have always been the healthy eating role model for Tom and my daughters. Have they followed my guidance? Not always, but more and more in recent years. There were times I just didn't know if the nutrition education I shared was making any difference as I observed Tom eating lots of sugar loaded food. I felt helpless as I watched him eat this food because I worried about his health. We have lived together for many years, and while I have been happy to educate, I didn't want to be the food police. I would share my view, modeling healthy eating myself and observe his choices. Since some of Tom's relatives have struggled with diabetes, he slowly, slowly, slowly became more open to changing lifelong habits. Upon retirement, he embarked on a quest to lose weight and eat healthier food. I feel relief witnessing the new choices he is making as pounds slowly slip away, reminding me of the young man I married thirty four years ago.

Now you have some understanding of what healthy eating means to me, you can imagine looking through the lens I use to view other people's food choices. When beginning my work with David, I began by observing his eating habits to gain information over time. I realize since independence was the aim for David, much of his food was being selected from restaurants, which often offers not-so-healthy food options. When choices center around soda, burgers on white buns, and fries, with little to no veggies, I get concerned. I addressed the issue with David directly, observing his reaction and attempts to change, and the way he kept falling back into familiar habits.

I stewed and worried, hemmed and hawed until I gathered enough courage to call in the big guns: his mom. We addressed the soda issue first, which was most definitely an uncomfortable conversation for us all, yet it needed to be done. The realization that his mom has diabetes and drinking lots of soda is a sure way to move towards diabetes made an impact on David. He worked on changing his soda drinking habit by choosing water and sometimes one glass of lemonade. This was definitely a productive step forward. Addressing food choices is another issue which requires time and perseverance. I suggested watching Michael Pollan's movies"Cooked" and "In Defense of Food". We watch the trailers for short education pieces because David is open to just a bit of time learning about healthy eating. I do my best to keep my spirits up while attempting to teach healthy eating habits.

♥ **Eat Healthy Food:** When working with people to create healthy eating habits, there are times when uncomfortable conversations have to occur in order to bring challenges into the open for discussion. Do you feel the need for a tough conversation with yourself or someone you know? What strategies are you considering? How might selecting healthier food choices improve your life? Are there small changes you could make to support your well-being in big ways?

Pay Attention to Your Feelings

There were times when I would be getting ready to pickup David, rushing around to make sure I remember everything, and a text would show up on my cell phone:

David: How are you doing?

Me: I am fine, just getting ready to leave to pick you up.

David: See you soon.

I realized he was sending this message to check to make sure I was planning to pick him up. At first, these messages were cute, and I was patient. But the cuteness wore off when it became a pattern, and I began wondering if he didn't trust me. We talked about why he was sending these messages, and I asked him to send direct questions instead of pretending he wanted to have a conversation. The messages shifted to:

David: Are we working together today?

Maria: Yes!

These messages will sometimes come while I am driving to his house and I cannot read or reply to them safely. I have never forgotten to pick David up, and I wonder why he is texting me so often right before we work together. I ask if he has a calendar to write down the days we schedule our travels and he says he does have a planner he uses. I started sending him a text of the days and times we are together so there is no confusion. Finally, I asked him why he asks me if we are working together if we planned this day and time together. David says he wants to make sure I am not stuck in traffic somewhere or I had trouble getting to him. In order to address his behavior, I asked him what he thought I would do if I couldn't work with him one day. He said, "You would let me know," and I agreed I would definitely let him know. We then started joking about how he could text me asking: "Are you alive?"

Before picking up David two days later, I texted: "I hope you are alive because I am coming to get you!" He texted back: "haha I am alive and well." My frustration with his texts led to asking questions, which led to discussing options, which led to hearing his thinking and feelings, which led to humor! We understand each other better now and all will be well on this topic; although, we know there will be other emotional and social frontiers to explore in the future.

Here is another example. I just want you to know, David and I don't typically text between our meetings, which is a good thing for both of us. David had been texting me each week to ask if we could go to the bank before doing anything else during our Wednesday meetings. I answered factually at first, saying, "Sure." After this pattern repeated each week, I got a niggling feeling something else was going on beneath the surface, so the next time he texted me this same question, I realized some humor was needed and replied, "Your wish is my command." Followed by a genie emoji. Later that day, I talked to David about his role in this mentoring relationship. I said, "You are the leader of your life and our work together. I provide guidance to help you learn and grow in the areas you choose. I am kind of like a genie in a bottle who you can ask for wishes and I will do my best to make those wishes come true within reasonable means." David laughed at this analogy so I know he got the intended humor. Since David is not a bossy person and needs to learn to speak up for himself more, this analogy helps him go in the direction which is most beneficial. If I were working with a bossy person who needed to learn patience and respect, I would not have used this tactic. Medicine for one person can be poison for another.

Each situation is unique and individualized. I have to pay attention to what I am feeling as I ask David questions about his thoughts and emotions so a foundation of understanding is established. Since I am super sensitive, I may react more strongly than other people. This is certainly possible; however, I am the person he and his family chose, so we just go with what comes up in each situation between us. There is always a place of confusion for me, when I feel agitated but am not quite sure how to work through a challenging situation. I take time for observation and reflection. Once I feel ready to take some sort of action, it seems the issue works itself out relatively quickly. Resolution is often completed with humor and laughter.

♥ **Pay Attention to Your Feelings:** If something bothers you time after time, this is a sign there is an issue to be addressed. Is the issue for you to work on within yourself or is it a challenge to address directly with someone? Using humor is often helpful to create more easeful transitions.

Observe Family Dynamics

Understanding family dynamics is important with mentoring because so much of what people are like comes from their family. I would say this is especially true with a special gifts child because the parents are required to do a tremendous amount of work, even more than if they had a child with typical development. Most notably, at twenty five years of age, David still lives with his family, and in many ways, they are his major source of socialization.

For this reason, getting to know his family better will help me understand David better. In order to do that, I want to invite David and his family up to the lake where we have a cabin when there aren't many other people there. It would be nice to enjoy the beautiful water, sand, and nature together. I want to spend some time with Peter, David's younger brother, who is also on the autism spectrum and is non-verbal. I could gain greater understanding about what is happening with him. Also, I think Tom will really enjoy chatting with David's step-dad and mom. I will ask David what he thinks of this idea and we can make a plan. I am curious to ask David to describe his grandmother and what their relationship was like. His mom tells me I am similar to her, which really intrigues me.

❤ **Observe Family Dynamics**: Where would it be wise to understand family dynamics in your life or work? How do they affect the people you spend time with and your response to them?

Offer Ideas

Working with David is interesting because he can be quite engaging with a great sense of humor at times. He enjoys going on adventures, yet does not always have ideas of where to go. I enjoy making suggestions of what might interest him and seeing how the idea resonates with him. This is how our NYC trip came about.

As we sit in Burger King now, David eating a chicken sandwich, fries, and drinking water, I ask if he has ideas of what we might do together next week. He says he is still working on possibilities. I remind him of an idea we had discussed before: visiting all the libraries in the area. I talked about how Rose and I went to the Pine Bush Library, and then I remembered the Newburgh Library, which looks over the Hudson River and has lovely restaurants on the water. There are lots of great seafood restaurants as well as Café Pitti, which has a wood-fired oven for making pizzas and homemade gelato ice cream. Since David is half Italian and has never had gelato, he is excited for this idea. We are both looking forward to this trip.

When I enjoy this work, it is better for me and the people I am with. The choices are about what appeals to David and yet, since I will be with him, and I am driving, my opinion matters as well. My priority is putting each person first. I also keep in mind the instructions to put your own oxygen mask on before helping a child in a plane: it seems fitting that I need to be engaged and involved in this work in order to be most effective. It seems to me no matter what a person does, being passionate about it would increase happiness and efficiency tremendously. Imagine everyone doing what they love and getting paid as an extra bonus?

❤ **Offer Ideas:** When working with someone who is not sure of what they want to do, there is a fine line between giving options which appeal just to you and considering the desires of who you are working with. Finding a balance in this is important. It is okay to share your desires a bit, as long as this is not all the time. What common interests do you share? How might a trip to somewhere the person you are working with loves be made appealing to you as well?

Be Spontaneous

During much of our time together, David and I are quiet. We have time to be in the same space without the clutter of chatter, while our souls communicate in ways we are not even aware of. Often, something unique happens. One day, David and I were driving to explore a new library just after school let out. Bus after bus passed us, causing a whoosh, whoosh, whoosh sound. I imitate the whoosh and David starts doing this with me, which is great fun. Making sounds in a rhythm together makes our car ride feel like we are flying free. Soon we are driving on a section of road with many horizontal patch bumps and we are experiencing a whole new rhythm. David suggests we make a beat box rhythm for the bus and the bumps, and a creative activity we both enjoy emerges. When there are times of spontaneous fun, the contrast with our quiet times makes these moments extra special.

♥ **Be Spontaneous:** Embrace and appreciate moments when the sounds around you invite music to be made.

Use Stories as Teaching Moments

Yesterday, David got in the car and said, "I want to go to the Cottage Museum first." He got his phone out and became frustrated when he couldn't find the website he had discovered earlier. I got my phone out in an attempt to help him find this museum and couldn't find it either. I found the Franklin Delano Roosevelt Museum and asked if that interests him, and he liked this idea. David then got impatient because the directions to this museum were taking time to come up. I said out loud, "You seem frustrated," and he blurted out, "I just want to get going already." After the directions loaded onto his phone and he was ready to navigate, I asked if he wanted a suggestion for the future, which he said okay to, with a minor bit of annoyance because now I was delaying our departure even more. I suggested since he likes to be prepared for trips and leave right away, that he get directions up and ready to go on his phone before getting in the car. David agreed this was a good idea and even used it later this day. What a long way he had come in a short time— from getting in the car not sure even where he wanted to go, to making this adaptation. I shared how impressed I was.

The directions David uploaded to his phone through Google were really wonderful and clear. We took a new road I had never been on before: Canning Road, which meandered by farms, presumably growing foods to can, at least this is what I imagined in my mind. I noticed the traffic backed up on the highway we would be getting on soon. Quite surprisingly, by the time we were driving up the ramp to enter the highway, the traffic had thinned out and was flowing well. David used to be noticeably anxious with highway driving and had become so much calmer. I mentioned this to him and he said, "Yes this is true. I am still nervous with people coming in on the right." We talked about how important it is to be aware of when he does and doesn't experience anxiety.

David doesn't talk a lot. I always begin by asking him questions about his weekend, which he will answer pretty quickly. We don't listen to music in the car and on an hour-long car ride, there can be a lot of silence, which is okay. In these long silences, conversation can become fun social practice as well. I don't talk about myself much, but this day decided to tell David that Tom and I went to a *Zac Brown Band* concert on Friday evening. I asked if he would like to hear what that was like in the car or at lunch. He said he would like to hear the story during our car ride and here it is:

Tom treated me to a live concert since some of my friends had gone to see The Zac Brown Band in the past and had a good time. Bethel Woods is a beautiful setting, surrounded by farms all over. It was the original site of Woodstock. We arrived on a bus so we wouldn't get stuck in traffic on the way there or back. Walking on the grounds of Bethel Woods was exciting as we followed winding pathways lined with vendors on our way to the amphitheater.

We arrived at the event by 7:00 pm when the concert was due to begin and found a beautiful musician named Carolyn singing her heart out and giving a wonderful, engaged performance. The sloped lawn where we had decided to sit was sparsely filling in with people. I wanted to be up close so we could hear and see. At this point, the music was quite loud, so we found a spot towards the left side in the front, to the side of the loudspeakers. A family put their chairs a bit in front of us, seeming to be a nice group of people, excited to be together for this event. I really enjoyed Carolyn's music, yet over time it got harder and harder to hear as more people came streaming in.

There was a lot of activity. People were walking back and forth to the vendors, bringing lots of beers per hand with them. I said to Tom, "I think people will get quieter when the Zac Brown Band comes out to play." He didn't say much then, but he loves telling people my innocent remark when sharing our experience. Hey, all the concerts I have been to before were with Pete Seeger and Arlo Guthrie, and people were there for the music, for singing along, clapping, and dancing. This concert was nothing like I had ever been to.

The nice extended family in front of us had something brown in their hands that kept hopping out of their hands onto the ground, round and round. When it got to the kids, I saw it was a tiny toad. I went over to them asking if I could put it in a safe place for them. They were quite agreeable, and I brought the tiny toad to the tall grasses at the top of the hill. I seemed appreciative because he stayed still in my hand the whole time and seemed quite happy when he was hidden in the tall grasses. The security guard was fine with me doing this as long as I didn't stay on the hill.

The moment arrived when the much-awaited Zac Brown Band appeared on stage at 8:16 pm. The crowd was excited, and a good portion of people were singing along with the first song, dancing and attentive to the music, yet there was still this hummmm of other noise and talking and distraction going on, as people continue to parade back and forth between their seats and who knows where.

Tom tells me if things go bad to head up to the hill to the left. I am not sure what he is talking about and nod my head yes and take a walk up to the side of the stage for a better view, then back to our seat where beach balls are now being bopped around for people to hit up in the air and keep afloat. This is certainly a different activity from any concert I have been to. I enjoy playing along when the ball came near me, also quite frankly as a form of protection from being bopped on the head from a surprise beach ball invasion.

Not long after this game started, a fight erupted next to Tom. He stood up. I stood up. I saw a mom pulling on her son's arm to try to get him out of the fight, then another fight erupted and a rather large young man was lifted over the crowd in what looked like a chokehold. The "heading for the hills" wisdom Tom shared earlier was in the forefront of my mind as I collected our chairs and suggested to Tom this seems like a good time for us to head out. He was rather interested in the proceedings, and I learned later that he was considering throwing the ground cloth we brought over their heads to calm them down. I am glad he didn't follow through with this idea, and the security crew was able to solve the problems for the time being.

We headed to the top of the hill where there was quite a lot of space available, a lovely view of the screen showing the stage and we could actually hear better. It didn't take long to realize this was the designated smoking area, which was okay for a little bit because we were just so glad nobody was fighting around us. Could be the marijuana smoke chilled us out a bit as well, so we stayed until the intermission, when we decided to walk around. We ended up finding a bench by the entrance/exit to people watch

231

as first dribbles, then eventually streams of both sober and inebriated people walked and wobbled their way out with varying degrees of drama. It was a good place to people watch, that is for sure. We made plans for our "Zac Brown Band Celebration for Introverts" event that we would host in our living room the next year when we certainly would not be attending the concert at Bethel Woods! Both of us stayed in great spirits as we viewed this as an experience to learn from, and we revel in sharing the story with other people.

The vast array of behaviors I found puzzling formed the basis for great discussion points with David, like why would people attend a concert when they showed little interest in listening to the music? We talked about how the concert would have been a completely different experience if there wasn't any alcohol allowed. The point of me sharing this story and our discussion afterwards is I am very careful to ensure that anything I share or do is for the purpose of learning for David. He was engaged in the story, actively expressing his viewpoints, and our time talking was well spent. Since neither David, nor I for that matter, had ever been to a concert such as this, it was a new experience for us both to learn from.

David: My thoughts on the people at the Zac Brown concert. It makes me glad I didn't go because it sounds like the people at that concert were morons. I mean if you are going to get hammered and play beach ball over there when the purpose is listen to people perform music, why even go? It is a waste of money and tickets like that aren't cheap. I feel the same way with people who won't shut up at a movie theater. To me it feels like they just go to these things to pass the time because they are bored at home. If you do get drunk off your you-know-what and you wake up with a hangover with no memory of what happened, you are just wasting your time and everyone else's time. I am only half joking about this, but they should have gone to Red Robin instead. It made a good story though.

Our trip to the museum went quickly and with ease. We crossed the Hudson River, David giving me directions the whole time, and when we got close to the museum, "The Voice" as we call the female voice giving directions for Google told us to turn right onto 9D, then changed her mind at the last minute. Since the signs were suggesting we follow the original directions to turn right, David turned off his directions and said, "Let's listen to real life now." Well, lo and behold, wouldn't you know we ended up at Eleanor Roosevelt's Cottage Museum, the very museum David had wanted to visit originally. How cool is that?

We enjoyed looking around, reading about what an amazing woman Eleanor Roosevelt was, watching a fifteen-minute video about her life, then enjoying a forty-five-minute tour through her cottage and the other buildings and gardens on the property. We had some wonderfully engaging conversations about what interested us most about Eleanor Roosevelt and her mission for improving human rights, not only in in the United States, but around the world. After lunch at Red Robin, on our drive to his volunteer job at the library, I talked to David about what Eleanor Roosevelt stood for in her life and asked what is most important to David. He said, "Not underestimating what a person can do." How awesome is this mission in life? With this, I will not underestimate what David can do in his life and will continue to patiently guide him to continue reaching for his goals.

♥ **Use Stories as Teaching Moments**: What a wonderful way to have interesting discussions and to glean wisdom from real life experiences. What stories might you share which could be interesting and valuable for learning?

Be Open to Inspiration

David wanted to go to a comic book shop and when he got in the car, he had the directions all ready to go, even though I showed up ten minutes early. Quite impressive! On my drive to pick him up, I had been thinking of the spiritual teachings of Matt Kahn, author of the book, "Everything Is Here to Help You"(2019). In his book, he explains how well yes, *everything*, even emotions like fear, are here to help us.

I wondered how David's fear of people not stopping when they are coming up to a stop sign was helping him. When we were driving on a road and a car came down a driveway or up to a stop sign, especially on our right side, he got extremely agitated, tensing and moving his body, putting his foot on the imaginary brake and saying "Whoa" or " Look out lady" or "Watch it mister" or "What do you think you are doing?" I feel so badly for him because his fear is strong and swift, even with what I might view as a minimal threat. I have learned to observe this behavior and simply ask him to share what made him fearful. When he speaks about what he is feeling out loud, I neutrally acknowledge his reaction and basically act as a supportive witness of his experience. We talked about this idea of his fear being something that is here to help him on our ride over to the comic book store. We also talked about how life is always changing, how we might wish that the fun, joyful, happy times would stay forever and the fearful, angry, frustrating times would go away quickly. Life is not like that. Every day is completely different. Nature is always changing. Mentioning this was a way to give hope that even his strong fear response may change over time. I just put these ideas out there, suggesting maybe there is some purpose for him feeling this fear, something for him to learn from and just left it at that. He was open to considering this possibility, which impressed me since many people might think the idea of fear being here to help us is just ridiculous. David looked around the store while I was lucky enough to sit on the stepstool and do my paperwork.

While waiting for our food to be served at a wood-fired pizza place, I turned over the placemat filled with ads to find four calendars for 2019 through 2022. David commented that isn't much time. I asked where he would like to be in 2022. After some silence, he said he would like to be more confident. I asked for more details, which weren't forthcoming at this time. Patience, patience my dear, is part of this work. Rewards were soon to come after our meal when we filled out the surveys from our visit to the Eleanor Roosevelt Cottage and Museum. Below are David's comments about the visit:

The park was established because of its significance to the nation. In your opinion, what is the national significance of this park?
The Factory house was the most important because it helped the unemployed.

Is there anything else you would like to tell us about this park's facilities, services, or recreational opportunities?
The ranger was friendly and the exhibits of the house was fascinating.

Since I often don't know what David is thinking and feeling because he is not very talkative, reading how he experienced the park was really interesting for me. Knowing he understood and appreciated how the Factory House at the park is significant to the nation because it helped the unemployed, shows his capacity for empathy and compassion. Hearing he appreciated the friendliness of the ranger and how he found the exhibits fascinating is wonderful feedback for me. I wonder what he found fascinating today as I read this account of our adventure. These comments felt like a wonderful reward after many moments of silence, almost like a secret glimpse into David's soul, his thoughts and what was most important to him.

David added: "Everything that Maria has read to me about going to the Cottage Museum and Red Robin I remember as she does. The only thing I have no memory of is saying, 'Watch out, mister.' I do remember saying, "Watch out lady or Whoa but the "Watch out mister" is a blank for me." I guess maybe when I am that freaked out about highways and cars driving out unexpectedly, makes me forget about my comments and makes me lose focus on the task at hand.

And I was fascinated with everything at the museum and it was also a nice place to walk. But to be honest, I actually felt weird because I was the only young person in the entire tour. I was wondering if I should actually be there or not. Other than that, it was a really good day. One of my favorite moments was being at Red Robin, because they have really good burgers. That was only my second time being in that restaurant. After Maria brought me to the library I volunteer at, the rest of the evening was uneventful."

The subject of his fear came up again, and he was joking that it would be nice if the fear could just be toned down a bit. I said, just like turning the volume down on the radio. We were both hysterically laughing about this image we created together and somehow it felt like a door was opening to possibility…we will see what is to come…This work is about being in the present moment with the person I am mentoring. I might have an idea of what we might do that day and a clue as to what we might discuss, and then when we are together, the combination of our individual inputs—combined with the alchemy of inspiration, divine guidance, luck, whatever it is—can open us up to never-before-imagined possibilities. I feel so very lucky to be a part of this amazing process. It is funny, because at this point of writing, nothing concrete has happened and yet, I have a strong feeling some major breakthrough is going to happen. I will let you know when it does ☺

I sent this snippet of story to my long-distance writing friend Day Howell who shared her view:

What a lovely story. What catches my attention is the symbiotic mentoring that's happening. While you are the Mentor, you're receiving so much from your clients. The learning experience is almost like a warm ocean you're both swimming in together. I think with your open heart and awareness of the Divine, you've created a sacred space where you and your clients are both students. It's truly lovely.
What a gift!

❦ **Be Open to Inspiration:** When you are open to inspiration, the people you are with can sense this, even if neither of you are consciously aware of what is happening. Beginning a day with an open heart and mind is like clearing away weeds on a plot of land before visiting beautiful gardens for ideas. You may not know what surprises you might experience that day, but you are making space for something new.

Keep Trying Different Methods

One day, David said he would like to go to Richard's Dairy Shed, and he knew how to direct me without Google Maps' assistance. His directions were good, and he even watched the traffic to let me know when I could enter a busy road. Having David handle directions and telling me when it is safe to pull out is preparation for when he will oneday drive. While David ordered and paid for his triple-decker lemon ice cream cone, I waited at a picnic table overlooking a wetland. After finishing his ice cream, I asked if David wanted to look over his Life Plan and he agreed this was a good idea. I found the document through email on my phone and we reviewed it together, David reading the goals to me, then we discussed them. Towards the end of the document is this action plan:

> **Nutrition:** *I maintain an adequate diet that meets my nutritional needs, e.g., preventing choking, avoiding food allergies.*

> **Responsibility for training staff:** *Mom and Step-Dad are parents and are responsible.*

> **Supports:** *David has a normal diet. Staff needs to encourage David to make healthy food choices and to eat adequate nutrition for every meal.*

Staff needs to encourage David to make healthy food choices and to eat adequate nutrition for every meal. This sentence churned inside my head for some time: What is the definition of healthy food choices for David? I had no idea.

If you remember, I spoke to David and his mom about his food choices, especially his soda consumption. At the time, his mom was not happy to hear this report from me and scolded him, saying he knew better. David's dad was a documentarian and they had all watched *Supersize Me* together. Since David's mom is diabetic, they have whole grain bread at home and lots of healthy food. I explained I didn't want to be the food police. After this discussion, David said he cut back his soda consumption to one time a week as a treat and chose to drink lemonade or water on the other days.

However, I was really feeling like waving a white flag of surrender with David's eating because every time I took him to eat somewhere, he ate a burger and fries or pizza, or frozen yogurt or ice cream. Eating these foods as a treat occasionally is fine, but having them on a regular basis is not recommended as healthy eating. I wanted to officially resign as encourager of good eating with David because I was frustrated. I just didn't feel like progress was being made. I had other ideas, but couldn't figure out how to discuss them in a respectful way, because I was out of patience. Sarcasm, not my usual mode of thinking, started creeping in. In my head, I was thinking maybe David could find a fast food, soda-rich diet which helps people get stronger and we could discuss this approach. Oh dear, I sometimes feel quite hopeless about encouraging healthy eating. I decided to make one last ditch effort to share healthy eating inspiration and gave him a picture of a healthy plate, with half the plate filled with vegetables, one quarter of the plate showing healthy proteins, the other fourth with whole grains and a big glass of water on the side.

Because I was feeling frustrated, yet also really wanted to find a way to encourage healthy eating, the thoughts in my head were not being helpful. I decided to host a debate in my head after working with David that day between *Defeated Me* and *Encouraging Me* to see if there could be some resolution.

Defeated Me: I obviously can't teach him and I feel like a failure.

Encouraging Me: Okay Maria, let's slow down a bit. We are scheduled to attend a talk at Thrall Library titled, "Healthy Eating on a Budget" in July, so you are continuing to try different strategies.

Defeated Me: Aren't you enabling David's unhealthy eating choices by driving him to purchase burgers, pizza and ice cream?

Encouraging Me: Next time you work together, you could explain this predicament you are in, and maybe we can come to some sort of compromise.

Before speaking to David about enabling his unhealthy eating habits, I had the good sense to call Michael D, the Staff Support Liaison for ESS.

I explained the situation I was struggling with but did not give him David's name. I shared how I didn't want to be the food police and wanted to continue to build a positive relationship with David. Michael D provided me with much wisdom. He liked the idea of going to the Healthy Eating on a Budget class at the library. He explained what I can do: make suggestions and model healthy eating, recognizing participants may take five months or five years to make changes. In the end, it is David's decision as to what he chooses to eat when we are working together. If he continues to eat fast food, that is okay. I am not going to get in trouble for not doing my job.

Whew! I felt better knowing this. I realize seeing his Life Plan with official looking writing had made me feel nervous. Coming from the background of a teacher, it almost seemed like a syllabus I was to follow. The Life Plan is a guide, not an agenda to follow exactly. This is both liberating and perplexing—there is a feeling of not having clear bearings. I am grateful to not have strict guidelines because there is room for creativity. However, I also really want David to eat healthier food. It seems like my ego is getting involved, and I am allowing something not within my control to get me all spun up. David adds his thoughts here:

I haven't made the best food choices when I started working with Maria and I would choose burgers or pizza or what have you, not because I really didn't care and it wasn't to rebel. I have long days at college and on those days where I work with Maria, I have martial arts class on the same night. So since it would be past 9 when I got home to have my own dinner to fill my own appetite.

I didn't realize it at the time, but I think there was a soda addiction and with my mom and Maria pointing this out to me, it made me realize I should put some extra effort into having something else. For example, sometimes I have lemonade and mostly I have water. When Maria read this to me, I was feeling embarrassed and ashamed of my soda habit, but at some point, I decided to have soda on the weekends instead, to give myself a special treat, so my body won't be filled with as much sugar. And now I have smaller, healthier dinner choices such as omelets and a small amount of chicken. And since my parents and my mentor talked to me about food choices, I have more careful experiences with food and lately, I have been doing more physical exercises, outside of martial arts. In fact, I've used some of my martial arts practices to be physically fit because I don't want to be overweight. I mention weight because I have seen people who can barely go to a ShopRite, without any help from a motor cart that the store has and they have breathing problems. That is one of my fears.

I would like to say I didn't continue to stew over what to say when I next saw David because this is what I would have preferred. Truth be told, a lot of mental struggles occurred, which spun around faster and faster, the closer I got to the next time we worked together. Kind of like a whirligig which spins faster the more the wind blows. Back when I was on the Living Passionately Book tour, I stumbled upon a Whirligig Park in North Carolina and took this picture, now in black and white. How cool is this in toy form? How horrendous this is in mental anguish form.

Because I was acutely aware of these circling thoughts and really wanted to get them the hell out of my brain, I needed a solution. I decided to try saying a prayer Tosha Silver style, offering this whole situation with David over to the Divine.

Divine Beloved,
I turn these spinning thoughts over to you.

Teach me when to speak and when not to speak to David about his food choices.

Can you believe, the spinning thoughts released and I was able to shift my focus? Ahhh, sweet relief.

When I arrived at David's house, he was waiting outside for me. I don't usually see him this way, but for some reason, he looked so small, innocent and vulnerable. I did not speak to him about his eating right away, despite the fed-up teacher inside me wanting so badly to present a healthy eating lesson. After our hellos, he said he would like to go to the bank first to take money out of the ATM. He directed me there without Google maps, checking for traffic when pulling out of the driveway. I asked him how his recent vacation was and he said, "It was fun." I started singing the song "Tell me more" from Grease. This lightened the mood and David shared lots of details about his vacation, even expanding on how he felt when I asked him questions to understand his experiences. When talking about his vacation, it became clear what he enjoyed the most was the delicious food his family ate. I asked what he liked about the food he ate on vacation, and he said it was rich food. I learned rich food meant hot dogs, hamburgers, pancakes, ice cream, and other foods he doesn't normally eat at home. I asked if he felt the same way about the times we work together when he gets the opportunity to eat rich food he doesn't get at home often and David confirmed this was true. I asked him what kinds of foods he eats at home and he said cereal, apples, sometimes cold cuts. I explained part of his Life Plan is about learning how to eat healthy food. I told him I had spoken to an ESS support person without sharing his name, and I asked if I was not doing my job because David was eating so much fast food. David explained he thinks I am doing a good job because he does try some of my suggestions, like drinking less soda. David then asked what kinds of food I eat at home and when on vacation, so I had the opportunity to share how I eat very similar to the plate I showed him: lots of veggies and fruits, some whole grains, cheese, and seafood. I told him how much I love sweets and have learned to make healthier versions, like the frozen banana, chocolate peanut butter ice cream I eat a lot of in the summer. I explained I am not skilled at cooking fish well, so I like to order fish when I go out to eat. For example, last night, Tom and I went to an Ecuadorian Restaurant and I had grilled salmon with fried green plantains and a mango smoothie. This was a treat for me because the salmon and plantains are difficult to cook. I said when I traveled to Paris, I enjoyed the croissant and crepes, while also balancing these sweet treats with salads, quiche and other healthy foods.

This conversation was organic, with a natural flow of give and take. Nothing was forced and David opened the door to this opportunity for me to share some different strategies I use to eat healthy food which tastes delicious. How much better this felt and how much more productive our conversation was, rather than lecturing to a reluctant recipient. I also felt more relaxed and at ease and the spinning thoughts had blown away in the wind.

Later, when David chose to order his lunch from Wendy's, I decided to get a fruit smoothie, coaching myself that I was leading by example and that I didn't need to say anything to David about his food choices. He then wanted to get ice cream at Richard's Dairy Shack and assured me this is a treat and not a regular habit. He didn't want me to feel badly about his food choices, which was really thoughtful. I suppose this was a way for him to do what he wants while maintaining a pleasant environment. I understand this, and it is really okay. This is his self-directed program, and I am there to mentor and guide, not force anything to happen. What a wonderful learning experience this has been for us both.

♥ **Keep Trying Different Methods:** When something is bothering me and my mind is whirling faster and faster, gaining more anxiety and less wisdom with each passing second, often shifting focus by asking for input, saying a prayer or writing can help me calm myself down so I can be a more reasonable human being. If you don't give up and keep trying different ways to work with your mind and the person you are with, eventually something will shift and there will be a welcome opening.

You Are Important

One day, David and I had three hours scheduled together and he chose to go to the bank, to Barnes and Noble to pick out a book with a gift card he had, to Burger King, and then home. He wanted me to take him to the library for his volunteering and wait two hours for him to finish, but I had anniversary plans with Tom that evening which I was not willing to change. I was modeling speaking up for myself here and not changing my plans with David's last minute request. We talked about all of his options for getting a ride back, since he had made this request to me at the last minute. Uber was too expensive for his budget that week, the Dial-a-Bus is done at 5:00 pm, and a reservation has to be made at least a day in advance. David did not want to ask his step-dad to pick him up because he wants to be more independent, even though he told me his step-dad would probably say yes. Part of me wanted to debate the option of asking his step-dad. I held back because he gave a well-reasoned reply. I chose to respect this decision. Oh, but I also wanted David to value himself enough to speak up and ask his step-dad for a ride.

❤ **You Are Important** These examples show how David chose not to speak up for himself by not asking his step-dad for a ride and how I spoke up and did not change my plans at the last minute. Each of us is important, including you, the reader. Have you ever put yourself second in a circumstance where you could have embraced your worthiness and spoken up?

Foster Social Connections

Oftentimes, people on the spectrum have challenges in building connections with others, but everyone needs social networks, so this is a skill we practice. When I met with David for a quick hour before his library shift, he proudly told me—with a huge smile on his face—he had earned his orange belt in Taekwondo. While waiting for his spare ribs to arrive at the Chinese restaurant, his phone rang, and he excused himself to speak with a martial arts classmate. This classmate, a friend who now drives David home on a regular basis, was calling to say there was a weather advisory. They decided together to contact the teacher and determine if there would be class that evening. After a few minutes, the classmate called back and told David there would be class. I was so happy for David to have a connection with this classmate with whom he has this opportunity to engage socially and share interests. What a long way he has come in the short time we have been working together.

David: For a while, I did have a couple of classmates who drove me home and they were nice enough to do so. I remember Maria told me she talked to one of my instructors about it and my instructor told one of my classmates about this and that person agreed. And there was also another classmate who sometimes took me home. Like the first classmate was a male that was the same age as me or a little older. And there was a woman who was a few years older than me and she actually ended up driving me home more.

What else? (pause) For a while it went well and the people were nice and friendly. They were helpful and I made small talk because awkward silence with people I barely know didn't feel good so I did my best to make small talk. But then eventually since there are also people with their own busy lives, it was hard for them to pick me up and drop me at home. I mean in the first classmate wasn't able to because of things happening in his personal life and my other martial arts classmate has her own busy life and I decided it wasn't really fair of me to constantly depend on them because one time I was expecting to go to class but the person who was supposed to pick me up wasn't able to pick me up because of something that happened at work.

My other classmate didn't drive me home anymore. Not to be rude. She had nothing against me but since over time I started making enough money from my job and my insurance that I could get an Uber there. Some nights I get myself to class with Uber. Most of the time one of my parents will drive me and I end up taking a taxi home to be more independent and I'll say again, it wouldn't have been fair of me to rely on my classmates to get me all the time. It is a good thing too because I actually don't see them in class anymore. Maybe they attend classes on a different day or later. I can't say. It did turn out for the best because I am able to learn more and more on self-reliance.

Encouraging social connections takes patience, perseverance and time. Even though David is no longer being driven home by his classmates, the times when he was driven home, despite the moments of awkward silence, there were important connections being made. Maybe there will be a classmate who attends regularly and lives near David who would be willing to take a bit of extra time to drive him home. Maybe when David learns to drive, he will return the favor and give a classmate with special gifts a ride to and from class. The future holds so many possibilities.

❤ **Foster Social Connections:** How do you make time in your life or the lives of those you work with to help each other out and connect? Even though many people have their own car to conveniently go wherever they want, whenever they want, sharing rides and conversations is important for emotional health. We are social creatures who thrive through connection. Finding people who are a good fit for our personality and schedule may take time and many attempts, but these efforts are valuable for the collaboration and friendships which may form.

Communicate With Members of the Team

The Circle of Support meeting is very important for all of us team members in order to coordinate our efforts and help the people we work with. Sometimes, this can be quite challenging, however, as we all have different personalities and communication styles. I was finally invited to attend David's meeting, but I was very frustrated because I had accumulated a long list of questions for David's mom and I didn't want to have to bring up the communication challenges I was having at that meeting. On the morning before the meeting, we finally spoke through the phone, and she was extremely helpful. I learned the major goal she wanted for David this summer was for him to get his driving learner's permit, and fortunately, there was time to accomplish that before the summer was over. The other questions I had were related to David's goals through ESS. In the goals list, I had read several categories which indicated mentors needed to do training that I had not yet done, like practicing evacuations and emergency exits during a crisis. David's mom reassured me she and her husband were taking care of these requirements, and I didn't need to worry about them. These are state requirements that need to be on David's care plan, and I felt uncomfortable with the possibility of attending David's Circle of Support meeting asking why I hadn't been trained in these areas, potentially raising red flags about his parents not doing their job. The parents are most definitely doing a wonderful job with David, and I learned there is just bureaucratic wording which needs to be included. I was relieved to be able to let go of worrying about these topics.

Food, of course, was another area of concern I wanted to revisit. I asked David's mom what she wanted David to learn about healthy eating. She shared a dinner she had prepared for the family the other night—a salad with a store roasted chicken. This meal was inexpensive and fed four people easily, and it included a protein and a vegetable. It was a light, healthy meal which everyone enjoyed. This was the exact suggestion I'd had for David one time, which did not interest him at all, but at least his mom and I were on the same page! I also understand the conflict for David, who really enjoys rich meals. While his family does enjoy this kind of food when on vacations and for special occasions, David wanted to eat rich food all the time. Healthy eating was emphasized at home, but he was a young man who craved junk food, which he was not getting as often as he would like. His mom suggested David plan a family dinner one day a week and prepare a shopping list for the ingredients. This seemed like something we could do together, but it would be a challenge to find recipes which meet his desire for rich food and his family's desire to eat healthy.

I also shared what happened when David's martial arts class was cancelled the week before, when he asked me to wait for him to volunteer, then bring him home. Since I had plans already that evening, I was not able to honor his request. I explained the options I suggested— Uber, the Dial-a-Bus, or calling his step-dad— and how David rejected these options. His mom said she wished David had asked his step-dad because since working with me, they don't drive him to class very often, and they would be happy to do this for him when needed. She said David is too polite, and it is important for him to ask for what he wants. With this viewpoint, I could now work with David on speaking up for himself and asking for what he wants.

One other discussion was how David has learned to handle changes with greater ease. Now when he faces a challenge, he acts frustrated and annoyed, without melting down like he did in the past. Hearing this perspective was encouraging and helped me understand his behavior. I have observed times when David seemed annoyed with me when we had to do things a little bit differently than he had planned. Now I understand his minor display of annoyance as a sign of growth because he is not melting down like he did in the past. Anyone who is doing new things feels stress and discomfort at having to break old habits and venture into previously uncharted areas. His mom thanked me for working with David and said she was happy for how much David's world has expanded. This thirty minute conversation with David's mom provided many helpful insights, making my job so much more effective, plus allowed me to feel more at ease because I knew what was and was not important to focus on.

With a sense of relief to go along with my excitement and nervousness, I joined David's long-awaited Circle of Support Meeting at his home. I arrived ten minutes early, as David requested, which was great because I got to chat ahead of time with his mom and ask her a few more questions. I also had the honor of connecting with David's brother Peter in a deeper way than ever before when he nuzzled his nose into the crook of my neck, placed his hand on my shoulder and said something I didn't quite understand. I was also wondering about how things would go with other team members, who sometimes demand so much attention at the meetings. I said a prayer in my head:

May the words flowing through me be for the highest and greatest good of all.

At 5:30 pm, I heard other team members arrive. The presence of one team member, with the way she speaks softly about topics for David's benefit, calms and reassures me. Another team member tends to go off on tangents, taking the attention away from our meeting's focus: David. With all of this going on, I notice David waiting patiently to make an announcement, but with all the commotion in the room, no one noticed. Finally, I spoke up saying, "David has something to share with us." Eventually everyone's attention turned to David who shared he had gotten his learner's permit, which he proudly showed to everyone. We clapped and everyone spoke about how proud they were of David. His mom told the story of how David had come home, made dinner for the family and after everyone was seated he said, "By the way, I passed my permit test today." With love and fun, she said she punched him in the arm for waiting so long to share the news. One team member asked how David felt about passing his test and he replied he is proud of himself. Then, he shared more stories of his successes like how he earned his Orange Belt in Taekwondo and Hapkido. Team members took notes, asking for pauses every now and then so they could get all this wonderful news recorded for the report.

I continued to feel aggravated as some team members continued to come in and out of focus on David and his goals. I tried ignoring the digressions at one point and started a conversation with one team member about a question I had concerning David. This tactic did not work well because the story was retold so I wouldn't miss it! Yikes! How to get us back on topic!? Well, the conversation did eventually get back to David's progress, which was recorded in great detail. I learned how important wording was with these reports, and everything was recorded meticulously. David was making a lot of progress but also still needed support with his challenges: if the report is too glowing, and David seems too competent, funding might be taken away. Team members are masterful with their knowledge of how to navigate this complex system, and I really admire them for these skills. While walking out to our cars, One team member said to me, "Your work with people is quite extraordinary and very much appreciated." I thanked her and was wondering why she said this. I guess she sees a lot of mentors and my work must stand out. What a kind thing to say!

Do you remember when, not long ago, I was feeling stuck in working with David? Looking back, I see how making the effort to communicate with his mom helped him to move forward. Now he has earned his driver's permit (without special accommodations for his dyslexia), just passed his required five-hour driving course last night (once again, without special accommodations for his dyslexia), scheduled a day to get together with his friend Mark, and signed up for driving lesson orientation. He asked me what days I am traveling and I texted him those dates. Without communication between team members, these positive changes would never have occurred. David is taking charge of his life and doing so much on his own to make things happen.

While he was eating dinner before his five-hour course, I reminded David of a team member's question about how he feels now as opposed to two years ago when he was at home, not doing any of the activities he is now. David said he hadn't understood the question at the time and said, "I feel better now and have more purpose." I asked him to write this down so he can share this with her when he sees her at the next Circle of Support meeting. Oh, how wonderful this will be to witness, after all of the work his team has done to help David lead a more fulfilling life.

♥ **Connect with Members of the Team:** When it seems like you keep hitting a brick wall trying to do something or contact someone, you may just be one more try away from success, so it is worth an extra effort. How can you help to facilitate communication between team members? How might you overcome communication challenges?

Address Anxiety During Low Stress Times

When driving David to various places, he carefully watches traffic lights. If we are chatting about something when the car is stopped and the light is red, as soon as the light turns green, in a flurry of panic he announces, "The light is green now." Countless times, I have said, "Thank you," and moved the car through the intersection. Sometimes I feel annoyed at the extreme urgency to go exactly when the light turns green, but I have observed this behavior for many months and I am guessing it is anxiety driven. Since David is actually driving with an instructor now, I realize this urgency to go as soon as the light is green needs to be addressed.

While sitting at a red light one day, I explained when a light turns from red to green, it is not an emergency which has to be addressed immediately. If the people behind us have to wait a bit for us to get going, that is okay. They might be impatient, get aggravated and honk, which is also okay. I recognized it would be best to address this issue with him during a relaxed time, not when David is in an agitated state.

I have also been following this wisdom with myself. When my mind is busy, anxious and swirling with upset, I remember to sit down, write about what is bothering me and sort through what might be a reasonable solution. I used this recently when visiting Tom's parents, who can be challenging to communicate with. They often don't return calls and aren't comfortable with visitors. When I contemplated this problem, I decided to travel with Tom to visit his family, but allow Tom and his sister to visit their parents without me. This would reduce everyone's anxiety. I was able to attend a local yoga class, and met later with Tom's sister for lunch. Making these choices about what I really wanted to do, while also supporting Tom by making reservations at a lovely Airbnb for us, driving with him, and keeping him company, I feel happy and fulfilled. He is feeling supported by me and grateful to be able to visit his family. Everyone was happy with my solution.

♥ **Address Anxiety During Low Stress Times:** During low-stress times, a person is more open to suggestions and available to listen. There is no reasoning with anyone when they are upset. It is only once we are calm when changes can be addressed in reasonable ways. How might tense situations be relieved for everyone and different options explored?

250

Talk Or Write It Out

One day, I took David to an orientation meeting to set up his driving lessons. After filling out his paperwork, we were in the waiting room when suddenly, everyone was called to go in for the meeting. I asked David whether he would like me to accompany him or wait here. This question stopped David in his tracks. Clearly flustered by my question, he eventually replied, "I think I can do this on my own." Just like taking his driving permit and five-hour course on his own, David walked into the conference room for his orientation while I sat in the waiting room, using this time to catch up on paperwork.

When David came out, he said to me, "Don't do that again, asking me a question right before I go into a class." His anger felt really strong to me, and it stung. Although I replied in an outwardly calm manner, inside I felt so daggone hurt, but I set that feeling aside for the time being. Instead of getting defensive, I said, "You seemed a bit flustered by my question. I didn't know what you wanted me to do. Maybe if we talked about whether you wanted me joining you or waiting outside, I would know how to support you best." David agreed we could discuss plans ahead of time in the future.

Later in the car, David said it was his fault for not thinking about whether he wanted me to join him for the orientation. I do believe much of his frustration was because the class was confusing for him and it would have been better if I had been there. How could he know this ahead of time, never having attended something like this before? I realize now, David's anger, which he directed at me, wasn't about me at all. Writing this story helped me gain clarity on what happened.

It was time to lighten the mood. I started joking about how it might take twenty years before he actually got an appointment for driving lessons. We were howling in the car on our way to Wendy's, a great release after the frustration of facing bureaucracy and a seemingly endless trail of forms.

David: When we went to the building for any information on driver's license related topic, we went inside the building and I will say I had actually been to the building before. It had just been a while and was for different reasons which I don't remember why. But I vaguely remember having to go upstairs to sit and wait. I would say it was more my instincts guiding me and so I went upstairs since neither one of us knew exactly where to go. I looked at the sign and saw the SILEV sign. And so after having seen the sign, when Maria asked me if I wanted to go to the conference by myself or with her, it was close to the time when I was to do so and it caught me off guard. I made a quick decision I would and so I went to the room where there was a presentation a woman was giving about somethings. I wrote down some things but didn't understand what she was saying. I got frustrated. I did say, "Don't do that again." In that situation, we found out some information. I was annoyed the person who was in charge of the orientation did not have a lot of information and so after running that errand, Maria was driving me to Wendy's and I did feel bad about being annoyed and angry. I apologized. And the specific of the bureaucratic joke was, "I have to use the bathroom. You have to sign this form and that form to let me know you signed the other forms and then I ended the joke by saying, actually, I will just hold it. Okay, you can sign to let us know you are holding it in and sign another paper to say you signed that form." Other than my frustrations and agreeing it would be nice to ask me ahead of time to see if coming with me would be good and in hindsight, I should have asked her to come with me into that room and to be more calm, because she was doing what I told her earlier.

♥ **Talk or Write it Out:** When something feels off when working with someone, talk it out or write it out to get clarity first. This is the only way to come to an understanding and create ways to prevent challenges in the future. Reading and writing this book together has been a wonderful way for David and me to understand each other better.

Decompress to Allow More Positive Communication

I felt proud of myself for feeling David's anger and not getting angry with him in return. I did a good job of understanding where his frustrations were coming from and addressing what could be done to avoid this challenge next time, but to be completely honest, there was still a residue of hurt lingering in my heart when I arrived home. Writing this story in the evening seems to be clearing out the remnants of the heart hurt.

Speaking of arriving home, I was enthusiastically greeted by Lacey and Coco, eighteen combined pounds of pure love, acting like it had been years since they last saw me. Coco is bark crying as Lacey imitates his anguished sounds. After plugging the car in to be charged, Tom let them out of the gate for lots of licks and jumps and leaps and spins of joy. Tom then got a kiss, and we went into the yard to share stories from our day. I was starting to feel better, when I made the mistake of checking my emails and found this one sent to David's mom, his broker, and me from Dawn, his care manager from ESS:

> *Good Afternoon-*
> *I hope all is well. It has been brought to my attention that you are not filling out your name on the payee section of the expense reports. We are paying them (to you) as we know you are David's only staff. Please ensure moving forward that we have all of the necessary information filled out on the expense reports to avoid delay in payment.*
> *Let me know if you have any questions.*
>
> *Dawn Silverstone*
> *Self-Direction Coordinator*
> *Encouraging Self Support*

At first, I decided not to reply, then after a few deep breaths, I replied to all:

> *I will look at the form to figure out what I haven't filled in Dawn.*
> *Thanks for letting me know!*

I am so careful to treat people with the utmost respect. When I get an email written about me, but not even addressed to me, sent to two other people about me and how I messed up the forms yet again, my feelings get hurt. I start picking on myself, saying over and over again, both in my head and then to Tom, "I am so sensitive. Why do I let these kinds of things bother me so much?" (Note from Zhenya: Lovely Maria, what makes you sensitive is also what makes you compassionate, kind, and attentive to the people you help. Like any strength, it can feel like a weakness sometimes. But it is a blessing to others. I love you just the way you are. (Thank you so much for sharing these insights, Zhenya! ~ Maria)) Tom was very sweet, talking through the challenge points:

- The embarrassment of messing up and being called on it in front of people.
- How hard I work to do a good job and fill out the paperwork correctly.
- The insensitivity of the way Dawn addressed this problem, without using my name, interestingly enough, since not writing my name was the problem in the first place.

Tom then went through a list of things I had not done:

- You didn't hurt anyone.
- You didn't falsely fill out forms, trying to embezzle money.
- A train didn't crash.
- Nobody got laid off.

He certainly had a lot of good points. Interestingly enough, on the inside, I am deeply hurt by the way Dawn addressed this problem, and it feels terribly insulting, yet on the outside, I realize this is a minor "ESSue" (Get it? ESS- issue? Haha.) and has more to do with a person lacking in compassion and people skills, who is probably quite stressed and not being thoughtful in the way she communicates. After our discussion, I sent this additional reply all email so I could have more information to know what I messed up and how to do better the next time:

Dawn, could you please send me a picture of the forms I didn't fill out correctly so I can learn for future forms?
Your help is much appreciated!

After having written this story, once again I feel calmer, and I can breathe more deeply. I wasn't completely over this exchange because I woke up at three o'clock am still trying to sort through my emotions, so I wrote some more in my journal then read Chapter 7 (Mastering Relationships) of the book "Whatever Arises LOVE That," by Matt Kahn. He teaches the healing power of a compliment, where we can practice bringing a more positive viewpoint to any conversation. I realized this was exactly what I was doing with Dawn by keeping my responses upbeat and not getting defensive or angry about her insensitivity directly to her. I felt proud of myself for bringing love into communications with her and vowed to continue practicing with our exchanges. After writing, reading, and reflecting, I was ready to head back into bed and slept in until 7:00 in the morning, as opposed to my typical 6 am wake up.

Upon checking my email later that day, Dawn had sent me a picture of the timesheets in which I didn't put my name with these spots highlighted in yellow and asked me to let her know if I had any questions. My response was:

Oh gosh the yellow highlighter really helps. I never noticed that line to fill in before. Thank you so much Dawn!

And that was that. I now pay extra attention to that line on the forms where they want my name printed in addition to my signed name at the bottom of the form. A few days later, Dawn sent an email to all of us with updated timesheets for David. When I went to print them, there was light grey lettering in the background that said, "DRAFT: DO NOT USE" Fortunately, I saw this before printing a bunch of copies. I carefully considered how to handle this. I didn't want to embarrass Dawn in front of everyone, so sent this email directly to her with nobody else copied:

Thank you, Dawn!
I went to print the new timesheet and, in the background, it says Draft, do not use. Do you have another version which we can use?
I appreciate your help!
>> *Maria*

She wrote back right away:

Yikes, thanks for catching that. Let me take a look.

And she quickly sent us all a copy of the corrected timesheet and thanked me individually. I hope modeling kindness will help Dawn learn different ways to communicate with people respectfully.

❤ **Decompress to Allow More Positive Communication:** Hurricanes have this peaceful center where all is well, called the eye of the storm, where despite the powerful winds, rains, thunder and lightning raging around it, there is peace. When caught in the middle of a storm of strong emotions coming from another person or yourself, how can you embody the peace which is present in the eye of a storm? How could an exchange be made more positive and respectful for all involved?

Be Understanding When Being Ignored

There are times mentoring people when my feelings get hurt because people on the autism spectrum have challenges understanding situations from other people's perspectives. Since I am sensitive, I often feel what another person is feeling strongly in my body as if I am that person. Sometimes I forget the people I work with have a hard enough time figuring out how they feel, so it is just not possible for them to even consider my feelings. When I don't take this personally, I am a better mentor. Here are two examples to illustrate this.

When planning with David for a day he was going to spend time with his friend Mark, David said he would like to be at Mark's house by 2:00 pm. I asked David when he wanted me to pick him up. He said 7:00 or 8:00 pm. For me, this would have meant spending a total of one hour driving in my car without pay, being paid for one hour when David was in the car, plus waiting for five hours not being paid. Since a situation hadn't come up like this before, I asked one of David's support team members if it is my job to wait for David for five hours while he spends time with his friend, and she confirmed this is not my job. Fortunately, David's parents were happy to pick him up and drive him home. I was able to consider this situation objectively and realize that while I was willing to spend an hour driving without pay, followed by driving one hour with pay when David was in the car, I was not willing to spend another five hours waiting for David without pay. I did not take it personally that David had not considered my time in this situation. I simply found out what was expected of me, and made a plan so David could spend time with Mark, while I took care of myself.

Although I didn't feel hurt in this particular situation, sometimes I do feel hurt. For example, I had just returned from a month-long trip and hadn't seen David for over five weeks. This was a long separation after having worked with him on a weekly basis for over a year. I thought about David during my trip, and he was the only person I work with for whom I brought a souvenir: a piece of lava from a volcano we visited. I was excited to share stories with him about the volcano. We scheduled our work together a week after my return, so I was rested and recovered from the exhaustion of travel. I picked him up at the agreed upon time and learned he wanted to travel to New Paltz, a college town nearby with interesting restaurants and bookstores. David had cut his finger recently, and his attention was very much focused on his bandaged finger. He was in some pain, and worried about needing to change the bandage. While driving, I asked lots of questions about what he had been up to the last five weeks. Distracted by his finger, he answered my questions as briefly as possible. With the piece of lava in my pocket, I felt a volcano of angry lava building inside of me because David never asked about my travels, despite us being together for over two hours. I certainly could have shared stories without being asked, but we are working on social skills, and it was important for David to initiate this conversation. Imagine what problems his lack of interest would cause in a friendship or close family relationship. Since people on the autism spectrum have challenges with social skills, this was a prime learning opportunity. I was so freakin' mad at him because I value our friendship greatly, as you may be able to tell by now.

I reminded myself to take some slow deep breaths and consider the best way to handle this situation. Can you imagine how it would feel having to remind a friend that we haven't seen each other for five weeks? Once I was calm enough to speak with some semblance of reason, I asked David if he knew where I had been over the last five weeks. He immediately perked up and asked how my travels were. I shared the adventures Tom and I had at Rangitoto, giving him the piece of lava, which had traveled about eight thousand, eighty-eight miles, first in my hand, then in my backpack and suitcase. It was rolled along with my luggage through many airports, trains, shuttles, and walkways to make it into his hand on this January day. I also brought my computer in order to show him pictures of the volcano. David showed some interest, but I was careful not to linger too long as his attention was still very strongly on his finger. Here is his account of how the day went:

David: On the week before, I did play around with the idea of wanting to go to New Paltz to explore a different place because I don't go there very often. And also, when we went to the restaurant, I remember feeling relaxed and hungry and it was my breakfast because this was a morning trip, if I remember correctly. The food was delicious. It did not occur to me to ask Maria about her trip to New Zealand, not because I did not show any interest. I forgot to ask. My brain was on cruise control. I was too relaxed and it didn't dawn on me about her trip until she brought it up by asking me if I wanted to know what happened on

258

her vacation. It was in a shock of my forgetfulness I asked her about her trip.

She told me about the volcano and shared about what she saw there. She grabbed a small paper bag and then she gave it to me. I took the rock out and she told me it was from the volcano. Thankfully, she did not go on it when it was erupting. It was inactive. I thought it was cool this rock came from a different part of the world and from New Zealand, no less. And so, after breakfast, we went to a book store to explore. We looked around a bit and when we were done, Maria drove us to a comic book store. I actually looked in there by myself and bought a Spiderman Graphic Novel and a single issue, of which superhero I don't remember. After that, Maria drove me home.

I feel a bit embarrassed about getting so upset because David did not ask me about my trip until I gave him a little nudge, because his behavior was completely normal for a person on the autism spectrum. Since I feel emotionally connected with David, I expected more from him and yet, this has been an amazing opportunity for a teachable moment for both of us. Will he remember this time I stayed so calm and patient after not seeing him for a long time? Will he remember to ask a friend how they enjoyed their adventures in the future? Will he remember a relative's birthday without reminders from family? Since I still have not had training on how to foster social skills, I am learning as I go. I wonder if there is something more I could be doing as a mentor and hope there will be opportunities for training in this area available in the near future.

♥ **Be Understanding When Being Ignored:** Being ignored doesn't feel good, does it? How do you handle circumstances when nobody is paying attention to you? Are you able to know your value and worth whether you are being noticed or not?

Take a Break

David was an adventurous eater when we first began working together. I loved discussing the types of food he liked and suggesting different types of restaurants for him to try. Every now and then, he would ask to go for pizza or burgers, and that was fine considering the great majority of meals were at new and exotic places. I don't know exactly when the shift happened, but slowly the novelty of going to new places slipped into visiting burger joint after burger joint after burger joint each and every week. In order to care for my own body's needs, I learned to bring healthy food for myself if we would be working together for a long period of time. I spoke to David about his predictable choices for what we did each week: I picked him up, we went to the bank to deposit coins, then he ate burgers, fries and lemonade or soda, then he went to Barnes and Noble to look around and finally, I dropped him at his evening martial arts class.

When he had bronchitis, I didn't question the sameness of this routine, because I imagined this was comforting to him, but when he was feeling better, I addressed the patterns I had noticed. Right after this discussion, David chose to go to Burger King for dinner. There comes a point when I just want to roll over on my back and wave a white flag of surrender! I don't share my sentiments with him. I understand my suggestions may be heard but not acted on immediately. In fact, I may never witness the results of suggestions I have made, and this is just something I need to recognize and accept.

David is not overweight like some of the customers at Burger King, like the woman who could barely shuffle in, leaning on a sturdy walker to get her fill of food which is slowly killing her. I just couldn't think of anything positive to say, so I kept my opinions to myself and choose to talk about other topics while he eats. I am able to be patient on the outside while steaming in anger on the inside. I could have completely given into my anger and rampaged about how fast-food restaurants are poisoning people, making them fatter, dumber, and addicted to unhealthy food, as evidenced by the obese and sick people who frequent these places. I chose to refrain, which was a wise move. One of the few bright points during the coronavirus pandemic was not frequenting these fast-food restaurants with David. It was nice to have a break from this aspect of the work.

♥ Take a Break: Some learning takes time, so when you feel resistance to moving forward in an area, instead of pushing harder, take a break and shift your focus to working on something different. This will give everyone a chance to gain new perspectives, and perhaps suggestions made in the past will now take root.

Fostering Leadership Skills

We worked together through phone calls and video chats during the initial outbreak of coronavirus. David learned how to video chat for his college classes without my assistance and to set up a Facebook video chat with my guidance.

I had started learning Qigong on my own and taught David as well. Since he had been studying martial arts for two years, Qigong was easy for him to learn, and a peaceful practice during these challenging times. David really enjoyed the Qigong flows. I would teach them to him first, then he would decide how many repetitions we did. He learned very quickly and I started asking him which flows he would like to do. I invited him to start teaching me and I watched as he gained more confidence and leadership skills. David researched some Korean martial art flows, which he taught me. He also shared stretches he did with his martial arts class during warm-up. Over a very short amount of time, David learned to teach me a full Qigong class, which was unexpected and quite inspiring. We discovered he had some strong teaching skills that had been lying dormant for some time. The seeds of teaching skills were there the whole time. They just needed a little bit of water in the form of attention and sunshine, in the form of encouragement to grow and flourish. I asked David if he might consider teaching Qigong with his college class and he said, "I might consider it." This felt like great progress to me because if David says he will consider something, what it really means is he is ready to give this a try in the future, which is huge.

Fostering Leadership Skills: Are there times when you teach someone a skill, when you can then pass the role of teacher on to them?

Take Action to Care for Yourself

In the beginning, communication with David's mom was excellent. She offered guidance, suggestions, and support that were valuable to me and David. She was excited for David's adventures and new learning. I had considered possibly mentoring David's brother, Peter, who had many more challenges than David. I only considered this because I thought I would have family support and good communication. I imagined it could be amazing. I thought about the challenges and rewards of working with someone who was mostly non-verbal, finding ways to communicate, seeing how much he might be able to open up and become more connected with people. With my brother Evan, the opportunity to communicate verbally never happened. With Peter, there was potential and a flicker of hope, along with intriguing possibility of two-way communication.

The entire family was very supportive after the car accident, further strengthening my trust that back pay issues would be resolved. Month after month, David and I worked together with no word about what was happening with the back pay owed to me. I felt awkward asking and finally built up the nerve to ask about the status of the respite money coming in and my pay being upgraded to the hourly wage we initially agreed upon. I lost so much sleep over this issue. I felt embarrassed having to ask.

Deep-seated issues of unworthiness festered inside me. If these people who felt so connected to me and seemed to appreciate my work with David didn't think I deserved to be paid the full amount, what had I done wrong? Over time, I noticed my thoughts getting darker and turning inward towards depression. Slowly, after many sleepless nights, I realized that I had bypassed the anger I felt with David's mom for not honoring the heart-filled work I did with her son by communicating with me and I turned this anger upon myself, leading to feeling depressed and negative.

Finally, after more than a year of mentoring, my pay was doubled to the proper amount and some back pay was given to me. Several times, David's mom asked me how much back pay they owed me and over time all the funds owed were paid. However, the money was much less important to me than effective communication. If I could have had monthly updates, keeping me in the loop, I would have felt differently. I was patient for a long time, but maybe I was taken advantage of because of being too patient and kind. Instead of speaking up right away, I let this drag on and on. At one point, I decided I needed to let David know what was going on. I told his mom I was going to inform David about the situation and learned that she kept him posted on the pay progress, but not me! At least this time, I felt that anger and didn't turn it on myself. Over time, communication with his mom died out. She would not give me input or ideas on working with him, nor would she return calls or emails. I tried reaching out to David's step-dad to keep me in the loop but that never happened. I dearly missed being part of David's Circle of Support Team. I was not invited to meetings and did not understand why. Being excluded really felt horrible to me, a person who thrives on building heart centered connections with people.

I fully realize they had a lot on their plate: two sons on the autism spectrum, along with their own health issues and more. I came to accept communication was not going to improve and started working more with David's communication and leadership skills. We bonded more closely and became a dynamic duo team, working together to help David build confidence and life skills so he could be more independent. His mom started communicating through David about anything she wanted me to know, which boosted his organizational and communication skills. We worked together through phone calls and video chats during the initial outbreak of coronavirus. David learned how to video chat for his college classes without my assistance and to set up a Facebook video chat with my guidance.

Through video conferencing, we were having amazing breakthroughs in a relatively short amount of time during a global pandemic. However, I was once again excluded from his Circle of Support Meetings. I felt angry, sad, frustrated, bereft, and completely bewildered. I had a session with my teacher Dechen and asked her for guidance. She suggested I write a letter to the Circle of Support team sharing David's learning. David's explanation as to why I wasn't invited was his budget was discussed, and it isn't anyone's business what his budget is. I listened to his explanation and despite feeling a bit offended, said calmly to David, "Okay, that makes sense." While I totally understand David and his family may not want me to be present while discussing his budget, I also realize there could be different times during the meeting which are for the family and budget people and another part of the meeting where I can share his learning. Here is the letter I sent out to everyone:

Dear Circle of Support Team,

I have not been invited to David's Circle of Support meetings and feel like my observations are of value to have a full perspective of his learning. I want to share these celebrations with all of you. I spoke to David about writing this report, which we started together, then I added more details. This letter is arriving a few days after you all got together.

Here is the progress I have witnessed David making over the past few months:

- David has mastered using technology for video chats with school and our work together.
- David has been reading and researching historical textbooks to keep his learning going even after his college audit class is over. He is self-motivated. We have interesting conversations about what he is learning independently.
- David reports the meals he has been learning to prepare for himself and family every Wednesday, with Mom and Step-Dad's guidance.
- David has enjoyed learning Qigong exercises for both fitness and relaxation. He has taken a leadership role by researching Korean Martial arts moves which he teaches me. David has embraced learning Qigong, being a co-teacher and even taught me a complete class when we got together in-person. This illustrates his ability to learn quickly and become a competent leader in a short amount of time. He remembers the flows from week to week without using anything written down. David has even made up his own flow which he named, The Double Wave. This flow is a great way to release tension between the shoulder blades. In all of my years teaching yoga and Qigong, I have never had a student create their own flow or pose. David shines brightly with extraordinary talents.
- David learned visualization techniques to imagine his work at ShopRite going well. He also has tools from Qigong to help with anxiety.

- David has asked for us to practice meditation together. He chooses the amount of time we sit in silence, anywhere from 5 to 15 minutes, depending on the day.
- David makes a plan for our work together. He decides what he would like us to discuss and work on, keeping an eye on the clock so we stay within the time period he has chosen. David is also open to suggestions, even asking for suggestions at times when he is not sure what to do. He is showing great organizational skills and also has made strides in leading conversations.

- David is doing a good job communicating his family's wishes and tasks to be done for the FAPTO hours which Jasmine and you all have so generously submitted and had approved for me.

If this report is helpful to you all and you would like us to prepare one before the next Circle of Support meeting, I am happy to do this. I will wait until David informs me of when this would be needed and hope we will be given ample time to complete it.

Thank you for all you do to support David as he becomes more and more independent!

Sincerely,

Maria Blon

One team member replied to my letter right away, emphasizing what great progress David has been making. She also said David can invite anyone he wants to his meetings. Nobody else responded at all. My frustrations bubbled up in this poem:

Reflections
Nobody's respondn'
I feel quite despondent
What am I to do?

Being excluded from David's meetings felt awful. I care so much about him and want to be included. I realize how much stress this is causing me, but I have many options, and one option is to stop mentoring David. Since his family does not seem to want to work with me, this is not an ideal situation. Yes, my heart breaks even considering not mentoring him, but also there is a flicker of hope that I might be freed from this emotional torment which has been with me for way too long. Another option is to let go of the thoughts that were causing me so much emotional turmoil. My extreme sensitivity is a valuable tool when working with young adults who have special gifts. I want to learn how to be sensitive enough to feel emotions, learn what they are telling me, and take action quickly. I have to stop blaming myself when other people are not treating me with respect. It seemed like time to pluck the weeds choking out the flowers of loving thoughts that are meant to be blooming in my heart and mind. Let me also give myself credit for having the courage to face these uncomfortable emotions and share the most vulnerable parts of myself with whoever reads this book.

♥ **Take Action to Care For Yourself:** Is there an area of your life where you feel you are not being treated with the respect you deserve? Even though speaking up seems scary, sharing your worthiness to be included is important. I do hope you generate courage to share your value, because you are important and deserve to be heard.

Embrace Openings

At the end of working with each individual, I fill out a form and record what goals we worked on in our time together. Recently, I had finished working with David and received these new goals:

> *1) Encourage healthy eating habits-cooking & shopping. Expanding the intake of healthy foods. Trying new recipes. Learning new cooking techniques.*

> *2) Encourage David to swap to wholegrain foods such as brown rice, whole meal bread and rolled oats in order to help reduce the risk of developing heart disease and diabetes.*

> *3) Encourage David to eat Fruits and Vegetables. The goal is to fill half his plate with fruit and vegetables at every meal. Fruit and vegetables are naturally low in saturated and trans-fat, and rich in dietary fiber, vitamins, and minerals.*

Since I wasn't invited to circle of support meetings, this was a surprise for me, and I am not sure who created them. After David had finished his semester of college, I asked if he wanted to read over and discuss his goals. When we got to these three goals, I asked who created them and he didn't know. I asked if these were goals David wants to work on, and he said, "Yes, I would like to work on these goals and learn to eat better." I found this so interesting because as you know, I had spoken to David many times about healthy eating, which he agreed he wanted to do, yet what I observed was he was not making healthy choices when eating out with me. I told him he practices healthy portion control, which is something we both agree on. I explained in order to improve David's eating habits, we would need to know what his eating habits are now and offered the idea of either writing down what he eats over the course of a week or even better, taking a picture of what he eats for a week. David didn't jump on this idea, so I asked what his priority was for working on improving his eating and he said this was a medium priority. How we would find ways to work on improving his eating with a medium priority basis, I am not sure. Yet I hope something will happen by simply having had this conversation and having these goals written for us to work on. I feel grateful for whoever wrote these goals and look forward to seeing where they take us.

❤ **Embrace openings:** After taking a break from a frustrating topic for some time, keep your eyes, ears and all senses open to possibilities for opening discussion on this topic when you feel the time is right. Sometimes, an invitation will come directly to you, which I hope you embrace and move forward with in a new way.

Recognize When You Come Full Circle

As I continued working with David during the coronavirus pandemic, our relationship stayed steady in many ways, yet, there were subtle shifts occurring all the time. David agreed to work with me in his yard during the summer with the safety precautions of wearing masks and gloves. I was happy to see him in-person, so this was a nice change of pace. Wearing gardening gloves is something I enjoy and that option was acceptable to David, so it worked out well. Before the summer was over, he asked if I would be able to drive him to a park near his home so we could go for a hike. We both wore sneakers, shorts, summer shirts, masks, and gloves while sharing a glorious summer day, filled with warmth, lush green leaves, ponds brimming with water and soft trails to wind our way through the woods. After climbing a big hill and coming down to a bench on the side of the trail, David asked if we could sit for a bit and work on these stories. It was such a lovely setting to review the adventures we have taken together and for David to hear the thoughts and feelings going through my mind, with the opportunity for him to contribute.

The following week, he would be starting the final year of *"A Helping Hand"* program at the local community college, so I was acutely aware of how precious this remaining time together was. Since he was taking classes online five days a week, plus auditing two college level classes and attending martial arts classes two evenings a week, his schedule was full, and I didn't expect he would want to work with me until he had a break from school. I was surprised to hear from David in late September, asking if I could work with him two days a week. He also wanted to know if I could drive him to his martial arts class. This was a tough question for me to answer because my daughter was expecting her first child in the beginning of October. More than anything, I wanted to be able to hold my grandson after he was born and to be trusted by her to care for him when she went back to work. I couldn't imagine sending a baby to daycare when the coronavirus was still out of control in the United States. New York was doing relatively well under Governor Cuomo's leadership, but I chose to be extra cautious for our future grandson and mother who was eighty-three years old at the time. I had to tell David I was not able to drive him anymore, which was a tough decision to make and then share with him. I didn't think he would want to work with me if I couldn't drive him, and I was surprised when he decided to work with me two afternoons a week anyway. His schedule seemed packed, and I wasn't sure how this would be for him, but David delighted me by rising to this challenge with confidence and grace. I was eager to continue working on the book with him and so our work together began again.

David continues to develop his leadership skills, creating a schedule for what we do together each time. Typically, it includes the following:

- Catching up on what we are each doing briefly
- Reading his stories in this book to him for him to add his perspective, which is sometimes included in what you are reading and sometimes is just between us
- Practicing Qigong together, with David leading
- Silently meditating for five-to-fifteen minutes with David timing us
- Sharing stories of something funny or silly which happened to us in our lives

These activities fill the hour and a half we spend together in delightful ways. I feel lucky to receive peace and engagement through meditation and Qigong with David. He is gifting me with experiences I taught him. Our work has come full circle as I receive enrichment from him during a time of tremendous chaos swirling around the globe. In our time together, we are learning to focus on the goodness of the present moment as we connect and deepen our relationship. I don't have clearly defined goals for what our work together is or will be and yet, I trust the next lessons will show up at just the right time for each of us and we will embrace this learning together with the grace and confidence we have shared with each other.

David: In the summer of the coronavirus when Maria and I started working outside in my yard, I, like everyone else, didn't know the limitations of this virus but I knew to wear a mask and gloves. And then on our first day of working together in-person since the start of this virus, we actually worked on parts of this book and we also worked on some exercises, some Qigong moves and some martial arts moves to show Maria because I didn't know what to do during some of those exercises. I wore the surgical disposable gloves, which were really hot because of the weather. During our sessions, I decided to include some meditation

271

because it was the most relaxing exercise during our sessions. And then this would continue for summer, until August when I started college again early. And we agreed to hold off on working together again because I didn't know how busy my schedule would be. When I got my schedule for the school year, I took a picture with my cell phone and sent it to Maria's number and I reached out to Maria saying we could work together on Mondays and Wednesdays like we did before through our computers. And she agreed and sometime before that she told me she was expecting to have a grandchild, which was nice news to hear and I asked if she could drive me to my martial arts school on Mondays and Wednesdays after our sessions and I forgot all about her unborn grandchild (and that was my bad). She told me she wasn't able to drive me because I told you what she was expecting. I apologized for forgetting and understood why she was not able to take me to my martial arts class. The reason why I did this is I didn't want to rely on my parents all the time or spend too much money on the Uber (its like a taxi but you just pay with your credit card) I thought Maria would drive me like a regular taxi (minus the me paying her part), but I should have remembered that she has a life of her own and that was presumptuous of me to presume anything like that. But I wasn't mad. It did give me a chance to learn how to budget my rides a lot better. And at this point, as this book is written, we are still workin' through our laptops.

When I was little, it was at a time where there weren't a lot of programs for people like me on the spectrum and whenever and even if there were programs, it was very limited. I had trouble communicating verbally and I had and still have some sensory issues with a lot of loud noises. When I was diagnosed, a professional told me that I wouldn't have the capability to show affections or be able to understand anything complex or simple. My mom did not listen to that professional, so she made a maximum effort to get other professionals to help me to overcome my obstacles. She actually did a lot and she never gave up, never gave up on me. (Huge smile on David's face). As you know by now, I am able to form all sentences, to have a sense of humor

272

and to feel sympathy for someone who is treated unfairly. (Another big smile on his face) That's my comment for now.

I don't perceive David as being presumptuous asking if I could drive him to his Martial Arts Class because this is something I did for him for many months. I felt badly not being able to help him out this way, but because of so many unknowns with the coronavirus, I needed to be extra careful for my future grandson.

❤ **Recognize When You Come Full Circle:** Take time to appreciate the growth that the person you work with has achieved. Allow them to take the lead and create teaching experiences for you as they attain greater mastery of the skills you have been working on. How could you facilitate this type of leadership opportunity?

Appreciate the Efforts of Caregivers

The immense love, strength, faith, and perseverance David's mom has shown to advocate for her son for his entire lifetime, makes my heart swell and tears well up in my eyes whenever I witness him talking about how his mom, "never gave up, never gave up on me." At every meeting I have attended with her and David, she always says with so much love emanating from her heart and tears pouring from her eyes, "David is a superhero." The superhero who has been the wind beneath David's wings is his magnificent mom. All parents of children who have special gifts are superheroes. Being a mentor, working with individuals with special gifts is challenging and rewarding work as you have witnessed through these stories. Parent's contributions to raising these angels who have come to teach us so much, bump this work up to a much higher level of commitment and do not receive any monetary compensation for their devotion. While there is now a little bit of respite money so parents may take a break from caretaking, I believe they should be paid for the work they do to advocate for and raise their child. In the past, children with special gifts were sent to institutions, often funded by the government. Giving parents the support and resources they need to raise their children at home is better for everyone and is more cost effective. The more people who work with the specially gifted population and recognize the intensity of this work, the greater chance there is for more enlightened ways to support everyone involved.

♥ **Appreciate the Efforts of Caregivers:** Who are the heroes in your life and how do you share your appreciation for them?

Notice the Fruits of Learning

One day, we had the following exchange:

Maria: How do you benefit from our work together, David?

David: What I benefit with our work is that I am able to learn on how much and what kind of tip to leave at a restaurant and other economic skills like that. And I am able to have other life skills.

Now I ask myself what I have learned from working with David. One thing I have learned is I can be funny sometimes. I don't typically think of myself as a funny person, and yet, in combination with David, we have had some great laughs together. Reading over these stories, there are times when I feel immense pride for my patience and the way I have followed my intuition in our work together. I can't believe the challenges we have experienced and worked through together, like totaling my car, encountering rogue long horned cows at night, and having rocks thrown at the windshield. I also feel tremendous gratitude for what seemed like magical events which led to breakthroughs for us both. There are other times when I feel sad at the emotional torment I've experienced and sometimes an exhaustion at having to read and relive them again. But then there is also relief knowing I am not tormented by those specific circling thoughts that have kept me from sleep many nights; although, my mind has chosen other thoughts to obsess over and keep me awake sometimes. I must remember to give myself some credit as I am learning, situation by situation, to break free from these obsessive thoughts more quickly by addressing issues as directly and as soon as possible. Thankfully, I am experiencing longer periods where my mind is at peace.

The issues I wrote about related to David, his mom, and other people have given me opportunities to handle myself during challenging times. I have learned new strategies for dealing with situations which I imagine will come in handy in the future. Writing a letter to David's Circle of Support team was a creative way to share what David is learning, even though I was not able to attend the meeting when it was happening. I am learning more and more to simply be present with David when we work together, allowing him to lead the way, which is so much more relaxing than over-planning and worrying before each meeting. I don't do much, if any preparation ahead of time, which is very different from the way I managed my teaching and mentoring in the past. I am learning to be in the flow and enjoy his Qigong classes, meditation time, hearing his thoughts and sharing stories when he asks me, sometimes offering a story that I think could be helpful for his learning in a certain moment.

I realize David is connected with and cares about me in his own unique way. When he hears about times when my feelings were hurt, he will sometimes clarify he did not intend to be hurtful, which is very sweet and true. David enjoys sharing details from our time together and I learn more about what he was thinking and feeling during those times. I most strongly feel the immense love and gratitude David has for his mom, who has believed in him and helped him to thrive beyond anyone's expectations. We must give David credit as well for his drive to continue learning and working through obstacles with determination, good humor and intelligence. I feel grateful for witnessing the power of love to heal and am honored to have played a small part in David's life and growth. I believe David will support himself and be able to live independently of his family. With his intelligence, skills, humor, kindness, and dashing good looks, I can imagine him finding meaningful work which he enjoys and friends to have fun with.

David invites me to most of his Circle of Support meetings now. He really wants me there. He shows this by making sure the Zoom link is sent to me and checking in several times to make sure I received it. Then on the day of the meeting, I receive this text message from David, "Are you looking forward to tonight's meeting? And did you get the Zoom link?" Oh wow, he really wants me to be there and is such a gracious host. At the meeting, the Circle of Support Team were impressed with and grateful for the ten-page document David and I worked on to set SMART goals for his wishes to learn to drive, live on his own, travel and much more. The team was thrilled to know what David's dreams are and to have concrete plans written down. Since many of the people they work with have limited verbal skills, knowing, rather than guessing what the individuals want takes out the guessing work they often need to do in order to advocate for them. One member jokingly offered to travel to Spain with David so she can help with translation. Another member suggested he go with a tour group for greatest enjoyment and learning. At each section of David's Life Plan, which we were reviewing together, they asked for my input, which felt like such an honor. Now my perspective was being asked for and valued. What a relief and reward for work well done. I am so glad I believed in myself enough to speak up repeatedly to share how much I wanted to attend David's Circle of Support meetings. This had felt terribly painful and hard at the time. I am proud of myself for working through this discomfort by speaking up confidently, because now, I feel like the luckiest mentor in the world.

❤ **Notice the Fruits of Learning:** Look back on a time in your life where you worked hard, appreciating all you have accomplished and learned. Give yourself credit for not giving up, staying engaged, and doing your very best.

Our Work Carries On

I continue working with David and since we both received vaccinations for Covid, we are able to go on adventures in the car once again, which is great fun. David will be doing an internship at the Walden Library and taking audit classes at the college. We have started reading and discussing "A Bear Went Over the Mountain", which is a fun new activity for us. I do not have as much time to work with David these days and want him to receive support from another mentor. When my daughter Anna had a party where she invited family and friends to paint murals on the fence in her backyard, I met her friend Johan who has been working with people who have special gifts his whole life. He is a gentle, sweet, artistic man who seems to be a perfect match for David. David interviewed Johan and they appear to be a great fit. Johan wants to invite David to his apartment to show him how to cook healthy, delicious food with an instant pot and air fryer and they were talking about going to a Comicon festival together. Scheduling an interview with David's family is taking time, yet I feel hopeful Johan and David will begin work together soon and I can step back a bit in order to begin working on developing training opportunities for mentors. I want to keep working and staying in touch with David, but not as often as in the past. I am so excited to hear about his internship and hope this may lead to a paid position for him.

Epilogue

Sometimes, the work we do in the past revisits us in unimagined ways. These days, I am doing less mentoring of Rose, B.D., and David and have taken on a new cause: speaking up about the systemic racism in our local school district. This is a big, complex problem, not only in this district, but also in schools across our county, state, and country, one which needs to be addressed at a deep emotional level in order for healing to occur.

I was feeling hopeless one morning when we ran into a seemingly insurmountable legal roadblock in a case of a young black man with special gifts who, instead of being treated with the love and respect he deserved, experienced tremendous trauma by the way he was treated at his high school, on a day when he was struggling emotionally. That very afternoon, a former college student of mine, Daniel Villegas, whom I have kept in touch with over the last 20 years, joined our activist group for a meeting to share what he can offer to young people in the schools and the community at-large. Hearing his enthusiasm to encourage youth to believe in themselves and to learn to speak their truth in creative ways helped shift my perspective to one of hope and new possibilities.

When I shared the story with Tom of how Daniel gave me hope after this meeting, I remembered a day when I tried something different while teaching Danny. Because the transformation in this young man was so meaningful to me, Tom encouraged me to write the story down. Here is the poem, which tells the story in a few words, while still manages to convey some big lessons of realization for me and for all teachers and mentors.

From Danny to Daniel
A fidgety student in back of the class
Comes in late, maybe with a bit of sass
Can we focus on problem solving?
Or is math not so exciting?
Focus comes in and out

"Chatting again!?," I just want to shout
What can I do to capture
His attention so he'll have a future
Full of promise
And success?
I invite him to the front of the class
Encouraged his drumming, connecting it to maths
A moment in time
Where his spirit so divine
Shone brightly
Life carried on so nicely
Chance meetings now and then
Over many years until when
I witness him as a man
Showing youth how they can
Find meaning and connection
Between their lives and education
So glad I chose to hold
My tongue instead of scold
That young man so full of energy
Now giving what is absolutely necessary
Empowering youth to be
Brilliant, empowered and free

This story poem shows how making a connection with a person, offering a small gift of flexibility and kindness can have a huge impact. Sometimes just a little bit of love can ripple out into a life and continue touching countless lives in ways you will never know. Having faith that what you are able to offer in each moment is enough and is of value. Sometimes big problems can't be solved in the moment, so we need to find ways to stay hopeful and trust, keeping our hearts and minds open to possibilities. Solutions will come over time, even to the big challenges we are brave and bold enough to address. So, my friend, keep dreaming big and when you feel overwhelmed, use the tools shared here which will help you to stay open and hopeful. I will be doing these practices right along with you. My wish for you is that you and the people you work with experience the same blossoming of peace, success, and hope which Rose, B.D., David, and I experienced working together.

Appendices

Hearts Blooming Mottos

While reviewing these stories, there have been several themes emerging which could be used when discussing these stories and offering community discussion spaces and courses for mentors and spiritual seekers. There may be a workbook coming out in the near future which provides additional guidance on collaboratively or individually using the Hearts Blooming Tools. Here are our Mottos:

- *Set healthy boundaries*

- *Let go, open up*

- *Listen, observe and reflect*

- *Be creative*

- *Be bold*

- *Believe in yourself and the people you support*

- *Celebrate often*

- *Keep learning*

Simple Ways to Express Feelings Creatively

In reading these stories, it is clear the mentorship process can take a toll emotionally and sometimes physically. In trying times, expressing yourself creatively can be a tremendous help. Also, sometimes people may struggle to communicate clearly through words, and creative expression offers a way to share feelings they might never express directly. Being creative helps us step out of our logical, thinking mind to access our intuition, which is a deep reservoir of wisdom and inspiration. There are so many different ways to create! Here are a few ways to express yourself with creativity which don't require you to attend art school or conservatory in order enjoy the process.

♥ **Poetry:** There are many different styles of poetry to experiment with. I love poetry because emotions can be expressed in a few words, yet in powerful ways which the author and readers can relate to and feel. Take time to experiment with different types of poetry.

A simple style to start with is haiku. These often nature-based poems have a pattern of three lines of writing: the first with five syllables, the next with seven syllables, and the last with five syllables. Try reading this out loud and notice what you feel in your body.

Not sure what will be
Leap off cliff, splash, crash, geyser
Yikes, woohoo, big smile

♥ **Make a Collage:** Step out of your thinking mind and simply feel what images or words you are and are not attracted to. Here are the supplies you will need: a variety of magazines, a large piece of paper or posterboard, scissors, double sided tape or a glue stick, a table or floor to spread everything out and uninterrupted time to play.

Take a few deep breaths, feeling your feet on the floor, your bum on the seat, and notice the air going in and out of your nose. Set your worries aside and be present in this moment. Look through the magazines and cut out pictures or words which you feel attracted to and enjoy the explorations. After you feel complete in selecting your pictures and words, look through them and start arranging them on the large paper, eventually choosing where to glue or tape the pieces on. Have fun and enjoy creating a collage which is appealing to you at this moment.

🖤 **Make Nature Sculptures:** Explore outside and collect the treasures you find. Don't worry about creating something which will last forever, create something fun in this moment, then let it go. Here are a few different ideas to try:
- Stack rocks in unexpected places along a trail.
- Draw in the sand, adding shells and rocks as part of your creation. You could even make a quick design in between waves, then watch the design as it washes away.
- Arrange leaves and sticks in a pattern pleasing to you. Over time, the wind will blow them away, but that is part of the process of nature and life. Instead of picking leaves or sticks from a live tree, use ones which have already fallen on the ground.
- Build and decorate a fairy house, maybe at the base of a tree or in a pile of rocks.

🖤 **Write or tell a story:** Describe a challenge you are experiencing as if it is happening in a different era, location or even in a comic book scene. Have fun creating characters with exaggerated personalities, the evil villain, the innocent victim, the courageous hero. Be outrageous and enjoy the process.

Here is an example of a fantasy story I wrote when frustrated by a leader in our local school district. I made a video of myself reading the poem. The feedback I received was interesting because some people thought I was talking about another leader in our country at the time.

There once was a captain of a ship
Hired to educate and uplift

He encountered oceans storming
Predicted by observers warning

Open your eyes
Pay attention to the tides

Of change all around you
His supervisors said we adore you

Old ways not working
As the captain was failing

His grip on the wheel grew tighter and tighter
Observers say this can be done better

If you would open your eyes
Admit you are not being wise

Loosen your grip on the wheel
Allow your heart to feel

Together we can make it right
Even through the darkest night

As a team we see what to do
Captain, your eyes are closed, we don't want you

To lead us astray
We know a better way

Step aside, allow us to show
How as a team, we can learn and grow

The captain of this ship eventually completely let go of the wheel when his dysfunctional ways were exposed. The story in the paper said he had been planning his retirement for some time, but those who know what happened behind the scenes, know a different story. At least he is not leading our school district anymore and there is an opportunity for a new start. This poem helped me deal with my frustration at the time in a way which was fun. Sometimes, we can't change what is, yet can shift how we handle the situation.

♥ **Dance:** Wherever you are, inside, outside, under the water, on a roof, dance to music in your head, on your phone, in the wind or in the silence. Don't worry about how you look, enjoy moving in ways which feel fantastic to you.

Connecting Spiritually with Evan

In the summer of 2014, Evan was very sick, spending most of his summer in the hospital, primarily in intensive care. During this time, I went through an intense grieving period where I just kept crying. I could not stop. But I didn't understand why I was sobbing so often. Evan has never been able to speak with us, yet I continued to speak with him in my head, while feeling his spirit in my heart. Tapping into this presence, I decided to write a letter from Evan, thanking us for all that we had done for him in his life. The words for this letter flowed through me very quickly. I read it to my husband Tom, bawling the whole time. Then, like magic, my grieving ended. I think Evan was asking me to be his voice so that when he died peacefully on Friday, August 22nd, I would have this letter to read at his memorial service.

Here is the letter from Evan to all of us:

Evan from heaven
What have you come to teach us?
To be patient, kind, compassionate, loving, grateful and accepting.
How?
Evan wants to say thank you to the important people in his life:

Mom, I am the luckiest person in the world having you as my mother. I appreciate the gentle love and care that you have given me for these 33 years of my life, during which I have received the best care possible. I am truly blessed. You have helped the doctors learn how to heal me, because you know me better than anyone.

Dad, thank you for caring for me, feeding me, clothing me, accepting me, loving me, bringing me on adventures to the beach, restaurants, music, and gardens. I am glad that when you felt stressed out, holding me calmed you down.

Maria, you have treated me with love and kindness while walking me, holding me, feeding me and talking with me. I am happy that because you have cared for me, you have learned to teach people about caregiving while living a balanced and passionate life.

Paul, thanks for being my fun older brother. I liked lying on your bed, listening to your music. Thanks for dancing with me to help me stop crying.

Ella, you were the best nurse dog, letting Mom know when I was having a seizure and keeping me company.

Molly and Ivie, thank you for joining Mom to visit me at Allegheny Valley School. I am glad they allowed dogs as visitors.

Thank you to all the people who have cared for me through my life: Teachers, Babysitters, AVS Staff, Doctors and Nurses. I am blessed to be so loved.

Evan, thank you for all that you have taught us. Say hi to Dad, Sarah, Granny, Grandpa, Grandmom and Grandad. Have a wonderful time being a free spirit, back at your home in heaven.

Love,
*   your sister Maria*

After Evan passed, I was at a pond where I spent a lot of time connecting with Evan's spirit. I closed my eyes and, in my head, asked, "How is Evan doing?" I saw an image of a pink box with big bow on top. The box opened and a bunny hopped out. Initially, I didn't understand what that was about. Then I asked if Evan was fishing with Dad (our Dad loved to fish). I saw Evan and Dad sitting on a grassy bank next to a gently flowing stream. Dad had his arm around Evan. They looked very peaceful.

I continued to walk, trying to understand what the box and bunny were all about, then it hit me all at once. I made a stuffed bunny in seventh grade and asked Mom to bring it to Evan at the hospital. The nurses loved the bunny and would put it under his arm. When Mom went to say goodbye to Evan after he passed, she said Evan was hugging the bunny. I started crying at that point, realizing that Evan was thanking me for the bunny and it seems there is a live bunny with him and Dad up in heaven.

Contributors

Having my mentoring journal edited into this book has been a fantastic experience. Peggy and Zhenya have added words, sentences, even paragraphs, which when I read them, I wonder how they knew how I felt and what I was thinking. There were many times I was aware something needed to be added or taken away, yet I just couldn't figure out how to make this happen. I am so very grateful you each knew how to navigate us through these confusing times in your own unique way. Thank you both for your expert editing, encouragement, and support through the creation of this book we have polished together!

Following is more information about the contributors to this book:

Editor Peggy Gilbart specializes in helping an author improve their written work without compromising their unique voice. Currently, Peggy is part of the editing team at YouSpeakItBooks.com.

Editor Zhenya Goma currently serves as Writing Specialist for the University of Texas-Austin's On-Ramps Rhetoric program. Although most of her experience has been with academic texts, the process of working with Maria to create a new type of spiritual book was very fun and rewarding! Maybe this is a new passion! You may contact Zhenya at zgoma86@gmail.com.

Spiritual Teacher Dechen Rheault is a gifted seer, empathic and energy healer with clients spanning the globe. Working remotely, she can communicate with a person's soul, helping loved ones know their deepest wishes, even if the person may not be able to speak. For loved ones who are non-verbal, this heart connection may bring comfort and valuable insights when making decisions about their care. For more information and to contact Dechen, go to: yourwisdomways.com.

Writer Mary-Jo Salvadore's academic credentials are a BS degree in education K-12 with a Master's degree in Special Education. She taught (Business Dept.) for 27 years. She was the Co-Director of the Academy of Finance for 15 years. Mary-Jo continues to mentor B.D. on a weekly basis.

Tom Blon, my best friend for almost 40 years has been the reason so many of these stories can be read by you. Countless days, upon returning home after mentoring, he was ready and eager to hear me share the challenges and triumphs experienced that day. Often, he would encourage me to write the story down, for which I am exceptionally grateful. Tom has also read through the book at its different stages and offered valueable feedback. I am so very lucky to receive your patience, presence and encouragement throughout this whole process. Thank you!

Coco and Lacey have been companions for the entire book writing process. They love being near me. If I am writing at my desk, Lacey sits behind me in the large circular green velvet throne-like chair, while Coco rests in his bed underneath, sort of like double decker dogs. When I was recording the audiobook in the attic, because that is the quietest spot in our house, they were quite insulted to be excluded, yet all seemed to be forgiven when I came downstairs. Following a robust celebration upon my return, I lifted them onto the couch to edit the audio, each taking their favorite spot: Coco between my legs and Lacey off to the side. What animal friends are your companions in life?

Maria Blon is an ever-changing, expanding woman who will probably be passionately doing something new each time you meet her. She lives in New York with Tom, Coco, Lacey and her garden plants, animals, compost and many glorious worms and bugs. You may reach out to Maria about offering classes, presentations and discussion groups at 2mariablon@gmail.com. Thanks to Anna Blon for this artistic picture.

Be well my friends and may your hearts keep blooming!

Made in the USA
Columbia, SC
24 November 2021

49691930R00159